Youth Mainstreaming in Development Planning

Transforming Young Lives

Commonwealth Secretariat

Commonwealth Secretariat
Marlborough House
Pall Mall
London SW1Y 5HX
United Kingdom

Published by the Commonwealth Secretariat
Edited by Editors4Change
Typeset by NovaTechset Private Limited, Bengaluru & Chennai, India
Cover design by Commonwealth Secretariat
Cover photo by Daniele Romeo/Alamy Stock Photo
Printed by Charlesworth Press, Wakefield
Icons by Freepik from www.flaticon.com

Wherever possible, the Commonwealth Secretariat uses paper sourced from sustainable forests or from sources that minimise a destructive impact on the environment.

Copies of this publication may be obtained from

Publications Section
Commonwealth Secretariat
Marlborough House
Pall Mall
London SW1Y 5HX
United Kingdom
Tel: +44 (0)20 7747 6534
Fax: +44 (0)20 7839 9081
Email: publications@commonwealth.int
Web: www.thecommonwealth.org/publications

A catalogue record for this publication is available from the British Library.

ISBN (paperback): 978-1-84929-164-4
ISBN (e-book): 978-1-84859-958-1

Foreword by Director, Youth Division

Youth Mainstreaming in Development Planning: Transforming Young Lives is a key part of the long-term commitment of the Commonwealth Secretariat to working with young people, to champion their rights and develop broad-based strategies to incorporate their capacities, participation and interests in the youth sector and beyond.

For more than 40 years, the Commonwealth Secretariat has focused on enhancing the capacity of youth sector actors to deliver youth empowerment strategies. Initiatives have included building the technical capacity of youth ministries and departments, supporting universities to deliver youth work education and training, and creating and strengthening youth-led networks and youth worker networks, among a range of other policy and practice approaches. This co-operation within the sector, and the remarkable achievements of Commonwealth member countries, has resulted in significant gains in realising young people's empowerment and rights.

Youth Mainstreaming in Development Planning envisages strengthening the wider influence of the sector in establishing holistic, youth-centric development planning across all sectors. This will contribute to young people's social, political and economic empowerment and open doors for their inclusion and contribution in broader development strategies.

The publication addresses a noted gap in guidance for youth mainstreaming. It is intended to trigger dialogue and mobilise consensus around visions and strategies for youth mainstreaming, and provide practical tools and techniques that help make young people and their interests visible in development planning. It continues the commitments made by the Commonwealth in the *Plan of Action for Youth Empowerment (PAYE)* to support cross-sectoral work with, and for, youth. This commitment has been reaffirmed through the years in high-level dialogue, including at consecutive Commonwealth Youth Ministers Meetings in 2008 and 2013, and the Commonwealth Heads of Government meeting in 2009.

We hope that *Youth Mainstreaming in Development Planning* will be a useful and impactful resource that informs youth mainstreaming strategies designed and implemented by the youth sector, by national/subnational planners and by other discrete sectors.

For the Commonwealth Secretariat, this publication marks the beginning of planned collaborative engagement with young people and the youth sector, as well as other sectors, to realise the potential of youth mainstreaming. This work with, and for, youth, will further strengthen young people's opportunities for living in dignity, good health, peace and economic security, in a society that respects and values intergenerational equality and justice.

Katherine Ellis
Director, Youth Division, Commonwealth Secretariat

Foreword by Chair, policy and advocacy, Commonwealth Youth Council

New initiatives in youth policy formulation and their translation into programmes and practice have played a significant role in engaging young people meaningfully in development processes. But there remains room for improvement to integrate a holistic, youth-oriented approach and provide an enabling environment that captures the experiences, skills, expertise and aspirations of young people.

The Commonwealth Youth Council (CYC) welcomes the timely publication *Youth Mainstreaming in Development Planning: Transforming Young Lives*, which will enrich and inform the sustainable engagement of young people in intergenerational spaces, at all levels of decision-making and as key actors and agents of change.

The CYC sees the handbook as a useful resource to engage with governments and other stakeholders working with young people, to better inform policy decisions and quality of engagement and to ensure that we achieve tangible outcomes and real change in the lives of young people.

The handbook provides a strong foundation for understanding and building on the concept of youth mainstreaming. It speaks to those who are new to youth work and youth empowerment strategies, as well as those who are experts in this area. This guide also does an exceptional job of clarifying any level of uncertainty on the relationship of youth mainstreaming to the Sustainable Development Goals.

The Commonwealth Youth Council, National Youth Councils and other national and regional youth bodies are poised to take away a wealth of knowledge from this publication. The CYC commits to integrate the concepts and tools of this handbook in its work and mobilise stakeholders to do the same. We are committed to the empowerment of a dynamic sector of individuals – who make up 60 per cent of the Commonwealth's population!

Nikolai Edwards
Vice Chairperson Policy, Advocacy and Projects, 2017
Commonwealth Youth Council

A Cross-Sectoral Approach: Youth Mainstreaming

Effective ways to bolster youth development include developing robust, stand-alone youth policies and integrating young people into sectoral policies of line ministries. In recent years, a cross-sectoral approach to youth policies has emerged both as an imperative for effectiveness and as a pragmatic answer to two challenges: the increasingly large youth population in many countries, especially the developing countries, on the one hand; and the poor implementation and funding of youth policies, on the other. A cross-sectoral approach also helps to support the development of young people so that they can achieve their full potential in all spheres of their lives. Additionally, mainstreaming is a recognized methodology for ensuring effective policies for specific social cohorts, as shown by the successful example of gender mainstreaming.

Nevertheless, cross-sectoral approaches come at a cost: they require increased dialogue, planning and coordination within governments, and even beyond, when considering multilevel governance mechanisms, as in the case of decentralized or federal states. Strengthening the youth expertise of sectoral ministries and subnational governments is a winning strategy to build strong alliances on youth issues.

From: "Policies and programmes involving youth", Report of the Secretary-General to the Commission for Social Development at its fifty-fifth session (E/CN.5/2017/5), United Nations, 21 November 2016, pages 4–5.

Courtesy of the UN Department of Economic and Social Affairs (UNDESA)

Preface

What does this publication do?

This publication serves as a set of analysis and implementation guidance to support youth mainstreaming (YM) initiatives and fill a noted gap in the sector on this topic. It comes in three parts, Part I: Concepts and Discussions, which facilitates pre-planning dialogue and discussion, Part 2: Implementation, which provides practical guidance and tools for implementing YM, including short case studies, and Part 3: Full Case Studies, which provides more detailed examples of YM within sectors.

Besides this, the tools and discussions put forward a vision, and stimulate us to examine our own views and practices around justice, equality and participation, and bringing young people, along with other marginalised social cohorts, to the forefront in development planning.

Who is it for?

This handbook serves:

- the youth sector[1] – ideally the key driver of YM as advocates and providers of technical assistance;

- national and subnational all-of-government planners – who lead inter-sectoral development strategies, particularly national development strategies;

- all sectors – (social, political and economic) that are involved in planning, including multiple intra-sector players, such as youth, youth networks, non-governmental players, academia, professional associations, the private sector and other key players; and

- organisations – putting in place YM processes and mechanisms.

Institutional commitments to youth mainstreaming

The Commonwealth began a dialogue on systematically incorporating youth mainstreaming within the Commonwealth Secretariat, as well as among partners, in 2007 when the Secretariat stated its intention to pay 'particular attention' to women and young people and observed that 'to mainstream youth, through education, knowledge and awareness is a huge global challenge ... the litmus test of development is whether [mainstreaming] has a transformative effect on women and young people'. Its publication, *the Commonwealth Plan of Action for Youth Empowerment (PAYE)*, placed a further strategic focus on youth mainstreaming.

The 2008 Commonwealth Youth Ministers Meeting consolidated this commitment and recognised that youth ministries need support and resources to 'enable ministries to more effectively lead the multi-sectoral youth mainstreaming approach to youth development and empowerment'.[2] This commitment was further reaffirmed in the Commonwealth Heads of Government Meeting of 2009.[3] The Baku Commitment to Youth Policies, which highlight the importance of 'a holistic approach to youth development, through increased collaboration across policy sectors'[4] and 'transversal and cross-sectoral co-ordination and work, as well as efficient and effective national-to-local implementation,'[5] indicated the widening of this global recognition of the centrality of youth mainstreaming.

Development organisations such as the African Union Commission,[6] the World Bank,[7] the United Nations Educational, Scientific and Cultural Organization[8] and the World Programme of Action for Youth have also committed to institutional youth mainstreaming. This has significant implications for replication of YM strategies across other global development and lending institutions, and for the way these institutions help shape change for youth.

Notes

1 The youth sector comprises all players whose central strategies are based around policies, programmes and research around youth empowerment, and will be further discussed in Chapter 6.
2 Commonwealth Youth Programme 2008, 3.
3 Commonwealth Secretariat 2009, 1.
4 United Nations 2014.
5 Ibid, 3.
6 African Union Commission 2016.
7 Le Cava and Ozbil 2016.
8 UNESCO 2002. See also UNESCO 2006.

References

African Union Commission (2016), 'African Union Commission Holds Youth Mainstreaming Workshop', available at: https://www.au.int/en/pressreleases/31593/african-union-commission-holds-youth-mainstreaming-workshop (accessed January 2017).

Commonwealth Secretariat (2009), *Investing in Young People: A Declaration on Young People*, Commonwealth Heads of Government, Commonwealth

Heads of Government Meeting (CHOGM), Republic of Trinidad and Tobago, 27–29 November.

Commonwealth Youth Programme (2008), 'Provisional Agenda Item 5A', Commonwealth Youth Ministers' Meeting, Colombo, Sri Lanka, April, Commonwealth Secretariat, London.

La Cava, G and Z Ozbil (2016), *Approach Paper: Mainstreaming Youth Issues in Europe and Central Asia*, World Bank, Washington, DC, available at: http://documents.worldbank.org/curated/en/722281468251379269/Approach-paper-mainstreaming-youth-issues-in-Europe-and-Central-Asia (accessed November 2016).

UN Educational, Scientific and Cultural Organization (UNESCO) (2002), *Mainstreaming the Needs of Youth*, available at: http://unesdoc.unesco.org/images/0012/001254/125433e.pdf (accessed January 2017).

UNESCO (2006), Section for Youth. *Youth Mainstreaming Training Kit*, UNESCO, Paris.

United Nations (2010), World Programme of Action for Youth. New York.

United Nations (2014), *Baku Commitment to Youth Policies*, 1st Global Forum on Youth Policies, October 2014, Baku.

Acknowledgments

We wish to thank everyone who has been directly and indirectly involved in informing the vision and shape of this publication. Special acknowledgement is due to the Government of Malaysia, which provided an initial grant to commence field research, to Dharshini Seneviratne from the Commonwealth Secretariat Youth Division, whose passion and expertise has guided the project through to completion, to the Secretariat staff and external experts who provided valuable insights, and to the young people who contributed to a rich dialogue around the concepts and guidance and ensured the incorporation of youth interests throughout the process and product.

Katherine Ellis
Director, Youth Division
Commonwealth Secretariat

Contents

Contents

Contents

List of figures

List of tables

List of boxes

Acronyms and abbreviations

AGPO	Access to Government Procurement Opportunities (Kenya)
ASEAN	Association of Southeast Asian Nations
AUC	African Union Commission
AYAC	Australian Youth Affairs Coalition
CHOGM	Commonwealth Heads of Government Meeting
CPRC	Chronic Poverty Research Centre
CSO	civil society organisation
CYC	Commonwealth Youth Council
CYMM	Commonwealth Youth Ministers Meeting
CYP	Commonwealth Youth Programme
CYPSPRC	Commonwealth Youth Programme South Pacific Regional Centre
DBKB	Youth in Executive Development Work Diploma
DFID	Department for International Development (UK)
DoH	Department of Health (South Africa)
DYDW	Diploma in Youth Development Work (Commonwealth)
FFD	financing for development
GDP	gross domestic product
GoJ	Government of Jamaica
ICT	information and communication technology
IF	Intergenerational Foundation (UK)
IYRES	Institute for Youth Research (Malaysia)
KBS	Kementarian Bela & Sukan (Ministry of Youth and Sports, Malaysia)
ODI	Overseas Development Institute
MBM	Malaysia Youth Council
MDG	Millennium Development Goal

M&E	monitoring and evaluation
MoYC	Ministry of Youth and Culture, Jamaica
MWYCFA	Ministry of Women, Youth, Children and Family Affairs (Solomon Islands)
MYP	Malaysia Youth Policy
NGO	non-governmental organisation
NSC	National Sports Council
NYC	national youth council
NYCC	National Youth Consultative Council
NYDF	National Youth Development Framework
NYP	National Youth Policy (Jamaica)
ODI	Overseas Development Institute (UK)
PAYE	Plan of Action for Youth Empowerment (Commonwealth)
PBM	Malaysia Youth Parliament
PYDF	Pacific Youth Development Framework
SDG	Sustainable Development Goal
SINYC	Solomon Islands National Youth Council
SINYP	Solomon Islands National Youth Policy
SPC	Pacific Community
SRH	sexual and reproductive health
SRHR	sexual and reproductive health rights
STI	sexually transmitted infection
TYPF	The YP Foundation (India)
UDHR	Universal Declaration of Human Rights
UNCRC	United Nations Convention on the Rights of the Child
UNDP	United Nations Development Programme
UNESCAP	United Nations Economic and Social Commission for Asia and the Pacific
UNESCO	United Nations Educational, Scientific and Cultural Organization

UNICEF	United Nations Children's Fund
UPFYA	Uganda Parliamentary Forum on Youth Affairs
UPM	Universiti Putra Malaysia
WPAY	World Plan of Action for Youth
Y-BAGAS	Youth Budget Advocacy Group of Awutu-Senya District
YDI	Youth Development Index
YFS	youth-friendly service
YM	youth mainstreaming

Executive Summary

Youth mainstreaming

Youth mainstreaming is a critical part of pursuing a vision for an egalitarian world. It helps embed young people's aspirations into development planning and ensure equality between youth and adults. In its best form, it connects democracy initiatives to equitable development outcomes for young people and communities.

Young people constitute one quarter of the world's population, and one third of the population in developing nations. This signals a vibrant and hopeful resource for the world. But young people are more than numbers. Their struggles for social justice and equality are increasingly visible and articulate. They have demonstrated their progressive vision for the world in multiple ways, be it as citizens, as voters or in organised youth movements. They have the greatest stake in equitable and sustainable development, and are also well positioned to contribute meaningfully to this.

At the same time, we are witnessing global and national moves that work against young people's vision for themselves and the world. In the global north, young people are reported to be poorer than their parents. In the global south, while abject poverty has decreased, the dividends of economic growth has not reached poor young people whose actual numbers are increasing. In a context of rising inequality and diminishing social support systems, young people form a large proportion of the world's unemployed, and they have challenges accessing affordable education and basic services. Mainstreaming youth interests and capabilities are becoming even more critical in this context.

Youth mainstreaming is about:

- ensuring youth-centric institutions and processes in development planning within and across all sectors to realise equitable development for youth and society;

- ensuring youth participation in all spheres and levels of development planning, without which positive and equitable outcomes for youth are not possible; and

- acknowledging the implications of intergenerational relations among youth and adults, and young people's unique developmental rights and evolving capacities in conceiving and delivering policies and plans for them.

Implementation requires attention to:

- moving beyond youth projects, programmes or 'youth activities', to holistic attitudinal, strategic and financing shifts in engaging, planning and delivering for, and with, youth;

- strong partnerships across stakeholders including diverse youth groups and the youth sector, and an ability to involve and respect all stakeholders committed to youth rights;

- ensuring that youth mainstreaming does not reinforce inequality and injustice;

- local, national and international contexts and analysing global systems, ideologies, policies and practices, as well as the localised realities of our nations and communities, including the ways these influence our ability to deliver on youth-centric policy and planning; and

- youth data that allow the articulation of youth cohort involvement in sectors, and outputs and outcomes for youth, including for subgroups.

The publication

Youth Mainstreaming in Development Planning: Transforming Young Lives aims to meet requests from member countries for timely, relevant guidance on integrating youth rights into institutional planning.

'Transformation' (a radical change for the good) suggests an ambitious goal, and often requires re-evaluating the ways we work, partners we work with, and the ultimate results we want to achieve for, and with, youth. By 'development planning' we mean all aspects of the planning cycle, including policy and strategy development and translating strategy into programmes, and thereby, outcomes for youth.

The publication echoes United Nations Resolution No. 70/1, which released the Sustainable Development Goals (SDGs), titled *Transforming Our World: The 2030 Agenda for Sustainable Development (Agenda 2030)*. Global transformation is possible only if young people contribute to, and benefit from, this transformation. While we acknowledge that youth aspirations may go beyond the SDGs, they still provide a strong foundation for our work given the SDGs' central commitment to reducing inequality, the goal of mainstreaming.

The publication is divided into three parts:

1. **Part 1: Concepts and Discussions** defines youth mainstreaming and aligns it to broader human rights, legal and development frameworks including the SDGs, and to social and policy contexts. This section encourages pre-planning dialogue and discussion around youth mainstreaming that is critical for reaching consensus on process and goals.

2. **Part 2: Implementation** provides practical guidance for the implementation of youth mainstreaming through discussions of planning and operational imperatives, including analytical tools, checklists and short case studies, some of them based on experiences influenced by the Commonwealth's strategies. Public financing and the role of donors are also addressed.

3. **Part 3: Full Case Studies** complements the briefer case studies throughout the publication with fuller studies of youth mainstreaming initiatives in the sectors of poverty alleviation, health, employment, finance, justice and urban planning from across the Commonwealth and elsewhere. These help provide concrete examples of the concept in practice, including challenges.

Use of the publication

The publication is a resource for the multiple stakeholders who will play a role in youth mainstreaming. These comprise the youth sector, including youth ministries and government planners, the non-governmental and voluntary sectors, academia, professional associations, youth collectives and youth-led organisations, the private sector, donors and others. It balances conceptual discussions with practical implementation guidance to meet diverse stakeholder needs.

The significance of the three parts may vary according to the role of the stakeholder (in research and analysis, planning, implementation, monitoring and evaluation, playing a watchdog role) in the process. However, they are strongly interlinked, and should be cross-referenced to receive the full benefit of the guidance. The publication itself helps you do this.

The process: Consultations, considerations and review

The development of this publication began with a roundtable discussion in 2013 involving youth development professionals, government officials, staff and young people via the Commonwealth Youth Council. It is also informed by youth mainstreaming practices in selected member countries as a result of the Commonwealth's strategic publication *The Plan of Action for Youth Empowerment (PAYE)*.

Since then, the process has included the incorporation of the SDGs and UN commitments made in *Agenda 2030*. It is also informed by influential processes that resulted in *We the Peoples: Celebrating Seven Million Voices,* of which 58 per cent of respondents were young people, and the extensive process undertaken by the Department for International Development (DFID)-Civil Society Organisation (CSO) Youth Working Group for *Youth Voices for a Post-2015 World*. It reflects the interests of visible rights-based youth activism and the priorities set by the Commonwealth Youth Council. The publication has undergone professional review for relevance and utility by young people, senior independent consultants and public sector officials representing all Commonwealth regions.

A living document: Feedback is welcome

This is an initial guide to draw in government officials and partners to engage in discussions and implementation of youth mainstreaming. It will be adapted and improved with learning from Commonwealth pilots and other initiatives. The Commonwealth welcomes stakeholders to communicate the strengths and challenges of this guidance, and ideas for improvement. In particular, we are aware that the guidance is primarily targeting public policy processes, government and civil society. How could we better target the private sector, media partners or academic institutions for youth mainstreaming?

Contributors

Lead author: Dharshini Seneviratne

Editor: Sarah Huxley

External review and advisory:

- Mereia Carling, Social Development Adviser – Youth, Social Development Division, the Pacific Community, Fiji

- Nikolai Edwards, Trinidad and Tobago, Vice Chairperson, Policy, Advocacy and Projects, Commonwealth Youth Council

- Bernice Hlagala, Director, Youth Development at the Presidency, Department of Planning, Monitoring and Evaluation, South Africa

- Sarah Huxley, Independent Consultant, United Kingdom

- Pauline Léonard, Associate Social Affairs Officer, UN Programme on Youth, United Nations Department of Economic and Social Affairs (UNDESA)

- Roshni Nuggehalli, Researcher, and Director, Youth for Unity and Voluntary Action (YUVA), India

- Latha Pillai, Director, Rajiv Gandhi National Institute of Youth Development (RGNIYD), India

- Febna Reheem, Asst. Professor, Dept. of Development Studies, Rajiv Gandhi National Institute of Youth Development (RGNIYD), India

- Nilanthi Sugathadasa, Former Additional Secretary, former Ministry of Youth and Skills Development, Sri Lanka

Internal reviewers:

- Katherine Ellis, Director, Youth Division, Commonwealth Secretariat

- Layne Robinson, Head, Programmes Unit, Youth Division, Commonwealth Secretariat

- Oliver Dudfield, Head, Sports for Development and Peace, Youth Division, Commonwealth Secretariat

- Rafi Karkar, Assistant Research Officer, Research and Policy Unit, Youth Division, Commonwealth Secretariat

- Tiffany Daniels, Assistant Programme Officer, Programmes Unit, Youth Division, Commonwealth Secretariat

- Lawrence Muli, Assistant Programme Officer, Programmes Unit, Youth Division, Commonwealth Secretariat

Research support:

- Tiffany Daniels, Commonwealth Secretariat

- Wijeya Jayathilake, Independent Consultant, Sri Lanka

Part 1

Concepts and Discussions

Successful policy is enriched by dialogue, debate and consensus. This part helps you do this. It discusses a definition of youth mainstreaming, concepts that define our approach to youth and youth empowerment, and societal, structural and institutional enablers that inform planning. The youth sector, which generally carries the technical expertise for youth mainstreaming, is also a key area of discussion.

Chapter 1
What Is Youth Mainstreaming?

This section looks at:

- a definition of youth mainstreaming
- concepts and approaches in youth empowerment and youth development, including in development planning
- key considerations.

1.1 Youth mainstreaming

Ensuring equity and justice for young people in global and national planning (as for any other group side lined in policy-making) is critical, and realises a fundamental human right. This is an important ethical and moral imperative, but it is also a political priority considering the explicit articulation of national and global equality for all, including for all ages, in the Sustainable Development Goals (SDGs).

Youth mainstreaming is a transformative process that is inclusive and consciously proactive, placing the capabilities and rights of young men and women alongside those of other marginalised community members in development planning. It is transformative because it radically improves young people's wellbeing and rights by translating co-created visions into youth-centric policies and programmes.

Mainstreaming is based on a guiding vision of all social groups benefiting equally from the fruits of development, and participating in that development in accordance with their full human potential.

Youth mainstreaming can be defined as:

> *Strategies for intergenerational equity and justice that enable young people's capabilities, participation and human rights to be an integral dimension of the analysis, design, implementation and monitoring & evaluation of policies and programmes in inter-sectoral planning across all social, political and economic spheres. It enables young people and adults to benefit equally from, and contribute equally to, development outcomes.*[1]

Youth mainstreaming, then, is a *strategy* to achieve the *goal* of equality. Therefore, mainstreaming is not an end in itself; social equality is. It links democracy initiatives to achieving equitable development for youth.

We can illustrate youth mainstreaming in the following manner. Figure 1.1 is aligned to critical goals in the SDGs that help us articulate youth mainstreaming – to be discussed further in Chapter 3.

It is important to keep in mind the end-goal of social equality for youth (the 'why?') as we review and reform our institutions for youth mainstreaming (the 'what?'). If we lose sight of this end-goal, our work will not be in the best interests of youth, and will not create equal opportunity and equal status for them.

Creating equal opportunities for young people means not that they need the 'same' inputs as adults or other generational groups, but that they need *specific* inputs (for equity and justice) relevant to their unique and evolving stage in life (see Annex 1), that enable them, including marginalised youth subgroups/age groups, to achieve equal social, political and economic status with adults. Measures for equity result in social equality for all, including youth. (How we can concretely express diverse dimensions of creating equal opportunity for youth is further discussed in Table 3.1, the Equality Matrix for Youth.) Inequality and inequity are explained in Box 1.1.

Figure 1.1 The youth mainstreaming arrow

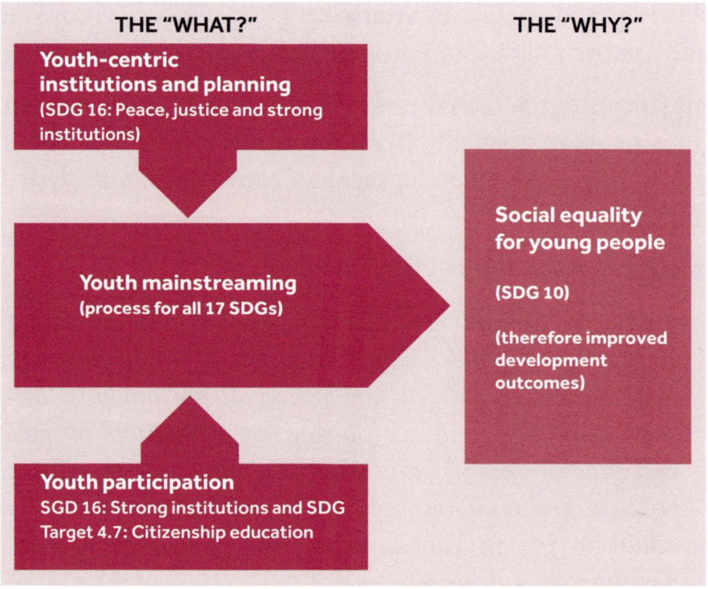

THE "WHAT?"   THE "WHY?"

Youth-centric institutions and planning (SDG 16: Peace, justice and strong institutions)

Youth mainstreaming (process for all 17 SDGs)

Social equality for young people (SDG 10) (therefore improved development outcomes)

Youth participation SGD 16: Strong institutions and SDG Target 4.7: Citizenship education

---

Box 1.1 Inequality and inequity

Inequality refers to the condition of being unequal, and can usually be expressed in numbers and percentages such as access to education, employment or freedom from poverty. Inequity, on the other hand, is related to injustice and unfairness. It is also often expressed in numbers, but is more often expressed in qualitative ways.

If youth unemployment is thrice that of adult unemployment, this is a clear manifestation of inequality for youth. This inequality has been shown to be a result of inequities in the employment sector pertaining to attitudes towards young people, the lack of consideration of young people's specific situation in life as those transiting from education to employment, and the lack of comprehensive youth employment strategies.

Equity and justice measures, in this sense, may be seen as mechanisms and processes which attempt to address this inequality. To take our example, this could mean comprehensive youth employment strategies that address youth-specific challenges in gaining employment. Equality is relative, never absolute, and much work needs to be done to maintain the gains that are achieved.

Indeed, the youth mainstreaming endeavour of equality is a key way in which young people express their vision for a better world; the DFiD–CSO document *Youth Voices on a Post-2015 World,* which informed SDG processes, expressed the views of young people from 12 countries across the globe. It articulated equality and freedom as the first principle ranked in order of importance. According to the report, 'The focus on equality and freedom highlights the current issue of widening inequality, which young people see as having a significantly negative impact on development'.[2] Equality for youth, and age-based discrimination, are particularly noted in the document.

1.2 Why 'youth' as a category?

From a historical perspective, 'youth' began obtaining prominence as a specific social category more than 400 years ago in the West (more recently in the global South), with the emergence of the printing press, the proliferation of ideas and the need for literacy. The education of certain age groups, particularly children and young people, therefore became a priority.[3] The increasingly fast-paced urbanisation and industrialisation of the nineteenth and twentieth centuries, and the widening gap between adults and children/youth, brought the notion of 'youth' even more to the fore.[4]

In political terms, on the one hand, young people became active as agents of social change as seen through civil rights and peace movements, student unions, environmental activism and so on. On the other, they were controlled as a group, as seen through policies to limit and circumscribe youth agency in the context of young people's social and political resistance.

We often look at young people through three different lenses:[5] (see Annex 1).

1. An age category: This is a common, yet inadequate, definition of youth. The complexity of defining youth through age is seen in the way age limits are set in different contexts. In the UN, the youth age range is 15 to 24; in the Commonwealth, it is 15 to 29. Youth age ranges across countries vary from a minimum of 14 to a maximum of 35, or above. Some countries also recognise that social and economic factors that determine qualities of a 'youth phase' may mean some flexibility in extending age limits at the lower or higher end in addressing youth needs and interests.[6] An exclusive focus on age categories has also been problematised for its tendency to ignore inequalities youth face because of class, gender and other forms of marginality.[7]

2. A transitional stage: The specific transitional aspects of the journey from childhood to youth in terms of developmental stages, first impressions, sexual maturation, entry into secondary/higher education and employment, and other specific generational experiences. Young people, *as youth*, have different development priorities from children, adults or older citizens, and these priorities need to be addressed.

3. A social construct: Young people are seen as 'a critical indicator of the state of a nation, of its politics, economy, and social and cultural life'.[8] Young people, particularly since the 1960s, have become symbols of hope, but also symbols of resistance around the world. Social constructs also ascribe subjective qualities to 'youth': negatively, as rebellious, disobedient etc. (even though young people may not see themselves that way), or more positively, as idealistic and courageous by virtue of their relative independence from established and formal institutional interests. The more negative constructs also contribute to intergenerational inequity, which we will discuss further in Chapter 2.

Young people's specific generational location is qualified throughout the publication as follows:

1. Younger youth groups, for example adolescents, as opposed to older youth groups, are, *in general,* more vulnerable in all contexts.[9]

2. Young people face greater combined forms of inequality when their age-specific experiences, which can in themselves be a source of marginality, are multiplied by their experiences based on their sex, race, class, economic, social, gender, caste, ability/disability, social stability/instability etc. (intersectionality).

3. Young people's marginality must be considered in relation to the marginality of other groups such as women, children, older persons, racial and religious minorities, sexual minorities, those living with disabilities, and so on. Youth mainstreaming is therefore part of broader strategies for non-discrimination and equality for all.

In terms of policy and planning, the most marginalised youth, particularly younger youth groups, i.e. those facing the greatest social, political, economic or geographical marginalisation,[10] are the least buffered by the impacts of social inequities, and non-responsive economic, political and social policies. It is their collective voices and concerns that are the most relevant in defining policy priorities for all, as well as in youth mainstreaming.[11] Equally, positive policy outcomes for marginalised groups in general also have positive outcomes for youth, and vice versa, which implies solidarity among such groups.

1.3 Foundations for youth mainstreaming: The Commonwealth Charter and UN human rights conventions

The discussions in this publication is underpinned by rights-based principles. The Commonwealth Charter, which defines the work of the Commonwealth, reinforces the core Commonwealth values of democracy, human rights and the rule of law. It has an explicit asset-based view of young people and recognises 'the positive and active role and contributions of young people in promoting development, peace, democracy and in protecting and promoting other Commonwealth values, such as tolerance and understanding, including respect for other cultures'.[12]

Commonwealth values reflect the values of international human rights conventions such as the United Nations Declaration on Human Rights (UDHR) and the United Nations Convention on the Rights of the Child (UNCRC), which explicitly articulates *children* as a cohort that is marginalised by virtue of being children, capturing the interests and rights of young people under 18.

A rights-based approach perceives young people as rights holders and the state and all institutions as duty-bearers. This sees citizens, including children and young people, as agents of change and partners in the development process – as articulated in articles defining their right to participation (Articles 18–21 of the UDHR, and Articles 12–16 and Article 17 of the UNCRC), which include articles on the right to information and self-determination.

These aspirations will help us develop detailed principles for youth mainstreaming, as outlined later in Chapter 14.

1.4 The paradigm of youth empowerment

Youth empowerment has three key dimensions, as visualised in Figure 1.2:

- Social empowerment – where young people have a sense of autonomy and self-confidence

Figure 1.2 Dimensions of youth empowerment

- Economic empowerment – where young people have control over owning and managing economic and other related resources, including being employed

- Political empowerment – where young people can formally voice opinions and influence social, economic and political processes.

Fulfilling aspects of all three dimensions are important in achieving holistic empowerment for young people. See Annex 2 for an elaboration.

Youth empowerment is defined in the Commonwealth as:

> *Enhancing the status of young people, empowering them to build on their competencies and capabilities for life. It will enable them to contribute to, and benefit from, a politically stable, economically viable, and legally supportive environment, ensuring their full participation as active citizens in their countries.*[13]

This definition highlights the importance of youth empowerment strategies in enhancing young people's capabilities, but also highlights the need for economic, social, legal and political enablers that contribute to this empowerment, including, importantly, through duty-bearers working with young people (with diverse capabilities and emerging power) in shaping these enablers and outcomes for equality and justice.

Box 1.2 highlights further the multidimensional nature of enhancing youth capabilities.

Box 1.2 The capabilities approach and youth empowerment[14]

The capabilities approach, developed by the economist and scholar Amartya Sen, is commonly used as a framework for understanding youth empowerment, including in the Youth Development Index (YDI). This approach focuses on 'a person's capability [opportunity] he or she has reason to value'.[15] The focus here is in the creation of opportunity, rather than how the person makes use of that opportunity. Youth empowerment strategies in this sense can be seen as strategies that enhance the capabilities of youth. This also refers importantly to the person's 'freedom to determine what they want and what they value'.[16]

The capabilities approach is an important complement to understanding youth empowerment, because it goes beyond instrumentalist measures of income or access to commodities, which are the focus of economic analysis. It also shifts the focus away from the means of living, to the actual opportunities of living.

(Continued)

Box 1.2 The capabilities approach and youth empowerment (*cont.*)

A privileged young woman from a high-income family, for example, who clearly has economic opportunities, may have fewer opportunities in other terms – such as freedom of expression in the household or in the university she attends. So she has more of one means of living well, but not others. The question here is the extent to which her opportunities can be enhanced in order that she, if so willing, can indeed have freedom of expression in other spheres. Youth empowerment can be seen as strategies and processes *that enhance these opportunities* for young people, irrespective of whether they make use of them or not.

1.5 Policy/attitudinal approaches

There are diverse policy/attitudinal approaches to youth empowerment and development. The challenge, while acknowledging this diversity, is to establish a common rights-based vision for youth mainstreaming, and to uphold commitments to youth-centric planning throughout policy and programme processes. Table 1.1 shows some predominant policy approaches. Some of these support achieving empowerment and equality for youth, while others work against this.

Table 1.1 Four policy/attitudinal approaches to youth

Approach	Description
Deficit approach	A deficit lens posits youth as a 'problem' and focuses on the 'correction' of these problems, such as drug abuse, crime, illiteracy and so on. This is still a predominant approach in planning for youth. It neglects examining the failure of structures that serve young people and focuses on young people's 'failures'. It also does not acknowledge young people's own agency as problem-solvers and creators of positive social change.
Youth for development approach (Instrumentalist)	This approach is often seen as 'instrumentalist'. It sees young people as 'instruments' for broader national development and often fails to perceive the centrality of a young person's own need for self-empowerment and building connectedness. When it does look at a young people's needs, it often prioritises issues of economic empowerment and employment at the expense of their broader social and political empowerment.
Equity and welfare approach	An equity and welfare approach focuses on basic human needs and the social and economic welfare of young people. It may look at aspects of equity and inequity for young people, such as youth poverty, the need for social safety nets etc. Where young people are proactive partners in shaping basic needs, it will also be asset based.

(*continued*)

Table 1.1 Four policy/attitudinal approaches to youth (*continued*)

Approach	Description
Asset-based / empowerment approach (rights based)	This approach focuses on young people as assets in transforming their own circumstances and, through this, working for a larger good. It is rights based in prioritising young people's agency in defining and shaping social, political and economic agendas, including ensuring equality for youth. While the equity and welfare of young people are central to an asset-based approach, young people are active agents in shaping this. This is the approach that informs this publication.

Everyone has a bias towards an approach; it is important to understand why you have that bias. What evidence exists to support your choice? Are some biases informed by fear? Or hope? Which brings better outcomes for young people?

Box 1.3 looks at a concrete example of the implications of different approaches in programmes for and with young people.

Box 1.3 Asset based or deficit focused? Programmes that address violent extremism

Some conventional programmes designed for young people which attempt to combat violent extremism are based on a deficit model that sees certain young people as a potential 'threat' to society. These programmes are often, though not always, based on the interests of national security, rather than youth empowerment and contribution.

Researchers have found that assumptions behind some such initiatives, i.e. that lack of education and jobs can result in youth and others turning to violence and extremism, is not backed by evidence, and often contradicts it.[17] In turn initiatives based on these assumptions aimed at counteracting violent extremism that may have implications for less than 1 per cent of the population, have not been shown to achieve the ultimate result of reducing violent extremism.

From a youth perspective, the way 'at risk' young people are identified, or the way they are engaged with, can create further stigma and alienation in societies in which certain groups of young people already feel insecure and alienated. Some programmes, for example, request staff in public schools to identify 'potentially at risk youth' based on behaviour within and outside the classroom.[18] This is despite the fact that there is little credible evidence of typical trajectories that a person follows to violent extremism,[19] and indeed of extremist thought leading to violent extremism.[20]

Proactive, asset-based programmes that address issues of extremism and violence, however, operate based on different assumptions. The United Nations Security Council Resolution on Youth, Peace and Security, 2015,

(Continued)

Box 1.3   Asset based or deficit focused? Programmes that address violent extremism (*cont.*)

focuses entirely on the critical role of young men and women in peacebuilding and countering violent extremism.[21] It has a strong asset-based perception of young people. At the Commonwealth too, peace-building paradigms are based on principles of dialogue and understanding[22] articulated in *Civil Paths to Peace: Report of the Commonwealth Commission on Respect and Understanding* led by Amartya Sen. This holistic approach acknowledges the complexities of violent conflict and looks at attitudes as well as broader structural factors that influence the creation of peaceful societies. The report of the Commission:

- acknowledges the positive roles that young people play in peace-building, and rejects the notion of young people as 'mere recipients of plans'[23] or young people as 'problems';
- promotes mutual understanding and respect among all faiths and communities in the Commonwealth in achieving peace;
- is based on 'the Commonwealth's agreed fundamental emphasis on human rights, liberties, democratic societies, gender equality, the rule of law and a political culture that promotes transparency, accountability and economic development',[24] which goes beyond seeing conflict as a result purely of economic grievances;
- addresses additional structural factors such as non-sectarian and non-parochial education (quality of education as much as access to education) for young people; and
- observes that promoting civil (non-violent) paths to peace is the responsibility of all parties,[25] including governments putting in place policies for equality, justice and participation.[26]

As much as youth are proactive, positive creators, they also observe and internalise confrontational, militarised cultures. If the world sends a message that violence can be addressed by further violence, then some young people may also adopt this thinking.

Where there is dialogic engagement with young people, within cultures demonstrating respect and understanding for all, and formal structures and policies that promote peace, there will be reduced risk of negative responses to violent conflict by young people. These will instead enhance the possibilities of including and valuing the voices of young people working for peace, and influencing conflict resolution. So, moving away from deficit approaches to asset-based ones is integral to a peaceful, equal world for all, including for young people.

1.6   Young people's developmental and safeguarding rights

Young people's rights mostly overlap with the rights of all, as will be the focus throughout this publication. However, their developmental rights and rights to protection and care (safeguarding), different in degree from younger children's developmental and safeguarding rights, are still pertinent for young people, particularly younger youth. This is because of their evolving and growing capabilities, both physically and mentally, and evolving independence and autonomy.

The UNCRC, the human rights framework that best refers to developmental rights of an evolving age group (children) with some overlap with the category of youth, refers specifically to the following:

1. Right to survival and development (Article 6) and right to a standard of living adequate for the child's (read 'young person's') physical, mental, moral and social development (Article 27 UNCRC). The UNCRC generally articulates child (in our case 'youth') development as a human right and highlights the child's right to development in the context of a positive family environment, reinforcing traditional and cultural values in fulfilling the right to child development, and linking the developmental rights of children to their best interest. Developmental rights of children with special needs (children living with disability) are also specifically addressed. It is the responsibility of the state, parents/legal guardians and other duty-bearers to ensure this. Elements of this can be inferred as critical for youth development, considering that youth are a cohort whose capacities are evolving.

2. Right to protection and care (UNCRC Article 3), applying both to parents and legal guardians, and to institutions serving children/youth. In our case, this applies not only to private domains such as the family, but also to public domains where interactions of young people, particularly of younger youth, can expose them to risks of safety and security, including in contexts of participation in expressing opinions of dissent within institutions.

Table 1.2 shows some examples of the incorporation of young people's developmental and safeguarding rights for three sectors.

Table 1.2 Young people's safeguarding and developmental rights in YM

Sector	Examples: Young person's right to physical, mental, moral and social development	Examples: Young person's right to protection and care
Poverty alleviation	Poverty and resultant trends of malnutrition and lack of housing and education can affect the physical and mental development of young people. **Implication: Integration of psychosocial and developmental (physical) specialism in poverty alleviation programmes.**	Poverty can leave youth, particularly girls, vulnerable to safety and security issues due to lack of protected living environments, and lack of access to secure sanitation. **Implication: Integration of youth safeguarding and confidentiality measures in poor communities, and poverty alleviation programmes.**
Justice	Incarceration of young people can have negative effects on their mental, moral and social development if not adequately addressed. **Implication: Integration of psychosocial and youth developmental specialism in youth justice programmes.**	Young people are excessively vulnerable to bullying and harassment in justice sector institutions, due to their age and evolving independence and autonomy. **Implication: Integration of youth safeguarding and confidentiality measures in justice programmes.**
Health	The active withholding of reproductive and other services from youth can have specific harmful effects on young people's physical and emotional development. **Implication: Integration of psychosocial and youth developmental specialism in all health programmes.**	For young people, issues of privacy and confidentiality in accessing healthcare are critical due to various levels of adult–youth dynamics and power relations, including with parents and healthcare staff. **Implication: Integration of youth safeguarding and confidentiality measures in health programmes.**

In not losing sight of the objective which youth mainstreaming attempts to reach, some considerations need to be kept in mind:

1. **Top-down, bottom-up:** Maintaining civil society's role

   Youth mainstreaming must be both top-down and bottom-up. On the 'supply' side, entire institutional frameworks including our economic policies, defence policies, social, healthcare and education policies are all accountable to young people, with youth ministries playing only one part in the whole picture. On the 'demand' side, young people's organisations and civil society have the responsibility of constantly engaging with institutions and providing the checks and balances necessary to ensure the continuing relevance of the youth mainstreaming process to changes in young people's lives.

Without robust engagement between society and institutions, no real change is possible. It is the demand from constituencies that energises responsive planning, as proved again and again in development practice. This relationship between government and civil society, particularly organised youth groups, will be further discussed in Chapters 7 and 8.

2. **Youth mainstreaming should not co-opt youth agendas:**

There have been, and always will be, concerns, especially among independent youth groups,[27] that 'mainstreaming' youth issues into centres of power and decision-making might result in institutions co-opting the youth agenda and taking away its 'radical edge'.[28] This then has implications for protecting fundamental freedoms, as well as incorporation of diverse voices in to the policy-making process as youth mainstreaming is implemented.

Youth mainstreaming requires a transformation of institutions and professional capacities to open up institutional scrutiny by and for youth (and other marginalised groups), but, before this, a transformation of mindsets and social norms that affords power and voice to young people in development planning across sectors.

3. **Maintaining the youth sector's relevance:** A call for youth mainstreaming does not, however, devalue the important work of youth-specific programmes and projects run by youth ministries, departments and youth development organisations, which in fact have a wealth of knowledge for other sectors to incorporate.

Moreover, the specific discipline of youth empowerment and development and the related profession of youth work (the profession referring to skilled youth engagement) need more investment than ever, while the technical contributions of the youth development sector to youth mainstreaming are clear. This will be further discussed in Chapter 6.

1.7 Conclusions and reflections

This chapter took us through a specific definition of youth mainstreaming that focused on setting in place processes of equity and justice to achieve equality for youth. It then examined various ways of thinking about youth and their issues, which can have an impact on the way we plan for them. It also reminded us of critical considerations in terms of acknowledging the role of multiple stakeholders, of working with youth sector stakeholders and ensuring that youth mainstreaming does not co-opt youth agendas.

**Box 1.4 Reflections on Chapter 1:
What is Youth Mainstreaming?**

- How does this definition of youth mainstreaming fit with your context? Are there any other aspects to consider?
- How did 'youth' emerge as a social category in your context? Why did this come about?
- Do policy processes you are familiar with adopt asset-based or deficit approaches to youth development, and acknowledge what everyone brings into the policy process?
- Is there a sufficient focus on young people's developmental and safeguarding rights in planning with, and for, them?
- How do we mainstream youth in all sectors while conserving the unique value of youth-specific interventions and institutions?

Notes

1 The foundation of this definition is the UN Economic and Social Council (ECOSOC) definition for gender mainstreaming, as it appears in ECOSOC 1997. It has been revised to highlight key factors the youth sector perceives as important in youth mainstreaming.

2 DFiD-CSO Youth Working Group 2015, 8.

3 'The social category was first formulated with the idea of nation-states, science, and religious freedom' (Patel et al. 2013, 3).

4 See, for example, Tebbutt 2016 for a historical study of youth in the British context.

5 Commonwealth Youth Programme 2007, 44–54.

6 Module 2 of the Commonwealth Diploma (Commonwealth Youth Programme 2007, 44) mentions an example from the Malawian Youth Policy of the time.

7 Ibid.

8 De Boek and Honwana 2005.

9 Particularly in contexts where the higher age limit for youth is often 30 and above.

10 See Commonwealth Secretariat 2013b, which provides tools for marginality mapping for young people around these five domains.

11 This is explicitly recognised in UN 2015, 3 – 'reaching the furthest behind first'.

12 Commonwealth Secretariat 2013a, 7.

13 Commonwealth Youth Programme and Institute for Economics and Peace 2013. 18.

14 This section is written with the support of material in Sen 2009, 231–8.

15 Ibid., 231.

16 Ibid., 232.

17 'A study of terrorist attacks from 1986 to 2002 found no correlation between low GDP [gross domestic product] and incidence of terrorism, a finding that has been replicated again and again across different measures and time frames. A 2016 study found that countries with higher economic prosperity and lower inequality were more likely to see residents travel to Syria as foreign fighters, rather than less, and that unemployment was "not highly correlated" to overall foreign fighter activity' (Berger 2016 quoting Benmelech and Klor 2016).

18 Brennan Centre for Justice N.D.

19 See, for example, Brennan Centre for Justice N.D.

20 Berger 2016, 3. Also see Anyadike 2016.

21 United Nations 2015.

22 Sen 2008.

23 Ibid., 12.

24 Ibid., 9

25 Ibid. See, for example, page 22 on the 'War on Terror'.

26 Ibid. See pages 25–26 on government roles in promoting peace: 'It might involve articulating clearly that government itself stands for the principles of respect for individuals as human beings, and that all people have the right to be treated fairly and with dignity. Governments can also a) adopt policies that tackle gross unfairness and injustice, b) create systems which give citizens and their preferences a strong voice, and c) acknowledge the role of the international community in shaping universal values and promoting positive change'.

27 Commonwealth Youth Programme 2008, 11.

28 This term is used in relation to gender mainstreaming in Rai 2003, 19.

References

Anyadike, O (2016), *Does Countering Violent Extremism Work?*, available at: https://www.irinnews.org/analysis/2016/08/10/does-countering-violent-extremism-work

Benmelech, E and EF Klor (2016), 'What Explains the Flow of Foreign Fighters to ISIS?', National Bureau of Economic Research, No. w22190, available at: http://www.nber.org/papers/w22190

Berger, JM (2016), *Making CVE Work: A Focussed Approach Based on Process Disruption*, International Centre for Counter-Terrorism, The Hague.

Brennan Centre for Justice, New York University School of Law (N.D.), *Countering Violent Extremism: Myth and Fact*, available at: https://www.brennancenter.org/sites/default/files/analysis/102915%20Final%20CVE%20Fact%20Sheet.pdf.

Commonwealth Secretariat (2013a), *Charter of the Commonwealth*, Commonwealth Secretariat, London.

Commonwealth Secretariat (2013b), *Youth Development Index*, Commonwealth Secretariat, London.

Commonwealth Youth Programme (2007), *Module 2: Young People and Society*, The Commonwealth Diploma in Youth Development, Commonwealth Secretariat, London.

Commonwealth Youth Programme (2008), *Report of the Stakeholders' Meeting on Youth Mainstreaming*, Commonwealth Secretariat, London.

Commonwealth Youth Programme and Institute for Economics and Peace (2013), *Commonwealth Youth Development Index: Methodology Report*, Commonwealth Youth Programme, London.

De Boeck, F and A Honwana (2005), *Makers & Breakers: Children & Youth in Postcolonial Africa*, Africa World Press, Trenton, NJ.

DFID-CSO Youth Working Group (2015), *Youth Voices for a Post-2015 World*.

Patel, A, M Venkateswaran, K Prakash and A Shekar (2013), *Ocean in a Drop*, Sage, New Delhi.

Rai, S M (2003), *Mainstreaming Gender, Democratising the State*, Manchester University Press, Manchester.

Sen, A (2008), *Civil Paths to Peace: Report of the Commonwealth Commission on Respect and Understanding*, Commonwealth Secretariat, London.

Sen, A (2009), *The Idea of Justice*, Allen Lane, London.

Tebbutt, M (2016), *Making Youth: A History of Youth in Modern Britain*, Palgrave, London.

United Nations (2015), *Security Council Resolution on Youth, Peace and Security*, United Nations, New York.

UN Economic and Social Council (ECOSOC) (1997), *Agreed Conclusions for Gender Mainstreaming*, A/RES/52/3, available at: http://www.un.org/en/ecosoc/docs/2006/resolution%202006-36.pdf

2

Chapter 2
Why Youth Mainstreaming?

This section helps us understand:

- youth disengagement

- intergenerational inequity

- how these social inequities result in tangible unequal outcomes for young people

- why mainstreaming benefits all of society.

2.1 Young people need to feel engaged

Young people constitute one quarter of the world's population, and one third of the population in developing nations.[1] They have led drives for equality and justice through youth social movements throughout the world. They have been at the forefront of political action, as in the Middle East and Africa in the recent past, and in the anti-corruption movement in India.[2]

On the part of decision-makers, there is an increasing recognition of the importance of young people's place in development, and increasing efforts to bring young people to the table in development planning.[3]

Yet, despite their active participation in development, and meaningful efforts on the parts of governments, youth still have less access than adults to formal decision-making processes, and to influencing policy. Translating good intentions into practical action has often been hindered by capacity and political constraints. This has resulted in a poor reflection of young people's rights and interests in planning.

Coupled with this is the intentional disengagement of young people from mainstream political and administrative processes, because of disillusionment with these processes. Young people's favoured modes of self-expression through youth social movements have often resulted in tensions between youth and policy-makers.

Youth mainstreaming is partially about bridging this gap in engagement, and creating youth-friendly spaces within policy domains for their greater participation.

2.2 Intergenerational equity and justice is lacking

Just as gender mainstreaming was built around a lobby for equal male–female relations, youth mainstreaming advocacy is built around equitable intergenerational relationships and the fostering of mutual respect between adults, young people and other age cohorts. There are no purely technocratic solutions for bridging generational gaps, but solutions that are built on positive attitudes towards, and respect for, young people that translate into policy domains.

Intergenerational equity suggests addressing the multiple ways in which young people can be discriminated against by virtue of their age in both the private and public domains. Non-discrimination policies often clearly prohibit discrimination based on age, and the SDGs unequivocally call for an end to age-based discrimination. However, clear evidence of the manifestations of this discrimination within these domains is evident.

These may be explicit discrimination, or implicit discrimination – where a practice, policy or programme does not consider a specific factor affecting youth. Of course, some cultures and contexts will have clearly positive dispositions towards youth. In terms of institutions, attitudinal factors will affect provision (service delivery) and outcomes for young people.

Let's look at some domains in which young people interact and how intergenerational inequity is evident, including examples of legal/policy measures that either reinforce, or counteract, these inequities:

1. Society: Young people may be marginalised in communities in specific ways by virtue of attitudes towards them, labelling and stereotyping them as being irresponsible, lazy, rebellious, 'angry', and so on.

2. Family settings: Parental authority may undermine young people's concerns and interests. For example, in the public sphere, parental consent laws may affect a young person's ability to access healthcare and health-related information. Often, ensuring young

people's – particularly younger youth and girls' – rights to services has been written into law; for example, by providing adolescents with the ability to make independent decisions around healthcare access.

3. Educational institutions: Imbalances of power between students and education authorities are often reflected through limitations placed on student organisations, curbing of students' freedom of expression and sidelining student views on learning/teaching and educational governance, both in schools and universities. Similarly, young people's right to accessible education is often undermined by laws and policies that challenge affordable education provision. At the same time, positive legal provisions may dictate that young people have a formal place in educational governance and access to education as a right.

4. Workplaces: Junior staff at institutions may be marginalised in decision-making because of the perception that their views are immature and not based on 'experience'. As entrants to employment, they may in fact have difficulties entering the work force itself, despite possessing skills. In an era when young people are increasingly employed in informal economies, contracts that do not stipulate minimum work hours ('zero-hour' contracts) and extended probation periods affect young people's economic security further.

5. Public institutions: Young people may be discriminated against as receivers of services and benefits in public institutions, where a lack of responsive design of services for youth results in inadequate delivery. For example, moves taken in one country to withdraw housing benefits from youth aged 18–21 as a means of reducing welfare spending (the assumption being they can live with their parents) are an indication of how young people are the first to lose out in cuts to public expenditure. On a positive note, these challenges are often explicitly addressed through laws. For example, in prison systems in some countries young people aged 18–25 are given better protection and care than adults, although not to the same extent as children (aged under 18). They may be housed

separately from adults in prisons, in recognition of their specific developmental stage as youth.

6. Party-political domains: Young people, while being an age cohort who actively contribute to the life of a community and nation in more informal ways, are less well represented in formal structures such as local government and parliament. In some countries, eligibility to enter politics is at age 25, and there is rarely anyone below 35 in political leadership positions. This considerably affects ways in which young people's interests in all the above settings receive formal political mandates. From a voter perspective, some countries are pushing for the voting age to be moved down to 16 instead of 18, so that very young people's interests are adequately represented in party political domains.

Such social norms that affect youth are multiplied by their identities of class, caste, gender, disability and so on.

Research into youth unemployment, for example, has highlighted the institutional and political discourses that reflect intergenerational inequity and negative perceptions of poor, unemployed young people; these are based on a deficit view of unemployed youth, who are accused of 'languishing on benefits' (often an argument put forward to rationalise defunding social benefit systems). This is the perspective of an elite, according to the research, who are out of touch with reality. Young people want to work, rather than exploit social welfare:

> *Almost all young people would choose work over the dole –* *almost any work. You have to be completely out of touch not* *to know this.*[4]

Similarly, a poor young woman accessing a healthcare facility can potentially face many forms of discrimination due to her gender (gender discrimination) – for example, specific and often complex issues in reproductive healthcare; her poverty (entrenched attitudes about the poor); and her age (being perceived as young and irresponsible). Box 2.1 articulates a real-life example.

A poor young man in the criminal justice system will face similar challenges, particularly when they are treated the same as adults in conflict with the law, which overlooks their

Box 2.1 Young people's voice on health services

The first thing the nurse asked me was my age, and I said I am 17. She questioned if at this age I am sexually active because in her culture, girls who are 17 are still virgins. The fact that she questioned why I had come for contraceptives at such a young age, that is totally unacceptable. That means she is promoting teenage pregnancy. And after that I told myself I will never go back to the clinic for contraception.

(Note: In this country, all young people can legally access reproductive healthcare, including contraception, after the age of 12.)

— Young woman from a Commonwealth member country

Box 2.2 Young people's voice on the justice system

They need to just work with people and then that will help stop it if they actually do something about it rather than just go to prison, even for three months or a year or whatever it is. They ain't doing nothing. What you're doing, you're going into prison full of criminals and learning more stuff in there. So you're going to come out without anything and be back to square one, you'll just do the same thing, it gets you nowhere.

— Young male offender

specific developmental stage or their future potential. Box 2.2 exemplifies this.

Challenging this intergenerational inequity requires concerted efforts at dialogue and respect across generations,[5] including exploring new youth-centric policy directions. An example is provided in Box 2.3.

2.3 Intergenerational inequities result in inequalities for youth

The intergenerational inequities discussed above in relation to social norms and service provision lead to tangible inequalities for youth in terms of inequitable income, unequal employment opportunities, unequal health outcomes, challenges to functioning as full citizens and inequality across generations.

Reducing social inequalities is one of the core goals of the SDGs. Recent research indicating the extent of this inequity (62 individuals have the same wealth as 3.6 billion people[7]),

Box 2.3 The Intergenerational Foundation's Parents Against Student Debt Initiative

The Intergenerational Foundation (IF) in the United Kingdom researches fairness between generations and enhances positive relationships between all age cohorts, including youth and adults. Its initiatives contribute to collaborative intergenerational dialogue between youth and adults. The work of the IF has focused significantly on issues for young people in the UK, including youth and housing and student debt.

The IF's Parents Against Student Debt Initiative[6] brings parents together with young people in a common intergenerational call for a fair financial deal for students entering university. Initiatives have included a march by students and parents that helps bonding and adult understanding of the aspirations, challenges and frustrations faced by young people in the face of challenges in accessing affordable education.

The campaign builds a common bond between parents and students on issues such as fee hikes and increased interest in student loans, which are causing middle-class, but particularly poor, students to face a precarious financial future or decide to opt out of higher education altogether.

The IF's campaign calls on parents to show their solidarity with student by marching alongside them, writing to Members of Parliament (MPs) to stop further fee hikes and student accommodation fee increases, to reflect on student policies and becoming student-friendly voters for political parties offering fair deals, and generally working with students for fairer loan deals. Projects such as this can significantly enhance intergenerational understanding, respect and common causes.

and evidence of the failure of dominant economic paradigms to deliver for the most marginalised,[8] all indicate a need to look not just at economic growth, but at distributional equality[9] of financial wealth and other resources – including across age groups, as indicated in the SDG targets. This inequality affects young people in specific ways (see Box 2.4).

Box 2.4 Inequality increases youth poverty

Inequalities fuel poverty, undermining the impact of economic growth on poverty reduction. Age itself is a vector of inequality, excluding millions of young women and men from access to financial resources, work opportunities, social welfare mechanisms and decision-making spaces, despite their right to all of these.

– The Overseas Development Institute (ODI) 2013

Despite these goals and observations, in the global north, young people today are reported to be poorer than their parents[10]. In the global south, while abject poverty has decreased, the dividends of economic growth have not reached poor young people whose actual numbers are increasing[11]. In employment, for example, young people, especially young women, are globally the most affected by high unemployment rates, with youth unemployment rates nearly three times higher than those for adults[12].

Research examining youth unemployment in the context of institutional employment practices in the United Kingdom notes:

> *Unemployment is highest among the young simply because they are the most vulnerable when the job market shrinks. You can keep a firm or a branch of the civil service going for some time using only older employees. Rather than sack people or deny those at the top the pay rises to which they feel entitled, you just refrain from hiring new staff when people leave or retire, and expect those remaining to take on extra work – often for no extra pay.*[13]

These crises, according to the research, are exacerbated by

- social inequality that results in wealth accumulation, which reduces investment in job creation and therefore increases youth unemployment; and

- the removal of welfare rights at a time when youth unemployment is rising, which affects youth wellbeing even more.

This is the case in a developed country. The circumstances of young people in poorer countries, with fewer welfare safety nets, are probably even more compounded.

Young people are also disadvantaged in terms of access to housing,[14] credit and finance,[15] and are differentially impacted by health, justice, migration and other mechanisms and processes by their specific generational location as youth.[16]

There are also disparities of outcomes for different *cohorts* of young people. Outcomes for youth are intersected by their experiences and realities, as influenced by identities of class, sex, ethnicity, religion, sexual orientation, geographical location, disability and so on.

For example, despite important gains in education among young women, three out of five illiterate young persons are female, with some countries showing female literacy rates as low as 15 per cent as opposed to male literacy rates of 35 per cent.[17] Globally, in 2010, 56.3 per cent of young males participated in the labour force, against 40.8 per cent of young females. Where young women do participate in the labour market, they generally confront greater challenges in accessing jobs, i.e. they face higher unemployment than their male counterparts. When employed, they are also more likely to be in traditionally female occupations and unstable, part-time and lower-paid jobs.[18]

Agenda 2030 (UN 2015) explicitly noted that the Millennium Development Goals (MDGs) were off-track on maternal and reproductive health, among several other things, which significantly affect both young men and women, but young women more so. This is a call to look at youth mainstreaming through the lens of diverse youth groups, and to provide opportunities for them to participate in framing decisions that affect their lives.

Despite these observations, most development programmes have yet to fully explore solutions for the differential impacts policies can have on different groups, including diverse youth groups, resulting in greater fallouts from the development process and cycles of deepening inequalities.

2.4 Youth interests are the interests of a just and prosperous society

Advocating for young people's interests means that we firmly situate youth rights and youth interests[19] in democratic governance frameworks and their components, including broader participatory structures. Otherwise, we would merely be trying to right a wrong within the existing paradigms of power.

The development frameworks we advocate need to identify non-discrimination, not just for young people but for everyone, and to ensure gender equality and be free from class, racial, ethnic, sexual, disability, caste and other biases. This involves challenging the current climate of global restructuring, and challenging the erosion of rights entitlements that have already been fought for and won.[20]

Continuing inequality for youth means entrenching broader poverty, debilitating social and economic growth, and creating social conflict, all of which work against reaching the SDGs.

There are clear long-term benefits that go beyond the benefits for young people in working towards equality for them. Given the above observation then, youth mainstreaming is important not only because it is the right thing to do, but also because it can:

- **catalyse long-term change for everyone** – as sound development outcomes for young people benefit society as a whole across generations;

- **create efficiency and growth** – as responsive planning and consultation enable efficient resource allocation and create value for money;

- **reduce poverty** – as overall development outcomes lead to the reduction of poverty;[21] and

- **enhance social cohesion**[22] – as a content youth cohort creates collaborative, positive relations with communities and the nation.

(See Table 3.1, the Equality Matrix for Youth, in Chapter 3, for an elaboration of these broader benefits.)

The link between equitable programming and institutional efficiency has been recorded across sectors where research capacities have existed to create robust evidence, as in the case outlined in Box 2.5.[23]

Box 2.5 Investing in youth is investing in society

Investments for the [youth] age cohort is an effective development strategy because it generates changes that will last throughout their life-time, with higher absolute returns than investment in older adults.

The benefits to countries in terms of human, social and economic development include increased productivity, lower health costs, enhanced social capital, and greater individual and community resilience to cope with shocks. Investments in mechanisms for youth participation at every level can improve policy and programming, promote civic engagement and encourage good governance. Investment in young people is, in short, an effective way to meet development priorities amid the global contraction of development assistance.

– ODI 2013

Given all this, it becomes logical and inevitable for governments to focus on equality for youth, a significant cohort of the population in many developing Commonwealth member countries. It is the right thing to do. But also, the success of national development outcomes is premised on positive outcomes for young people.

2.5 Conclusions and reflections

This chapter rationalised youth mainstreaming as a means of establishing intergenerational equity and justice, including reiterating the importance of 'leaving no one behind' in development planning: in our case, youth groups, particularly marginalised groups. Rising global inequality affects young people in specific ways, and entrenches poverty and inequality, creating challenges to social cohesion and peace. This is exacerbated by young people's lack of engagement with decision-making processes. Comprehensive youth mainstreaming processes will be built around an analysis of how these trends affect young people in your own countries.

Box 2.6 Reflections on Chapter 2: Why Youth Mainstreaming?

- How do young people express themselves to government and other decision-makers in your context? Are these collaborative approaches, or is there tension between governments, stakeholders and youth? If there is tension, how can this be resolved?

- Is intergenerational equity and justice a subject that is discussed in your context?

- How does intergenerational inequality intersect with other forms of inequality such as class, caste, gender, disability and so on?

- What are the key manifestations of inequality for youth and beyond in your context?

- How does inadequate youth mainstreaming limit sustainable development in your context?

- How does this result in unequal development outcomes for youth?

Notes

1 The Global Youth Development Index and Report 2016 (Commonwealth Secretariat 2016b) highlights that three-quarters of the world's 1.8 billion young people aged 15–29 live in countries where youth development is categorised as 'low' or 'medium'.
2 Patel et al. 2013, 2.
3 Office of the Secretary-General's Envoy on Youth 2016.
4 Dorling 2015, 66.
5 See Nuggehalli 2014, which talks of the protagonism of young people and adult roles in enhancing this capacity.
6 Intergenerational Foundation (N.D.)
7 Oxfam 2016, 2.
8 Ostry et al. 2016.
9 Ibid., 41: 'The evidence of the economic damage from inequality suggests that policymakers should be more open to redistribution than they are. Of course, apart from redistribution, policies could be designed to mitigate

some of the impacts in advance – for instance, through increased spending on education and training, which expands equality of opportunity'.

10 See, for example, Crawford R et al 2015 and Organisation for Economic Co-operation and Development, 2014, available at: https://www.oecd.org/social/OECD2014-Income-Inequality-Update.pdf. Accessed February 2017.

11 The World Bank, 2016.

12 International Labour Organization (ILO) 2015. 'World Employment and Social Outlook: Trends 2015', quoted in Oxfam 2015.

13 Dorling 2015, 66.

14 See, for example, Clapham et al. 2012.

15 See, for example, Clapham et al. 2012. Also United Nations Capital Development Fund and Mastercard Foundation N.D.

16 See full case studies in Part 3 of this publication.

17 Commonwealth Secretariat 2016a, 3.

18 United Nations 2015, 1.

19 'Youth interests' should always be locally identified. Having said this, the My World Survey has received more than 5 million votes from 16 to 30-year-olds internationally. This age group identified the following as their top youth issues/interests affecting their lives: a better education; healthcare, better jobs; and an honest and responsive government. See United Nations 2015.

20 Rai 2003, 25.

21 Moore 2005, 21: 'Not only can poverty experienced in youth have implications across the life course of the young person, it can hinder the capacity of a young person to bounce back from deprivation suffered in childhood, and affect the long-term life changes of any dependents, including and especially the young person's own children'.

22 ODI 2009, 7.

23 An example of increased efficiency and cost effectiveness, as they relate to restorative justice for young people (which indicates youth-mainstreamed approaches within the justice system), can be found in a seven-year study by Matrix Evidence 2009, as reported by the UK Restorative Justice Council. This study explores the costs and benefits of alternative interventions for young non-violent offenders, with a focus on restorative justice. Research in this case projected that pre-court schemes save society almost £275 million, with the cost of the scheme being recovered within the first year and savings over ten years being more than £1 billion. Further studies such as this, examining benefits of youth-centric approaches within social and economic sectors, need to be commissioned to obtain evidence for youth-centric planning.

References

Clapham, D, P Mackie, S Orford, K Buckley, I Thomas, with I Atherton and U McAnulty (2012), *Housing Options for Young People in 2020*, Joseph Rowntree Foundation, available at: https://www.jrf.org.uk/sites/default/files/jrf/migrated/files/young-people-housing-options-full_0.pdf

Commonwealth Secretariat (2016a), 'Fast Facts: The Commonwealth', available at: http://thecommonwealth.org/sites/default/files/inline/Fast%20Facts%20on%20the%20Commonwealth%20-%2025%20Jan%202017.pdf

Commonwealth Secretariat (2016b), *Global Youth Development Index and Report* Commonwealth Secretariat, London.

Crawford, R, D Innes and C O'Dea (2015), *The Evolution of Wealth in Great Britain*, Institute of Fiscal Studies, London: available at: https://www.ifs.org.uk/uploads/publications/comms/R109.pdf

Dorling, D (2015), *Inequality and the 1%*, Verso, London.

Intergenerational Foundation (N.D.), *Join Parents Against Student Debt*, available at: http://www.if.org.uk/join-parents-against-student-debt

International Labour Organization (ILO) (2015) 'World Employment and Social Outlook: Trends 2015', available at: http://www.ilo.org/wcmsp5/groups/public/@dgreports/@dcomm/@publ/documents/publication/wcms_337069.pdf

Matrix Evidence (2009), *Economic Analysis of Interventions for Young Adult Offenders,* Matrix Evidence, Barrow Cadbury Trust, available at: https://www.barrowcadbury.org.uk/wp-content/uploads/2011/01/Matrix_Economic_analysis-T2A-2009.pdf

Moore, K (2005), *Thinking about Youth Poverty through the Lenses of Chronic Poverty, Life-Course Poverty and Intergenerational Poverty*, Chronic Poverty Research Centre, Institute of Development Policy and Management, University of Manchester, Manchester.

Nuggehalli, R (2014), 'Children and Young People as Protagonists, and Adults as Partners', in Westwood, J et al., *Participation, Citizenship, and Intergenerational Relations in Children and Young People's Lives,* Palgrave Macmillan, Basingstoke Hampshire.

ODI (2009), *Equity in Development, Why It Is Important and How to Achieve It,* ODI, London.

ODI (2013), 'Youth and International Development Policy: The Case for Investing in Young People', *Project Briefing* No. 80, May 2013, available at: http://www.youthpolicy.org/library/wp-content/uploads/library/2013_ODI_Project_Briefing_Youth_International_Development_Policy_Eng.pdf

Office of the Secretary General's Envoy on Youth (2016), 'How Leaders Brought Youth to the 71st United Nations General Assembly', United Nations, New York, available at: http://www.un.org/youthenvoy/2016/10/world-leaders-brought-youth-71st-un-general-assembly/

Organisation for Economic Co-operation and Development (OECD) (2014), *Income Inequality Update: Rising Inequality: Youth and Poor Fall Further Behind*, available at: https://www.oecd.org/social/OECD2014-Income-Inequality-Update.pdf

Ostry, JD, P Loungani and D Furceri (2016), 'Neoliberalism Oversold?', *International Monetary Fund (IMF), Finance and Development*, Vol. 53 No. 2, pp 38–41.

Oxfam (2016), 'An Economy for the 1%', *Oxfam Briefing Paper*, Oxfam, London.

Patel, A, M Venkateswaran, K Prakash and A Shekar (2013), *Ocean in a Drop,* Sage, New Delhi.

Rai, S M (2003), *Mainstreaming Gender, Democratising the State,* Manchester University Press.

World Bank (2016), "While poverty in Africa has declined, the number of poor has increased", available at: http://www.worldbank.org/en/region/afr/publication/poverty-rising-africa-poverty-report.

United Nations (2015a), *My World Survey*, available at: http://data.myworld2015.org/

United Nation (2015b), Transforming our World, the 2030 Agenda for Sustainable Development. (see references for this chapter for changes: UN 2015a, and UN 2015b)

United Nations Capital Development Fund and Mastercard Foundation (N.D.), *Policy Opportunities and Constraints to Access Youth Financial Services*, available at: http://www.uncdf.org/sites/default/files/Download/AccesstoYFS_05_for_printing.pdf

Chapter 3
The Sustainable Development Goals and Youth Mainstreaming

This chapter:

- discusses youth mainstreaming in relation to the Sustainable Development Goals (SDGs)

- expresses the notion of social equality for young people, the end-goal of youth mainstreaming, through an equality matrix for youth pegged to the targets of Goal 10: Reducing Inequality Within and Among Countries

- unpacks the implications of accountable and transparent institutions for youth mainstreaming in relation to selected targets of Goal 16: Peace, Justice and Strong Institutions.

3.1 The SDGs and young people

One of the main reference points for this publication is the 17 Sustainable Development Goals (SDGs) adopted in 2015, particularly their articulation of the primacy of social equality in Goal 10: Reducing Inequality, which is of direct relevance to what we are trying to achieve through youth mainstreaming.

Before narrowing down on the relevance of the SDGs to youth mainstreaming, it is important to remember that the goals make specific reference to youth in several targets. These are shown in Box 3.1.

However, our position is that the approach to every target of all 17 goals will have a specific, age-related, impact on youth. Our analysis will be based on an understanding that all SDGs are interconnected and indivisible, and that each SDG has an implication for young people in the way policy and programme decisions are made.

3.2 The SDGs and youth mainstreaming

As discussed in Chapter 1, youth mainstreaming is about achieving social equality for youth and adults through processes

Box 3.1 SDGs with specific references to youth

The SDGs that are generally seen as most pertinent to young people's empowerment and development fall into two categories;

- **Those that refer to age disaggregation or age groups:** Eight goals refer to age disaggregation or age groups in the goal, targets or indicators. These are Goals 1 (poverty), 3 (health), 5 (gender equality), 8 (decent work), 10 (inequality), 11 (sustainable cities), 16 (peaceful, just and inclusive societies) and 17 (partnership).
- **Those that specifically mention young people:** There are explicit references to youth, young men and women, adolescents, girls and women aged 20–24 in the targets or indicators of nine goals. These are Goals 1 (poverty), 2 (hunger), 3 (health), 4 (education), 5 (gender equality), 6 (clean water and sanitation), 8 (decent work), 13 (climate action) and 16 (peaceful, just and inclusive societies).

This is covered in detail in the Youth Development Index.[1]

for equity and justice. Consultations with youth leading up to the formulation of the SDGs highlighted their vision for a world where equality and non-discrimination were the norms. Equality for youth and society was the most important principle identified by young people in the DFID-CSO document *Youth Voices on a Post-2015 World*.[2] Moreover, youth between the ages of 16 and 30 formed 58 per cent of the millions who voted on themes affecting their lives in *We the Peoples: Celebrating 7 Million Voices*,[3] thus significantly influencing the results that placed education, healthcare, jobs and responsive government as the four key development priorities.

Transforming Our World: The 2030 Agenda for Sustainable Development[4] recognises the interlinkages between different dimensions of inequality. Mainstreaming marginalised groups, including youth, particularly marginalised youth, then becomes a critical precondition for reaching the goals, because of the SDG aspiration to 'leave no one behind', and because of the principle of universality and of reaching 'the furthest behind first'.[5] The SDGs also help us move beyond addressing the symptoms of poverty to ensuring participatory governance to achieve targets.

The 2030 Agenda also explicitly recognises the role of young men and women as agents of change, and their critical role as those who 'pass on the torch' to future generations in line with the SDGs' main theme of sustainable development.

> ## Box 3.2 Social aspirations go beyond the SDGs
>
> Social aspirations are often expressed in ways that are not measurable through SDG indicators. Some of these aspirations that are relevant to youth and not explicitly stated in the SDGs include ending child labour and undernourishment, ending illiteracy and violence, and expressing access to food and water as a basic human right. Some observations on the SDGs also note the need to better reflect human rights discourses, economic rules that inform equality, roles and responsibilities of rich countries and economic institutions, or discrimination against lesbian, gay, bisexual, queer/questioning and transgender (LGBQT) communities etc.[6]

However, even as we use the SDGs and targets as globally endorsed benchmarks, young people's aspirations often move beyond the SDGs (see Box 3.2), e.g. for education or fulfilling employment. Indeed, in this publication, we will integrate additional transformational paradigms of development that are not explicitly stated in the SDGs and targets.

Having established that, the SDGs are recognised as a significant move in defining and shaping a youth-centric global development agenda in that:

- mainstreaming youth plays a critical role in fully realising the SDGs;

- reaching the SDGs is of critical importance to young people's wellbeing and rights; and

- young people have also played a significant participatory role in shaping the SDGs to ensure their relevance to them.

This publication itself will utilise the SDGs as a benchmark in:

- defining an integrated vision for holistic youth empowerment and development;

- articulating equitable outcomes; and

- framing the context for case studies of good practice.

Now, we will examine how the SDGs articulate both the outcomes and processes of youth mainstreaming, reflecting elements of Figure 1.1, the youth mainstreaming arrow.

3.2.1 Equality (the outcome of mainstreaming)

The end-goal of youth mainstreaming is obtaining social equality for youth in relation to adults, as defined in the YM definition above. The SDGs made a landmark conceptual turn from a narrower lens of poverty alleviation in the MDGs to one that addresses the distribution of wealth and development outcomes, as indicated in Goal 10: Reducing Inequality Within and Among Countries. Equitable outcomes for all are specifically mentioned in Target 10.2, which calls to 'Empower and promote the social, economic and political inclusion of all' including for all ages. This focus on the generational imperative is significant.

The goal refers both to income equality and equality of development outcomes through health, education, justice and so on, for all people. Target 10.3 says 'Ensure equal opportunity and reduce inequalities of outcome, including by eliminating discriminatory laws, policies and practices and promoting appropriate legislation, policies and action in this regard' to achieve equality. Targets also call for striving for 'fiscal, wage and social protection policies' that contribute to social equality within and among nations. The commitment of the SDGs to 'leave no one behind' also highlights the interconnectedness of all SDGs to components of inequality (see Table 3.1).

All national development outcomes reported against the attainment of the SDGS will, therefore, be assessed for reaching the equality goal as much as growth goals.

3.2.2 Youth-centric institutions and planning (process 1 for youth mainstreaming)

Accountable, transparent and inclusive institutions and planning processes play a key role in facilitating youth-centric planning, and therefore contributing to youth mainstreaming. The SDGs clearly recognise this role of institutions, best articulated in Goal 16: Peace, Justice and Strong Institutions. Targets 16.6 (effective, accountable and transparent institutions), 16.7 (responsive, inclusive, participatory and representative decision-making), 16.10 (public access to information and fundamental freedoms)[10] and 16b (non-discriminatory laws and policies) are of particular importance (see Box 3.3). This institutional strengthening needs to be reflected in all legislative and policy processes and sectors in the implementation of all 17 SDGs.

> **Box 3.3 Articulations of youth mainstreaming in SDG indicator drafts**
>
> An earlier version of proposed indicators for Goal 16 on participatory decision-making proposed the following as an indicator: 'Proportion of countries that address young peoples' multi-sectoral needs within their national development plans and poverty reduction strategies'.[7] Even though this did not reach the final endorsed indicator list, this establishes the primacy of institutional strengthening for youth mainstreaming.

3.2.3 Youth participation (process 2 for mainstreaming)

Youth participation is the second critical process element for youth mainstreaming.

SDG Target 16.7 (responsive, inclusive, participatory and representative decision-making) has implications for the participation of all, and by inference youth, in decision-making that affects their life and society.

SDG Target 4.7 of Goal 4, Quality Education, reflects institutional roles in catalysing young people's social, political and economic empowerment (see Annex 2) and, therefore, their citizenship role, by supporting the creation of 'knowledge and skills needed to promote sustainable development, including, among others, through education for sustainable development and sustainable lifestyles, human rights, gender equality, promotion of a culture of peace and non-violence, global citizenship and appreciation of cultural diversity and of culture's contribution to sustainable development', in this case, for young people. This educative role is central to young people's ability to participate in the life of society.

So, in brief:

- all development goals have an impact on young people, even though only some explicitly mention youth;

- the SDGs will inform our discussions, as they are a framework which many young people have signed up to; but also

- youth may choose to go beyond the goals in terms of addressing injustice and inequality.

3.3 The Equality Matrix for Youth: Expanding SDG 10 targets

What is this social equality we are trying to achieve for youth? How do we express it in quantitative and qualitative ways? How do we integrate a youth lens to policy and planning processes that may not otherwise incorporate this lens? This discussion becomes important so that we constantly remember to what end we are transforming our institutions.

In Table 3.1, the Equality Matrix for Youth, we:

- Examine the most relevant targets of SDG 10: Reducing Inequality as a goal that best expresses what we are trying to achieve through youth mainstreaming across all goals.

- Examine the broad range of variables the goal addresses beyond traditional measures of income equality. It includes social, political and economic inclusion, fiscal and wage equality, social protection equality and a range of other determiners of social equality which are integral to youth empowerment.

- Align SDG 10 targets to the other 16 SDGs to demonstrate the comprehensive way in which the targets help us articulate social, political and economic equality for youth.

- Examine the greater benefits to governments and other stakeholders of youth-mainstreamed approaches to reaching development and social cohesion targets,

- Consider key implications for youth mainstreaming for each Goal 10 target in a broader sense.

- Highlight the centrality of partnerships for reaching all SDGs.

- Encourage discussion around the linkages of the SDGs and human rights frameworks.

3.4 Goal 16 and institutions for youth

Goal 16 provides a framework for strengthening youth mainstreaming through institutional processes across all 17 SDGs. Table 3.2 illustrates the implications for youth mainstreaming for the most relevant targets.

Table 3.1 The Equality Matrix for Youth (SDG 10: *Reduce Inequality*, its targets and its relationship to other SDGs)

Equality goal targets + related SDGs	Benefits of youth mainstreaming	Some implications for youth mainstreaming[8]
		17: Partnerships in all sectors for youth development/empowerment, youth data and budgets, youth participation, youth safeguarding
10.1: By 2030, progressively achieve and sustain income growth of the bottom 40 per cent of the population at a rate higher than the national average:		
a) Faster income growth for the poorest [also for youth] 1: No Poverty, 2: Zero Hunger, 6: Clean Water and Sanitation, 7: Affordable and Clean Energy, 12: Responsible Consumption and Production.	1: Helps to efficiently reach poverty reduction goals by addressing specific needs of youth groups 2: Creates efficiency and reduces burden on social welfare programmes 3: Demonstrates practised state commitments to social equality 4: Reduces youth discontent and disillusionment and therefore creates greater collaboration and social cohesion	Are the concerns and rights of young people in the bottom 40 per cent integrated into planning for income growth? Are these poorest youth groups able to influence policy? How advanced is life-cycle poverty analysis etc. that enables the analysis of intergenerational poverty so as to meet the interests of young people in the bottom 40 per cent?
10.2: By 2030, empower and promote the social, economic and political inclusion of all, irrespective of age, sex, disability, race, ethnicity, origin, religion or economic or other status. Target broken down:		
a) Social inclusion [including for youth] 3: Good Health and Wellbeing, 4: Quality Education, 5: Gender Equality, 11: Sustainable Cities and Communities.	1: Helps greater access of young people to public services 2: Helps make public services more relevant and responsive to all service receivers, including youth, and therefore more efficient, both financially and socially 3: Builds trust of youth in government and greater collaborative engagement 4: Creates a healthy, educated population 5: Reduces youth discontent and disillusionment and therefore creates greater collaboration and social cohesion	How is young people's social inclusion factored into planning for health, education, gender and the creation of cities and communities? Are young people, and young service users, more specifically, able to influence decisions in these places, particularly the most marginalised young people? Are they able to obtain affordable, accessible services with dignity and safety/confidentiality? Are young women's voices heard and respected within these spaces; are their concerns considered? Are young people able to influence the planning of cities and communities so that their needs are addressed in urban and community planning?

(Continued)

Table 3.1 The Equality Matrix for Youth (SDG 10: *Reduce Inequality*, its targets and its relationship to other SDGs) (cont.)

Equality goal targets + related SDGs	Benefits of youth mainstreaming	Some implications for youth mainstreaming[8]
		17: Partnerships in all sectors for youth development/empowerment, youth data and budgets, youth participation, youth safeguarding
b) Economic inclusion [Including for youth] 8: Decent Work and Economic Growth, 9: Industry, Innovation and Infrastructure.	1: Higher levels of youth employment and better working conditions irrespective of age 2: Builds trust of youth in government and greater collaborative engagement 3: Reduced youth discontent and disillusionment and therefore greater social cohesion 4: Enhances investments and wealth	Are young people's location in transition from education to employment, their role in beginning new families etc. factored into employment policies? Are young people able to participate as equals in trade unions, professional bodies and other bodies representing the interests of working people? Is industry, innovation and infrastructure focusing on young people's interests, including acknowledging young people's role in innovation?
c) Political inclusion [including for youth] 13: Climate Action, 16: Peace, Justice and Strong Institutions.	1: Greater meaningful youth participation in governance and electoral politics creates more relevant, responsive and efficient programmes for young people and for all 2: Potential financial and human resource savings due to focused, relevant programming 3: Governments demonstrate practised commitments to participatory decision-making and collaborative planning that help reach targets in Goal 16	Do young people have formal mechanisms within which to participate in decision-making in all development institutions and political institutions? Are young people adequately represented in party politics to represent youth and other interests and transform party political cultures? Where this is not the case, are affirmative action laws in place?

		17: Partnerships in all sectors for youth development/ empowerment, youth data and budgets, youth participation, youth safeguarding
10.3: Ensure equal opportunity and reduce inequalities of outcome, including by eliminating discriminatory laws, policies and practices and promoting appropriate legislation, policies and action in this regard:		
a) Equal opportunity/ equality of outcome [including for youth] Goal 5: Gender Equality.	1: Equal development outcomes for youth benefit all of society 2: Enables young people to be equal partners in social development 3: Builds a strong, cohesive society	Do social inclusion practices in 10.2 above result in equal opportunity and reduced inequality of outcomes for youth in all spheres, including education, healthcare, housing, justice, urban planning and so on? How is this measured?
b) Non-discriminatory laws, policies and practices [including for youth] 16: Peace, Justice and Strong Institutions.	1: Justice system supports reaching Goal 10, including for youth, ensuring equal justice for all 2: Executive commitments to equality and justice supports equality measures for youth and leads to social equality 3: Governments demonstrate transparency and accountability, thus building bridges and trust with youth 4: Provides foundational support for reaching equality	Are state institutions and all stakeholders accountable to young people? Is there sufficient assessment of laws, policies and practices for discrimination against young people, and sufficient movement towards creating enabling legislation, policy and practice for young people, with the participation of young people in all sectors and institutional settings? Which laws, policies and practices explicitly discriminate against youth? Is there adequate voice and influence around changing these?
10.4: Adopt policies, especially fiscal, wage and social protection policies, and progressively achieve greater equality:		
a) Fiscal policies [that favour youth] 16: Peace, Justice and Strong Institutions.	1: Contributes to greater transparency and accountability of financial institutions to youth 2: A youth lens helps to direct investments that result from good fiscal policy to where they are most required for young people, efficiently and effectively	Are there adequate measures in place to ensure fair fiscal policies and their transparent implementation? Are there progressive taxation regimes, whose returns are used to support programmes for equity, including for young people? Are the absence of equitable fiscal policies and lack of fiscal transparency affecting investment in young people in specific ways? If so, how? How are transnational capital flows regulated to ensure equity and justice?

(Continued)

Table 3.1 The Equality Matrix for Youth (SDG 10: *Reduce Inequality*, its targets and its relationship to other SDGs) (*cont.*)

Equality goal targets + related SDGs	Benefits of youth mainstreaming	Some implications for youth mainstreaming[8]
		17: Partnerships in all sectors for youth development/empowerment, youth data and budgets, youth participation, youth safeguarding
b) Wage policies [that support youth] 1: No Poverty, 5: Gender Equality, 16: Peace, Justice and Strong Institutions.	1: Provides decent employment opportunities for youth 2: A more content and productive youth workforce 3: Greater national productivity	Are wage policies fair to young people? If not, what is being done? How are young people involved in consultative processes that help create fair wage policies for all? Are young women specifically affected by unfair wage policies? How does this influence them?
c) Social protection policies [including for youth] 1: No Poverty, 3: Good Health and Wellbeing, 4: Quality Education, 5: Gender Equality, 16: Peace, Justice and Strong Institutions.	1: Reduces cyclical intergenerational poverty 2: Ensures equitable distribution of services and lowers social conflicts 3: Increases trust in government 4: Creates a content, collaborative youth population	Are social protection policies adequate, and are they adequately funded? Does the lack of funding for social protection affect young people in specific ways? Are young people actively involved, through formal structures, in influencing fair and equitable distribution of social protection benefits, as well as in dialogue to enhance investment in social protection? How are specific groups of young people such as women, ethnic and sexual minorities, young people living with disabilities, and so on, affected by social protection policies, or lack thereof?

A similar youth mainstreaming lens can be applied to 10.6: Voice of developing countries in decisions of economic and financial institutions; 10.7: Migration and mobility; 10a: Differential treatment for developing countries; and 10b: Official development assistance and financial flows to states with the greatest needs, all of which require the incorporation of youth rights and will indeed benefit from it. Similarly, the 11 official UN indicators ascribed to Goal 10 can be measured for young people as well (see United Nations, Sustainable Development Knowledge Platform, SDG 10 available at: https://sustainabledevelopment.un.org/sdg10).[9]

Table 3.2 SDG 16 and youth mainstreaming

Goal 16: Peace, Justice and Strong Institutions (youth mainstreaming process)	
Focus here: Accountable and inclusive institutions at all levels	
Selected targets	Implications for youth mainstreaming in all 17 goals
16.6: Develop effective, accountable and transparent institutions at all levels	Are there institutional policy guarantees for accountability and transparency to youth? Are institutions accountable to young people in responding to their aspirations and rights? Are there mechanisms in place to ensure transparency and communication with young people?
16.7: Ensure responsive, inclusive, participatory and representative decision-making at all levels	Does policy require public and youth consultations in decision-making? Are representative groups of young people involved in institutional decision-making at all levels? Are they able to **influence** decisions?
16.10: Ensure public access to information and protect fundamental freedoms, in accordance with national legislation and international agreements	Are there constitutional and structural gaurantees that ensure public access to information for youth in youth-friendly formats? Do young people have access to public information, including on access to public services, in youth-friendly forms? Are their fundamental freedoms to express opinions and participate in public life safegaurded?
16.b: Promote and enforce non-discriminatory laws and policies for sustainable development	Are laws and policies in place to ensure intergenerational equality with a specific focus on intergeneraltional equality for marginalised youth groups?

3.5 The Youth Development Index (YDI)

The Youth Development Index (YDI), developed by the Commonwealth, is a composite index of 18 indicators[11] that collectively measure progress on youth development through the five domains of education, health and wellbeing, employment and opportunity, political participation and civic participation. It compiles available global youth-related datasets to form an assessment of relative achievements across countries. The 2016 *Global Youth Development Index and Report*[12] measured progress in youth development for 183 countries, including 49 of the 53 member countries at the time of the report.[13] The YDI supports the disaggregation of data for youth in working towards reaching SDG targets and goals, and will be a useful tool at the national level for measuring the social equality of young people. Just as the gender equality goals

Box 3.4 Reflections on Chapter 3: The Sustainable Development Goals and Youth Mainstreaming

- In your context, have the SDGs been incorporated as a tool for national and subnational development strategies?
- How effective are the SDGs in helping us mainstream youth in planning, and in measuring changes for youth and everyone?
- Which human rights instruments/articles best reflect SDG targets and goals that you work with?
- How do young people's aspirations go beyond the SDGs' targets and indicators in your contexts?
- How can the YDI be used to measure/demonstrate equity/ equality for young people?

and targets in the SDGs help measure the ultimate outcomes for gender mainstreaming, the YDI will be a support in measuring equality for youth.

3.6 Conclusion

The Sustainable Development Goals are an important, though incomplete, reference point for the articulation, implementation and evaluation of youth mainstreaming, particularly their recognition of the importance of reducing inequality, which underpins the vision of mainstreaming. The SDGs can be complemented by the Youth Development Index (YDI) in examining outcomes for youth, given its focus on youth development.

Notes

1   Commonwealth Secretariat 2017, 17.
2   See Chapter 2: Why Youth Mainstreaming?
3   United Nations 2015c.
4   United Nations 2015b.
5   United Nations 2015a, 1 and 3.
6   For example, see Sengupta 2016.
7   UNDP/PRIO 2016, 8: Targets 16.1 on Peace, 16.3 on Justice, 16.7 on Inclusion and 16.10 on Freedoms.
8   These example implications involve multiple dimensions of social change, as reflected by youth aspirations that may go beyond those implied by the SDG indicators for these targets.
9   United Nations 2015c.
10 Plan et al. 2016 addresses youth-inclusive indicators for Targets 16.6, 16.7 and 16.10.

11 See the Equality Matrix for Youth, Table 3.1.
12 Commonwealth Secretariat 2016.
13 The number of Commonwealth member countries was 52 at the time of writing.

References

Commonwealth Secretariat (2016), *Global Youth Development Index and Report*, Commonwealth Secretariat, London.

Plan, Restless Development, Children's Environments Research Group, Queen's University and UNDP (2016), *Critical Agents of Change in the 2030 Agenda: Youth-Inclusive Governance Indicators for National-Level Monitoring*.

Sengupta, M. (2016), 'The Sustainable Development Goals: An Assessment of Ambition', available at: http://www.e-ir.info/2016/01/18/the-sustainable-development-goals-an-assessment-of-ambition/

UNDP/PRIO (2016), Expert Meeting on Measuring SDG 16, Report, Oslo, 28–29 January 2016, Voksenåsen Conference Centre, Oslo, Norway.

United Nations (2015a), *My World Survey*, available at: http://data.myworld2015.org/

United Nations (2015b), *Transforming Our World: The 2030 Agenda for Sustainable Development*, UN Resolution of the General Assembly, A/RES/70/1, United Nations, New York.

United Nations (2015c), *We the Peoples: Celebrating Seven Million Voices*, available at: https://myworld2015.files.wordpress.com/2014/12/wethepeoples-7million.pdf

3

Chapter 4
The Youth Mainstreaming Enablers Framework

This chapter:

- introduces the Youth Mainstreaming Enablers Framework, which helps us contextualise youth mainstreaming in the specific policy and institutional contexts we work in

- provides a concrete analysis of a context in education that enables discussion of the framework in a real-life setting.

4.1 Introducing the Youth Mainstreaming Enablers Framework

Outcomes for young people's wellbeing and rights are determined by enablers at several levels. Youth mainstreaming, in other words, occurs not in a vacuum, but within societal, institutional, policy and legal contexts that are relevant internationally and nationally. The commitments to structural transformation and partnerships for change addressed in *Agenda 2030*[1] need critical analysis of this big picture, along with pragmatic action.

Figure 4.1 (hereafter called 'the Enablers Framework') looks at some key enablers for youth mainstreaming. It helps us approach youth mainstreaming holistically in the context of societal (cultural norms), structural (formal/institutional) and organisational contexts. This discussion will help policy-makers situate youth mainstreaming in their respective contexts, including designing realistic plans for YM. This is elaborated on in Box 4.1.

In terms of our 'control' of the factors indicated in Figure 4.1, we would have greater control over organisational enablers than structural enablers. However, where structural enablers do not exist, or are not optimal, we can identify areas for long-term research and advocacy to influence donors and international banks, international conventions and legislation, and so on.

Box 4.1 Societal, structural and organisational enablers for YM

Societal factors: Social norms influence our engagement with youth, including all subgroups. What is their status in society? Are they seen as equal partners in the private and public domains?

Structural (macro) factors: Global to subnational social and economic policy systems/enablers influence organisational ability to implement youth mainstreaming effectively. This includes the way in which aspirational goals set by human rights conventions are translated (or not) into policy and programmes, or the broader way in which government and governance, including legislation and donor policy, are organised globally, nationally and locally.

Structural (meso) factors: This involves the more specific pre-planning political and investment commitments to youth mainstreaming, in terms of the direction of political will and public/donor spending towards youth mainstreaming, and a strong and facilitative youth sector.

Organisational factors: Youth-friendly, democratic organisational structures and processes are critical for effective youth mainstreaming. This enabler refers to these characteristics.

Box 4.2 How youth mainstreaming enablers/disablers influence the right to education

What are the enablers that influence 'mainstreaming youth' in an already predominantly 'youth-serving' sector such as secondary and tertiary education within the context of prevailing education and economic models? What are the societal, macro (global/national) policy and institutional imperatives that determine youth-centric education planning?

Recent developments throughout the world, in both the global North and South, have seen tensions between youth aspirations and education planning.[2] Cuts in spending for public education, for example, have meant that the lives of poorer and marginalised young people growing up now are far less hopeful than those who grew up ten years ago in terms of social and education mobility – be it in the developed or the developing world, with shortfalls even greater for developing world youth. This situation places considerable strain on achieving the aspirational goal of a right to education, as set out in the UDHR and UNCRC, and reaching SDG targets on education.

In some countries, where university tuition fees have increased dramatically and student loan facilities have been either scrapped or reduced, lower middle-class and poor students are finding it increasingly difficult to achieve their academic aspirations.

Student movements globally have highlighted the effects of the increased education cost burden placed on young people, and all young people's right to accessible education, including calls for racial and economic equality. Such

(Continued)

Box 4.2 How youth mainstreaming enablers/disablers influence the right to education (*cont.*)

movements often ask for an expenditure floor for education spending and accessible education as a human right. Often, student movements in one country have affected the growth of movements in others.

This lobby has also been prominent in countries that have exemplary, free tertiary education programmes, which are in danger of erosion in the long term because of policies that favour diversifying education providers beyond state providers, often without sufficient regulatory mechanisms for quality and cost.

In all these circumstances, while short-term measures have been put in place to redress the effects of spending cuts on young people themselves, successes have been limited. This is because of inadequate collaborative dialogue and political commitments, but also the broader economic, political and financing models which shape these policies, and which are often beyond the control of single governments. Meanwhile, in the context of rising income inequalities throughout the world, more and more young people are caught up in poverty and are unable to meet the financial demands of education – now increasingly transferred to families.

Analysis through the lens of the Enablers Framework, inequality and youth empowerment, shows us that:

- Increasing pressures on governments to cut public spending (macro-policy – global)
- Result in cuts in the most vital sectors such as education (macro-policy – national)
- Therefore affecting poorer and marginalised young people's right to education (access to services)
- In this way exacerbating social inequality based on race, class and so on (inequity)
- Resulting in student action (youth participation)
- Which, in turn, often creates tensions between education institutions and students, and violent backlashes by police and universities (negative organisational response)
- Along with negative attitudes towards young people's agency and participative actions by society (intergenerational attitudes and class relations)
- And the labelling of young people as those 'wanting everything for free' (a deficit lens), without a full comprehension of the context of their aspirations, life challenges and frustrations

Such analysis can provide indications of where financial, institutional, social, political and economic barriers or enablers of education attainment can be identified and addressed.[3] It particularly highlights the need to work with young people as partners in education planning; to ensure co-operation and shared decision-making between students and education decision-makers in both the public and private sectors; to protect the vision of Education for All; and to deliver optimally for youth.

Figure 4.1 The Youth Mainstreaming Enablers Framework

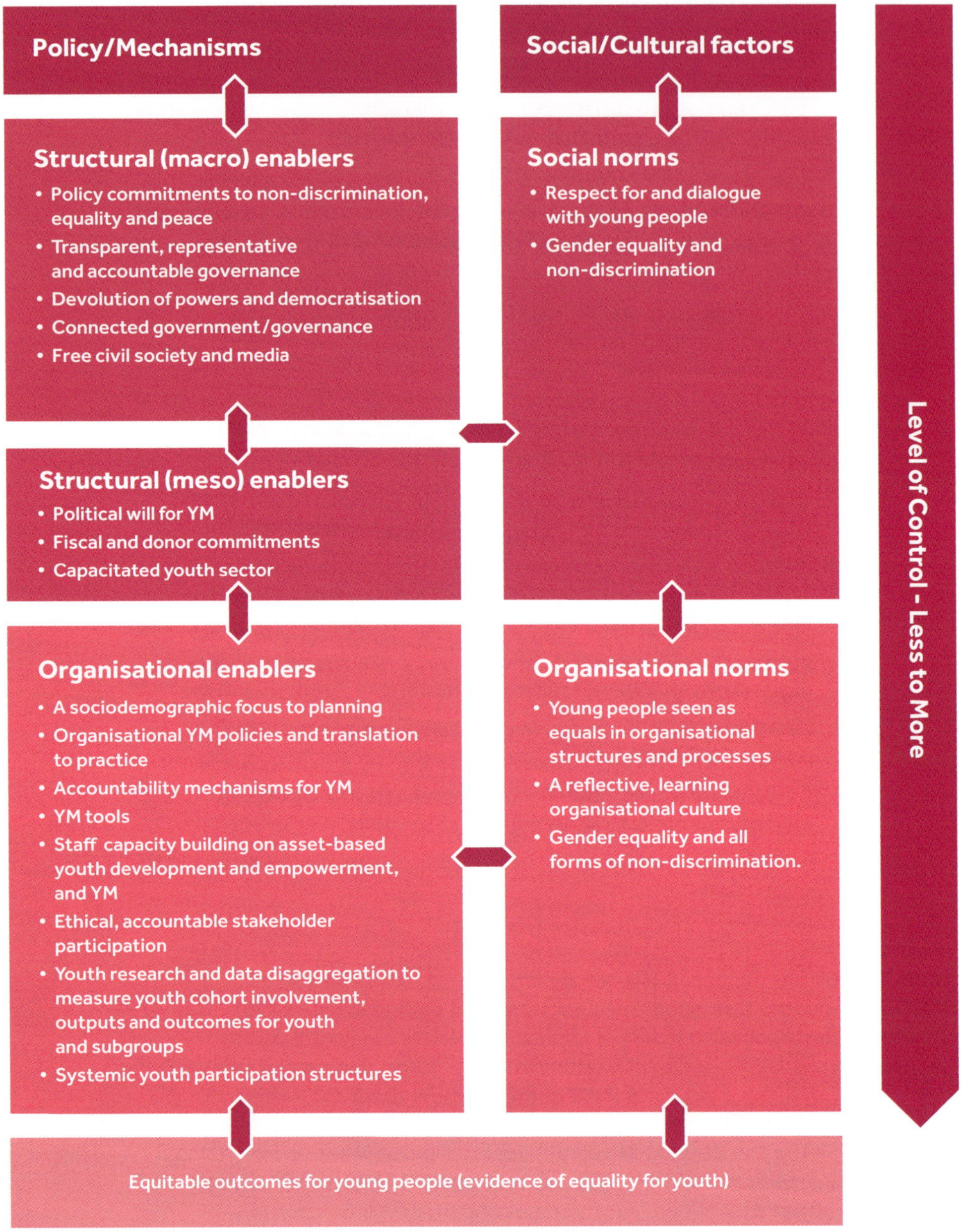

Policy/Mechanisms

Structural (macro) enablers
- Policy commitments to non-discrimination, equality and peace
- Transparent, representative and accountable governance
- Devolution of powers and democratisation
- Connected government/governance
- Free civil society and media

Structural (meso) enablers
- Political will for YM
- Fiscal and donor commitments
- Capacitated youth sector

Organisational enablers
- A sociodemographic focus to planning
- Organisational YM policies and translation to practice
- Accountability mechanisms for YM
- YM tools
- Staff capacity building on asset-based youth development and empowerment, and YM
- Ethical, accountable stakeholder participation
- Youth research and data disaggregation to measure youth cohort involvement, outputs and outcomes for youth and subgroups
- Systemic youth participation structures

Social/Cultural factors

Social norms
- Respect for and dialogue with young people
- Gender equality and non-discrimination

Organisational norms
- Young people seen as equals in organisational structures and processes
- A reflective, learning organisational culture
- Gender equality and all forms of non-discrimination.

Level of Control – Less to More

Equitable outcomes for young people (evidence of equality for youth)

This indicates that YM is gradual and ever-changing, and can build on strengths across time; it can in fact change face during different social, political and economic cycles of a nation/the world. YM, in other words, never 'works itself out of a job'.

Box 4.2 examines the implications of such a framework for a real-life example of young people's right to education.

Box 4.3 Reflections on Chapter 4: The Youth Mainstreaming Enablers Framework

- What are the enabling factors in your context for YM at the societal, structural and organisational levels?
- What are the challenges to effective youth mainstreaming and how can these be overcome?
- What are the short-term, medium-term and long-term actions required?

4.2 Conclusions

Before beginning a youth mainstreaming process in your country, it is important to assess how realistic your YM plans are by examining the context in which you operate. The Enablers Framework will help you do this.

Notes

1   United Nations 2015.
2   See, for example, Giroux 2014.
3   See also Thorat 2011.

References

Giroux, HA. (2014), *Neo-Liberalism's War on Higher Education*, Haymarket Books, Chicago.

Thorat, A. (2011), 'Private Education for the Poor in India', *Commonwealth Education Partnerships 2011/12*, Nexus Strategic Partnerships, Cambridge, 24–26.

United Nations (2015), *Transforming Our World: The 2030 Agenda for Sustainable Development*, UN Resolution of the General Assembly, A/RES/70/1, United Nations, New York.

Chapter 5
Policy Processes and Youth

_____

This chapter:

- examines how youth mainstreaming is not just about integrating a youth lens in a specific sector, but how it is also about understanding the interconnectedness between different policy domains, and broadly acknowledging the importance of considering sociodemographic factors in planning

- illustrates how these interlinkages have implications for the way we plan in a co-ordinated manner for youth.

5.1 Policy connectedness

The aspirations and frameworks discussed above ultimately translate into policies that inform our delivery for young people. Youth mainstreaming is not just about factoring youth capacities and interests into planning *within* a sector, but understanding how policies *across* sectors have an influence on each other, and can either strengthen or weaken other areas of policy/young people's realities.

Policies have differential impacts for young people, just as for other marginalised groups. YM policy and practice is also influenced by power, influence, interests, sensitivity in general to issues of social/demographic groups, and decision-maker/administrator relationships. This understanding becomes critical when planning across sectors and creating cross-sectoral dialogue.

5.2 Policies can affect young people differently

Policies can affect different social groups, including youth, in different ways. If these social groups are not specifically factored into the analysis, design and implementation of the policy, this differential impact will be a negative one; for example, young people form a disproportionate section of those globally unemployed. This is because the design of employment policies

Box 5.1 Housing policy and young people

The undersupply [of housing in the UK] is affecting the way young people experience the housing market in a series of real and significant ways, with knock-on consequences for their everyday lives and future aspirations ... [A]s homeownership and social housing move further out of reach for all but the richest and poorest respectively, young people are becoming more and more reliant on the private rented sector ... [T]hese experiences also impact on young people's sense of control and independence, their safety and security, their ability to build relationships and start a family, and their chance to put down roots and become part of a community.

– Institute for Public Policy Research 2012

has not adequately considered the voices and concerns of young people. See Box 5.1 for an example for housing policy.

5.3 Mainstreaming processes succeeds where all marginalised groups are considered

Youth mainstreaming is unlikely to be a standalone 'youth' lens where other social, political and economic marginalities are not considered. The success of YM will depend on capacities of policy-makers and planners to recognise the needs of different social/demographic groups. Where, for example, gender equity and other forms of equity for demographic and social groups/issues are not built into planning, it is unlikely that equity for youth will be built in.

5.4 Each policy outcome requires a range of players

Engaging in cross-sectoral work means looking at not only youth mainstreaming within a sector, but how your policy initiative will benefit from formal partnerships with other sectors.

For example, a range of policies will affect young people's access to affordable reproductive healthcare: ministries/departments with planning and finance portfolios would play a role in ensuring greater financing for the health sector's youth services; the education sector would educate young people on access to healthcare; community health groups would ensure outreach around preventative healthcare; and health services would provide the actual health support, minimised by the preventative actions of other sectors. This implies a co-ordinated approach to policy development, where policy initiatives related to the above are discussed, designed and implemented concurrently across sectors.

Youth mainstreaming, then, will mean adopting a youth lens in cross-sectoral policy co-ordination. In this way, the boundaries of policy areas often become blurred and cross-sectoral collaboration becomes inevitable.[1]

5.5 Each policy decision has impacts across policy domains

One policy decision in Sector A can create intended or unintended, negative or positive, outcomes in Sector B. For example, school expulsion policies can negatively affect youth crime,[2] as, being out of school, young people may be vulnerable to delinquency in contexts of poverty and other forms of structural deprivation. This, in turn, could influence expenditure and responses to youth crime in the criminal justice sector. It also raises the question of the basis of school expulsions, the devising of youth-friendly positive disciplining as opposed to 'punishment' in education contexts, and the need for young people's participation in decision-making within education settings; this would, in turn, positively affect both the education and justice sectors in reducing burdens on systems.

We will take another example from Country Y of a policy that was seemingly meant to benefit children in early childhood, but would have, if implemented, affected the autonomy of young mothers. This was the case of proposals in some countries with high female labour migration to restrict (mostly young) women's employment abroad if their children were below a certain age. It was indeed well-intentioned and meant to benefit very young children. However, women's rights groups pointed out how this also meant constraining women's economic choice and creating cyclical poverty in poor families, affecting children even more and affecting young mothers differentially. It then raises the question of how childcare is socially perceived, which gender norms inform policies and how these affect mostly young mothers; it also highlights the need for more gender- *and* youth-sensitive approaches to aspects of childcare provision.

5.6　Young people's interests may conflict with the interests of the status quo

In orthodox development environments, the interests of youth may be at odds with the interests of the status quo. Young people's movements, which should be at the centre of a youth-mainstreamed approach, have often disagreed with received development paradigms on education, health, social safety nets etc. and their concerns often go unconsidered in policy – as demonstrated in examples in this publication.

5.7　No policy is neutral to young people

Every public policy can have an impact on young people, including defence, social, fiscal and economic policies. For example, policies that prioritise high defence spending may result in funds being displaced from education and health, affecting social development outcomes for youth. A comprehensive youth mainstreaming approach requires that nodal youth agencies and all sectors can scrutinise and review each global, regional, national and sub-national to local policy proposal, as relevant, for its potential impact on young people, and ensure that evaluations assess the actual impact.

5.8　The policy process is not linear

We cannot assume undisrupted links from policy design to implementation. Often, those who design policies are removed several steps from those who implement them. In any mainstreaming process, it is critical to link policy-making processes to mid-level and field personnel, including young professionals, to ensure their ownership and during implementation. This applies both ways, as local government officers have much experience and knowledge to contribute to the design process. If we are to motivate middle-level managers and young professionals to carry out policy visions, then they must be involved in the entire process, not just the implementation stage.

Similarly, contexts in which policies were first designed may change during the implementation phase, and people and institutions that were at one point the champions of a policy may fade into the background with changing political regimes and power structures. The challenge is then establishing sustained links between the less transmutable elements in a process, i.e. civil society processes or relationships with longer-term administrative personnel, to ensure continuity.

5.9 Political economy defines policy decisions

The links between policy design, implementation and achieving outcomes are fraught with complexity and layers of explicit and hidden motivations. What incentives, restrictions and rules[3] do legislators, policy-makers and administrators have as they embark on their respective policy work? What motivates them? How do they balance job security, power dynamics and relationships as they work towards policy goals? These political economy considerations are integral to succeeding in youth mainstreaming.

5.10 Conclusions and reflections

Policy processes are complex and interrelated. An important step in youth mainstreaming is one that looks outward at the connectedness of one policy to others and to young people. We can no longer see ourselves as a single sector that only connects to other sectors for specific programmes, but as a sector that connects and collaborates meaningfully across all sectors, holistically and strategically, and in the long term.

Box 5.2 Reflections on Chapter 5: Policy Processes and Youth

- Does policy planning and implementation in your context consider interactions across sectors in planning in relation to outcomes for youth?
- What kind of dialogue does policy planning/implementation facilitate across sectors?
- Is this inter-sectoral interaction formalised through planning guidelines?
- What challenges and benefits exist in taking on this approach?

Notes

1   Cairney 2012, 97.
2   Ibid, 30.
3   See, for example, Hudson and Leftwich 2014 and UNDP 2012.

References

Cairney, P (2012), *Understanding Public Policy*, Palgrave Macmillan, Hampshire.

Hudson, D and A, Leftwich (2014), *From Political Economy to Political Analysis*, Development Leadership Programme, Birmingham.

Institute for Public Policy Research (2012), *No Place to Call Home*, IPPR, United Kingdom.

UNDP (2012), *Institutional and Context Analysis Guidance Note*, Oslo Governance Centre.

Chapter 6
The Role of the Youth Sector

This chapter helps us discuss:

- the role of the youth sector as advocates for, and technical experts in, youth mainstreaming

- the youth sector as a consolidation of different players with different kinds of youth expertise

- different analytical lenses that help us evaluate the youth sector in our contexts

- the specific youth empowerment paradigms the youth sector helps integrate into youth mainstreaming.

6.1 What is the youth sector?

The youth sector comprises the multiple players that focus on youth equality and empowerment as their main institutional focus. The sector's role is central to rationalising and providing technical support for youth mainstreaming. The more the sector forms a unified and collaborative identity among all players within the sector, and articulates a co-ordinated vision and strategy among its players, the stronger its influence on other sectors. A youth sector in a member country may comprise players such as those set out in Box 6.1.

6.2 Engaging with national development planning

For the youth sector to successfully mainstream youth:

- the above players need to be well-co-ordinated and should play a critical role in influencing national development agendas and frameworks; and

- the sector should drive the need for a youth lens in every aspect of national planning, including assessing the perceived and real impact of policies and programmes on young people.

A considerable number of Commonwealth member countries have some, but not all, of the entities listed in Box 6.1 generally

Box 6.1 Players in the Youth Sector

Government ministry/department for youth at the national and local levels
Generally, the state policy arm for youth.

Government youth service implementing bodies
These implement youth ministry/department policies for youth services and other related matters, including collaboration with other sectors.

Youth-led organisations
Often independent and sometimes served by umbrella bodies, youth-led organisations deliver youth programmes and advocacy driven strongly by youth interests.

Youth movements, including students' unions
These differ from youth-led organisations in being relatively more independent of institutional affiliations and more informal in structure. In education contexts, such bodies could be student unions. They often tend to be issue-focused.

Youth-serving non-governmental and voluntary bodies
These deliver youth programmes.

Youth studies and youth-work studies delivery departments in universities, colleges and training bodies
These deliver training and education for youth empowerment and youth work.

Youth research institutes
Such bodies may co-ordinate with the youth ministry and other youth sector bodies for research relating to youth development and empowerment.

Youth workers' associations and other professional bodies in the youth sector
These are the guardians of quality and integrity in the youth sector, including youth work. They often regulate youth work practice and youth sector management.

making up the youth sector; these are at different stages of evolution. Often, the central nodal point is the youth ministry or a government youth department.

Engaging with national planning processes and ensuring policy alignment require advocacy and technical inputs to youth mainstreaming:

- **advocacy inputs** may include obtaining political will for YM, and gathering evidence of the financial and efficiency benefits of existing youth mainstreaming initiatives to demonstrate the viability of youth mainstreaming on a broader scale; while

- **technical inputs** would include the provision of youth empowerment knowledge and training to all sectors, including youth mainstreaming in sector planning and supporting sectoral assessment of youth-specific dimensions.

6.3 Youth sector preparedness for influence

It has often been noted how the youth sector tends to be 'squeezed out' in dialogue and deliberation around broad development issues. Players in the youth sector have observed how 'youth' as a distinctive cohort, and youth development as a concept, are 'often subordinated to other agendas *unless* it was in relation to specific problems such as drop-out from education, unemployment, substance misuse or crime'[1] with many seeing young people through a deficit lens. Overcoming these challenges and promoting asset-based approaches to engaging with youth, and youth issues, will require several considerations.[2]

6.3.1 What importance does the youth sector have in national development structures?

What level of importance is provided for the sector in national structures? Youth rarely has a ministry or entity of its own, and is more often coupled with sports or skills development. This sometimes, not always, leads to the undermining of the core priorities of youth development work, as articulated in Table 6.1. In other cases, the sector has been put at the very helm of national planning under the stewardship of the Head of Government – where there is either the advantage of receiving strategic and resource priority or the disadvantage of becoming somewhat side lined owing to the multiple priorities of the Head of Government.

Increasingly, in conditions where care economies are underfunded, the youth sector has disappeared from national structures into provincial governance, which again precludes strongly articulated national visions for youth. While the devolution of this authority can result in the design of more relevant and responsive local-level policies, there is nonetheless the danger of an absence of a national direction and vision, causing the watering down of a strongly articulated youth policy and programming.

6.3.2 How strong is the youth sector's leadership?

Leadership is at the core of how an institution is handled, wherever it is located. Does the leadership of the sector have a clear, participatory vision for young people? Does it have the political will to lobby for funds and strengthen human capacity to deliver for youth across sectors?

6.3.3 Is the youth sector's mandate clear and accountable to all?

Does the sector have a clearly articulated vision, mission and policies, particularly in the form of a youth policy that links to and supports youth mainstreaming across sectors? Is the policy implemented, and monitored and evaluated adequately? Are these mandates accountable to all youth groups, including the most marginalised such as young women, poor youth and youth facing discrimination due to caste, sexual orientation, disability or other factors?

6.3.4 How strong and clear are the youth sector's policy positions?

How strong are the sector's policy positions on youth? Are officials able to articulate the sector's position on young people's empowerment, participation, access to health and education, full employment etc. and represent the vision of the institution? Do they have the capacity to intervene in all aspects of policy-making with clear, evidence-based policy articulations that influence its vision, design and implementation for young people in other sectors?

6.3.5 Does the sector support youth participation structures?

Does the nodal body of the sector support structures and processes that mainstream young people in decision-making, such as putting in place national youth councils (NYCs) and youth parliaments, including ensuring their participation in decision making at all levels? How effective are they? Is their independence assured? Is the sector seeking ways to improve these structures?

6.3.6 How well is the government youth sector linked to all youth networks and civil society groups?

Other than its own youth participation structures, is the nodal decision-making body systemically linked to youth networks and civil society groups that represent the legitimate concerns and rights of young people? Is the sector adequately aware that there may be youth interest groups that are not necessarily represented in state-supported youth councils and youth parliaments? Are there effective connections with these alternative voices? Are all genders, races, social and economic classes, and caste groups represented in youth networks? Is there respect for diversity and difference?

6.3.7 How strong is the youth sector's commitment to youth rights?

Is there political commitment to the rights of young people? Is adequate political will generated for meaningful youth empowerment? Is there adequate funding and lobbying for youth budgets in other sectors?

6.4 Functions of the youth sector

The following are some functions of the youth sector that will help put youth development practice at the centre of youth mainstreaming.

1. **Establishing a visible youth agenda**

   An explicit youth agenda, particularly through youth policies co-created with young people, is critical to affirm the youth sector's legitimacy. Youth policies can be an effective indicator of how successful partnerships and collaboration with other sectors have been in developing a truly youth-mainstreamed strategy within the youth sector, as well as how integrated youth mainstreaming is in national development planning, and will in fact work to strengthen youth mainstreaming in all sectors. The youth policy agenda, if disseminated in reader-friendly formats to young people and stakeholders, also allows a shared vision and purpose for youth empowerment. It is important that the youth agenda be monitored.

2. **Linking with civil society groups that support lobbying processes**

Special efforts should be made to link civil society groups to government planning processes in their diversity, as indicated in Chapter 8. This requires going beyond government-led youth groups to integrate youth social movements and unaffiliated youth (see Figures 7.2 and 8.1).

3. **Linking to local government stakeholders**

Ensure bottom-up processes for decision making with local government, as well as top-down processes for information dissemination and consultation.

4. **Ensuring youth services training for officials**

Invest resources in the training of youth sector officials in youth development work; offer financial and non-financial increments for qualifications; and offer youth development capacity building to all sectors.

5. **Developing new initiatives and methodologies to ensure youth mainstreaming in government policy-making processes**

Develop nationally relevant youth mainstreaming policies and strategies to initiate dialogue with all development sectors.

6. **Reviewing proposed legislation, policy and programmes in all appropriate areas to assess the potential impact on young people**

Ideally carried out through the research and policy units of youth ministries/departments or in strong collaboration with research units of other sectors, youth mainstreaming requires a constant eye on emerging policies and programmes in other sectors. Officials should have the capacity to assess the potential and real impact of these policies on young people, in consultation with organised youth groups and other civil society groups.

7. **Advocating for the disaggregation of quantitative data for young people within census boards and all sectors planning for young people**

   The youth sector plays a critical role in working with census departments or equivalent bodies in advocating for and directing technical expertise, to ensure data disaggregation for youth to enable the measurement of outputs and outcomes for youth.

8. **Youth research**

   Evidence is the cornerstone of successful advocacy for, and delivery through, youth mainstreaming. Ideally, the youth sector, perhaps in partnership with other research agencies, should be involved in creating substantive quantitative and qualitative data on young people, and consistently developing new knowledge in the youth sector.

9. **Disseminating good practice**

   Research and policy units should design comprehensive case studies and disseminate good practice on youth mainstreaming, while research and policy units across sectors should work collaboratively to ensure research to support an enabling environment for young people.

6.5 Mainstreaming youth development and youth work approaches

The youth sector must be the champion of youth empowerment practice and ensure that youth empowerment paradigms are integrated into the work of all sectors. It is predominantly, but certainly not exclusively, in the youth sector that expertise in these paradigms will prevail, given the training provided by youth work and youth studies programmes across the world.[12] Table 6.1 elaborates on some youth work approaches adopted by the youth sector to facilitate youth empowerment.

6.6 Conclusion

In an optimally functioning structure, the youth sector will be the driving force determining the vision, strategies and outcomes of youth mainstreaming in all other sectors. This will also include mainstreaming the unique qualities of the

Table 6.1 Integrating youth work approaches to youth mainstreaming

Youth work

Youth work is at the core of youth development practice. The Commonwealth defines youth work as all forms of 'youth engagement approaches that build personal awareness and support the social, political and economic empowerment of young people, delivered through non-formal learning within a matrix of care.'[3]

Attributes of youth work	Implications for multi-sectoral work
Building citizenship (protagonism/agency) and promoting human rights: A key function of youth work is supporting young people to be active as citizens. Citizenship building is 'a dynamic and relational process. It requires a commitment by society to reorder social relationships based on fundamental political values of freedom and democracy. To promote responsible citizenship in a meaningful and durable way, we need to better understand the nature of this social project of citizenisation and why it is often fragile and incomplete'.[4] The agency of citizens is core to human rights principles.	Ensure that young people are perceived and engaged with as citizens in cross-sectoral programme cycles where their agency and influence is respected. Ensure capacity building for young people in building citizenship with inter-sectoral support.
Developing leadership and life skills/employability skills: Youth work supports young people's ability to develop democratic leadership skills and engage with society in non-combative, constructive ways, while achieving the objectives of their own wellbeing. 'Employability skills' are a set of life skills that enhances young people's ability to engage professionally in work life, as well as contribute to, and benefit from, a decent and non-exploitative work environment.[5]	Integrate leadership and life skills work with young people into day-to-day activities with them, as relevant to your sector.
Encouraging associative life: Building connectedness with others helps strengthen team work, build respect for diversity and create social cohesion. It multiplies the effects of young people's influence on communities and society. It also contributes to building democratic leadership skills, as discussed above. Associative life can take place in multiple forms including through youth clubs, youth movements, international youth networks, informal groups and so on.[6]	Support young people to build collective strength. For example, in the employment sector, this could mean creating a supportive environment for young people's groups to address youth-specific employment issues, or strengthening the ability of young people, including young women, to have a voice in mainstream labour collectives.
Social and political education: Youth work helps the education/emancipation of young people (seen as a two-way process between the young person and youth worker, both learning together), including experiential learning through their everyday lives. It also supports young people to understand their individual and collective experiences in terms of the sociopolitical context which they inhabit. This 'educative engagement' with youth workers and their everyday experiences provides valuable life skills. Youth work also involves the 'fostering of critical thinking in young people, who are able to analyse their own social and political context in order to be able to act on them, including analysing class, gender, religion and other identity-related dynamics'.[7]	Support young people to develop and strengthen their social and political knowledge, in order to understand and influence the youth-specific dimensions of multi-sectoral work. For example, in the health sector, how do broader health policies influence their access (or lack thereof) to health, including reproductive healthcare? How do young people engage with these issues?

Creativity and expression/leisure: In the youth sector, enhancing young people's ability to express themselves through creative forms of theatre, the arts, literature and so on is a fundamental part of holistic empowerment. In youth work, leisure activities such as sports or adventure become a 'means' to an end of learning together with youth workers. For example, a football game can be a site where young people learn about leadership, team work and collaboration, as discussed above.

Information sharing: Information is at the core of supporting young people to empower themselves. Meaningful youth participation is not possible without adequate information about services/policies. Youth work ensures that the right kind of updated information is constantly shared with young people in youth-friendly formats and media.

Intercultural learning: Intercultural learning is a fundamental aspect of peace building and developing respect and understanding, and is a major thematic area in youth work, particularly in contexts of ethnic/racial hostilities and armed conflict.

Professional care: Considering young people's evolving capacities, 'professional care' refers to a youth worker's ability to provide detached care to the young men and women he or she engages with. Ways in which a youth worker performs the role of 'professional carer' are complex and dynamic.[8]

Professionalising youth work

A core function, then, of the youth sector is ensuring the professionalisation of youth work, including through the recognition of youth work as a professional category; the formation of professional associations that can define and protect the standards of the profession; setting competency standards, developing qualifications and certification in line with standards;[9] and validation and supervision, as well as embracing a common set of ethical standards.[10] The caveat at the Commonwealth is that professionalisation is strongly linked to values and principles, and a focus on specific forms of rights-based, asset-based and enabling youth work that is endorsed as professional practice.[11]

Encourage young people's creativity, and support leisure activities. For example, in the justice sector, young people in contact with the legal system and in prisons could be involved in creative expression and participation in sport – to facilitate personal growth and minimise future conflict with the law, drug misuse etc.

Ensure that information is shared with young people in youth-friendly formats and processes relevant to your sector. For example, in reproductive health, cater to young people's information needs in ways that are useful and attractive to them.

Look for and remedy intercultural tensions through youth work processes in your areas of work.

Work with the youth sector to integrate youth work and professional care functions for young people where relevant. For example, justice sector, youth in detention.

Higher education and training institutes need to work with the youth sector in identifying professional needs of youth workers and developing responsive training and degree programmes.

All sectors also need to develop an understanding of the value of youth work competencies in sector staff in implementing youth-mainstreamed approaches.

profession of youth work into the work of all sectors. The youth sector's own explicit identity as a consolidation of multiple players, and its ability to work collaboratively with the strengths of each player in the sector, will help the sector contribute to and oversee youth mainstreaming effectively.

Box 6.2 Reflections on Chapter 6: The Role of the Youth Sector

- In your context, is the youth sector well co-ordinated among the players discussed above?
- Which of the above players in the youth sector are active in your context?
- Are they provided with the capacity to support youth mainstreaming across sectors?
- If not, what needs to be done to strengthen the youth sector and its engagement with other sectors?

Notes

1 Council of Europe 2004, 74.
2 Adapted from Rai 2003, 26.
3 This is a revised version of the definition appearing in Commonwealth Youth Programme, Asia Centre 2012, 11. This publication also provides the basic tenets of youth work championed by the Commonwealth.
4 Kymlicka 2013, 92.
5 Nicholls 2012, 14–15: 'Employability skills are different from employment skills which build specific profession-related skills and competencies. Employability, rather than employment training, is usually the focus of youth work. It is useful to remember that, "the purpose of youth work is not to fuel the labour market ... the youth service is not a career service; it is not a direct employer of the young. It does improve employability, however"'.
6 The Commonwealth Secretariat's Commonwealth Youth Council and the Commonwealth Students' Association are two forms of such associative life developed in international youth work. In the youth sector worldwide, youth clubs and youth parliaments are a dominant form of national/local forms of associative life.
7 Commonwealth Youth Programme, Asia Centre 2012, 10.
8 Ibid., 15.
9 See Commonwealth Youth Programme, Caribbean Centre 2012.
10 For more information, see Commonwealth Youth Programme, Asia Centre 2012.
11 See also Ord 2012.
12 The Commonwealth Diploma in Youth Development Work and the upcoming University of the West Indies Degree in Youth Development, which form part of the Commonwealth Degree Consortium on Youth Work, are examples.

References

Commonwealth Youth Programme, Asia Centre (2012), *Professional Youth Work: A Concept and Strategies*, Commonwealth Secretariat, London.

Commonwealth Youth Programme, Caribbean Centre (2012), *Competency Standards for Youth Development Work in the Caribbean*, CYP Caribbean.

Council of Europe (2004), *Youth Policy in Norway*, Report by an international team of experts, DJS/CMJ, Council for Europe Publishing. Strasbourg.

Kymlicka, W (2013), 'Responsible Citizenship: A New Approach', *Commonwealth Governance Handbook, 2013–2014*, Nexus Strategic Partnerships, London, 92–96.

Nicholls, D (2012), *For Youth Workers and Youth Work: Speaking Out for a Better Future*, Policy Press, Bristol.

Ord, J (Ed.) (2012), *Critical Issues in Youth Work Management*, Routledge, Oxford.

Rai, SM (2003), *Mainstreaming Gender, Democratising the State*, Manchester University Press.

Chapter 7
Transformational Youth Participation for Youth Mainstreaming

This chapter looks at:

- the primacy of youth participation in all policy spaces and in development planning to achieve youth self-empowerment and social equality

- the need to re-evaluate existing participation mechanisms to ensure they are meaningful, and not tokenistic, and are delivering results for young people, particularly the most marginalised.

7.1 Participation as expressed in human rights and development frameworks

Institutionalised youth participation in driving youth empowerment and development is not an option, but a necessity, for responsive policy-making. It is an important means to transformative youth mainstreaming practices.

Youth participation is enshrined in human rights instruments, such as through Articles 12–15 of the UNCRC and Articles 18–21 of the UDHR. In the SDGs, participation is best articulated within Goal 16 – Peace, Justice and Strong Institutions, through Targets 16.7 (responsive, inclusive, participatory and representative decision-making) and 16.10 (public access to information and fundamental freedoms) (see monitoring indicators below in section 7.9). Youth participation is also recognised in the World Plan of Action for Youth (WPAY).

7.2 What is transformational youth participation?

In general, youth participation spans three broad dimensions of change: 1) enhancing young people's confidence and self-esteem through the process of participation, 2) changing power dynamics between young people and adults and, eventually, 3) impacting on policies and services.[1] These dimensions apply to multiple domains, ranging from personal domains such as family and friendship groups to public domains such as schools, universities, work places and public institutions. This chapter focuses on enhancing young people's engagement with the public domains of policy and planning in all sectors and national planning spaces. This could be through party political participation, through youth social movements or engagement in public policy-making spaces directly, as partners in planning.

Youth participation in decisions that affect their lives is the right of young people irrespective of contributions to a larger good; the positive personal and collective developmental benefits of participation should never be under-estimated and should be supported unconditionally, particularly at the local level. However, if young people's interests are to be meaningfully integrated into development planning, their ability to influence policy in a climate of powerful contending interests (some such interests working against youth empowerment), should be an important focus. In fact, this is a key responsibility of broad, representative youth networks and councils.

Transformational youth participation therefore refers to:

1. The self-empowerment of individual young people participating in processes that contribute to developing their self-esteem, protagonism/agency, and interconnectedness with others, including demonstrating co-shared leadership qualities, ability to respect diversity of identity and ideas, and to enriching their knowledge and critical thinking skills. (See also Table 6.1 on contributions of the profession of youth work.)

2. This self-empowerment leading to their role in all policy spaces as informed and legitimate representatives of well-defined groups of young people in transforming youth rights dialogue, policy, practice and outcomes for *all* young people.[2]

3. Solidarity among youth social groups, where adults and more privileged youth groups with access to decision-making domains ensure support for less privileged groups in accessing and influencing these domains.

4. Solidarity among youth age groups, where adults and older youth enable younger youth to enter and influence these spaces.

5. Free and voluntary participation, where young people choose whether to participate *or not*. Meaningful youth participation is hard won and young people will be motivated to invest their time and energy in public policy spaces only if there is a genuine offer of power-sharing, and where their voice can influence change.

For the end-goal of youth mainstreaming (i.e. equitable outcomes of development for young people) to be achieved, it is imperative that young people's participation eventually result in their ability to:

- influence equitable social relations within policy spaces in the social, political and economic spheres;

- influence equitable policy formulation; and

- influence processes of effective policy implementation to ensure this equity, including ensuring the allocation of budgets and transparent expenditure.

7.3 Why transformational youth participation?

Transformational youth participation transforms young people themselves, and that is a critical outcome. However, it also transforms society and enables social equality for youth and adults. Young people's unique perspectives on their development, based on their own experience, strengthens responsive programming for young men and women. Their grounded understanding and experiences as students, healthcare recipients, employees, labourers, young mothers and fathers, young refugees, immigrants and so on can dramatically transform the thinking behind, and approaches to, programmes that affect them.

As the Commonwealth document *Professional Youth Work* puts it, '…The motivations, desires and passion of young people will likely be the richest seams of their future accomplishments and social contribution.'[3] The relationship between youth participation and the quality of programmes for them must not be underestimated.[4] Work towards attaining the SDGs is, in fact, a useful framework for which participation structures can be aligned and be responsive.

From a political and economic perspective, the likelihood of donor investment in youth participation initiatives increases if initiatives demonstrate not only the benefits of participation to young people themselves, but also this link between youth participation practices and policy and practice outcomes.

7.4 Translating participation principles into practice

Youth participation is clearly a subset of general participatory institutional cultures and good governance, and will be difficult to achieve where broader participatory planning environments do not exist.

The principles of participation need to be embedded at the policy level, and at the levels of the young people, youth workers, the community, directors, managers and advisers in all participating agencies. Figure 7.1 suggests processes that can enable this in all sectors and national and subnational planning spaces.

Figure 7.1 refers to optimal youth participation in governance, where genuinely representative young people participate in

Figure 7.1 Optimal youth participation for equality and sustainable development

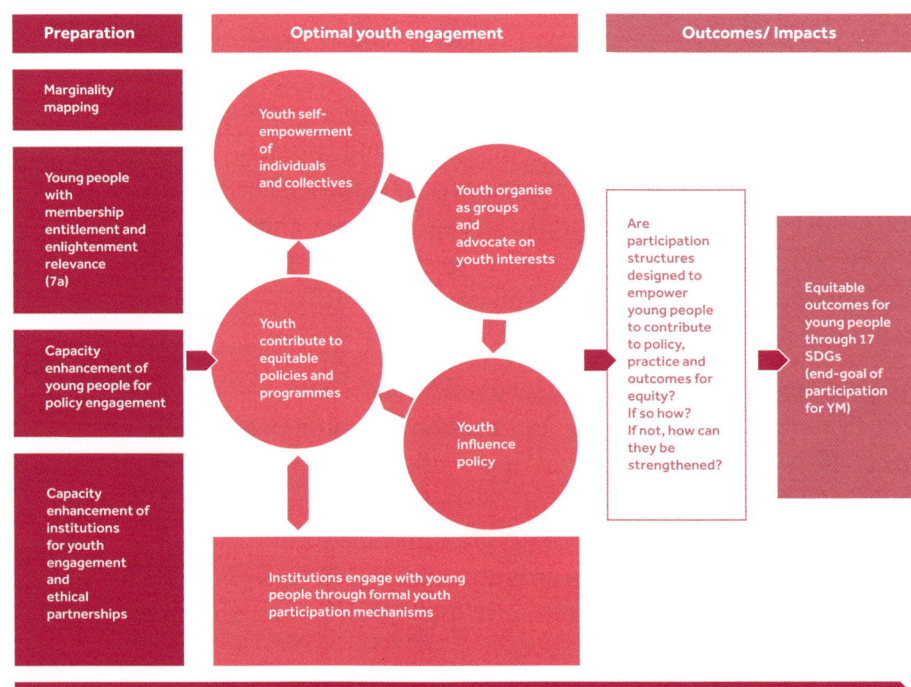

enabling institutions driving ethical youth partnerships and youth leadership, through youth-led research and evidence, in order to create change for all youth.

Not all of these components are required for beneficial youth participation, but this can be seen as optimal youth engagement.[5]

7.5 How do we enable transformational youth participation in our organisations?

Figure 7.1 has several implications for organisational governance in those agencies working on youth mainstreaming approaches. Below are possible steps an organisation can take to ensure this:

- Organisational policies that ensure youth participation at all levels.

- Organisational valuing of young people's knowledge and experience, and acknowledging this in designing responsive strategies and programmes for young people.

- Developing organisational guidelines for minimum standards in youth participation and support of youth networks/coalitions (see Annex 3).

- Developed and implemented marginality mapping processes (Annex 4) to identify those most marginalised and who will be the most affected by policies in your sector/organisation.

- Capacity building of staff and organisations to enable youth engagement (see also section 17.5).[6]

- Establishing formal participation structures in institutional decision-making processes to ensure systemic, rather than random, participation. This includes considerations of youth participation at:

  - the level of organisational decision-making in all sectors where youth participation best sits – i.e. within staff structures, on boards, in interview panels where staff are being recruited for youth-focused areas of work etc.; and

- all levels of the policy and programme cycle in all sectors – from assessment and planning to implementation and monitoring and evaluation (M&E).

- At the recruitment level, developing candidate assessment methods for attitudes towards young people and marginalised groups.

- Involving young people in recruitment panels to factor in their perceptions of candidates and their views on candidates' openness to youth and other marginalised groups.

While not all these criteria need exist to make an organisation youth-friendly, it is critical that we work towards achieving these targets.

Box 7.1 is an example of how youth participation was factored into the Australian Youth Affairs Coalition (AYAC).

Box 7.1 Youth participation at the Australian Youth Affairs Coalition[7]

The Australian Youth Affairs Coalition (AYAC) is the advocacy group for 4.3 million Australians aged 12–25 and the hundreds of thousands whose work it is to support them. At the time of writing, the body was no longer receiving state funding. The following involves principles and practices that it embraces in relation to youth participation, much of which is now disbanded to because of defunding.

One of AYAC's core roles is to create an effective link between decision-makers and young people, and also to play an advisory role to government and non-government organisations on the value of mechanisms for meaningful youth participation. A 2010 AYAC research report titled *Where Are You Going with That? Maximising Young People's Impact on Organisational and Public Policy* (2010)[8] investigated young people's participation and its impact in policy decision-making. The report demonstrated that young people can affect policy change, and need to be seen as such – as agents of change.

For AYAC, **empowering youth participation practices** involve:

a. simplifying policy development processes and clearly articulating opportunities for young people to contribute;

b. helping young people understand consultation and policy development processes;

c. using non-traditional methods of engagement and designing consultation mechanisms that are suited to young people;

d. creating solutions to barriers faced by young people in accessing consultation mechanisms;

(Continued)

Box 7.1 Youth participation at the Australian Youth Affairs Coalition (*cont.*)

    e. providing feedback and evidence to young people of the impact of consultation;

    f. embedding effective youth consultation in all public policy decisions; and

    g. using consultation strategies that also engage young people not traditionally engaged by the usual consultation mechanisms.

From a youth mainstreaming perspective, and before defunding, AYAC supported a range of Australian government departments – in education, health, the prime minister and the cabinet, political parties, sustainable development, the youth sector, human services and the taxation office – to build in youth participation mechanisms to policy dialogue.

At the institutional level, before defunding, AYAC actively engaged young people at all levels of decision-making and planning. Young people provided regular feedback and support for the work and approach that AYAC undertakes, through membership on AYAC's Policy Advisory Council, on the AYAC Board, on research reference groups and that project advisory groups. As a member says, at AYAC, 'youth participation is not simply "lip service" or jargon, but rather a genuine, practiced commitment across all areas of our work that any task begins by valuing, including and promoting the voice and perspective of young people'.[9]

7.6 How do young people participate?

How meaningful is young people's participation and how are they able to move beyond tokenism to having a voice, and so influencing policies and processes? The following outlines a few key ways of looking at the qualities of youth participation:

1. **Are young people's interests served?** Sarah White's youth participation framework 'interests in youth participation' outlines forms (from nominal to transformative) and functions (display to means/end). The framework discusses interests of participation of the originators of the initiative (top-down) and communities (bottom-up), of which the combined interests form the 'function'. Transformative participation in White, as in our case, refers to participation being both a means of empowerment and an end of social good (Annex 5).[10]

2. **Are young people invited to policy spaces or do they 'claim' spaces?** Gaventa's Power Cube (Annex 6), further discussed in Chapter 8, also helps us

understand different forms of participation, which can be through a) invited spaces or b) claimed/created spaces. Invited spaces often incorporate more mainstream youth voices, frequently represented by organisation-led youth participation structures, while claimed/created spaces represent less mainstream, alternative voices. These include independent youth movements, protests or, importantly, participation won through systematic lobbying for access to policy domains. Incorporating both forms of voice and influence is important for responsive policy-making.

3. **Is it informed participation?** The more informed and evidence-based the participation, the greater the likelihood of strategic policy influence. Informed participation can range from participation supported by information received from adults to information created by young people themselves. Youth-led information becomes the most robust form of knowledge young people can wield for influence. To enable this, young people can engage in their own knowledge creation through youth-led research (see also Chapters 9 and 17), where young people, often in partnership with adults, design, implement and analyse their own findings to produce grounded knowledge for policy change.[11]

4. **Are young people seen as partners/protagonists?** Successful youth participation is built around ethical youth–adult partnerships, in which both parties engage with and respect each other as equals, listen to each other's opinions, and everyone's contribution is acknowledged and valued. Building intergenerational partnerships helps us address power dynamics between adults and youth and build respect across generations. There are different conceptions of the notion of youth as leaders and agents, well articulated in the DFID–CSO guide *Youth Participation in Development,* which outlines the three-lens approach to youth participation where young people can move between being beneficiaries, partners and leaders.[12] It also proposes minimum standards for youth mainstreaming. The idea of children/youth

as protagonists, and adults as partners in the case of children and young people leading research, is further elaborated by Nuggehalli.[13]

Young people are aware of the complexity of meaningful participation processes, and the responsibilities it places on them, including adapting participation initiatives to the evolving capacities of, and opportunities for, different youth groups in their specific contexts (see, for example, Box 7.2).

7.7 Which young people participate, and what are the outcomes?

All young people's voices need to influence policy and practice. This often occurs through legitimate channels that enable all youth voices to be heard. Representation, particularly of the most economically, socially, culturally and geographically marginalised,[14] and of actual service users, will be the most practical and effective form of participation for all.

Indeed, research has demonstrated how privileged groups with access to decision-making arenas can help more marginalised groups reach these spaces.[15] In this way, solidarity among privileged youth/adult groups and marginalised youth groups means that those youth in positions of influence and with access to decision-making arenas facilitate the self-representation and self-empowerment of those with less influence in national and global policy domains.

This applies equally to older youth/adults ensuring the access of younger youth to policy spaces. Youth in the younger age brackets are often left out of decision-making domains because

---

Box 7.2 Meaningful youth participation

There is no country that get fixed like magic ... it is hard work, it is tedious and has to be consistent. In terms of young people, what I am really interested in is helping 15-year-olds improve local areas, helping 18-year-olds to engage in local government, helping 25-year-olds to engage with local political parties, engage in policy-making and in decisions that happen in local areas. Young people will not get involved in governance just because they decide because we are young you have to put us on the table, they will get involved because they are actually making a change. That's the thing we need to think, how do I as a young activist mobilise people in my street local area, mobilise people in my village, town to actually make a difference?

– Young woman from a Commonwealth member country in Africa[16]

of the complexity of adhering to parental permission regulations and safeguarding determinants. All these should be a key focus for youth networks.

7.7.1 Legitimate representation

It is those groups that are directly affected by a given policy, or those who represent such groups in meaningful ways, which serve impactful youth participation in policy domains. Amartya Sen identifies two useful criteria for deciding how representation works effectively. These are set out in Box 7.3.[17]

These may be useful criteria for policy-makers in working with young people on decisions of youth representation.

7.7.2 Distance from policy spaces/platforms/ acceptance

Who participates, and whose participation should be enabled, is also defined by:

- the distances from policy spaces of different youth groups (Figure 7.2); and
- their levels of acceptance within policy domains.

Box 7.3 Forms of youth representation

Membership entitlement: 'A person's voice may count because her interests are involved'. This would mean the membership of that person in a group affected by a development trend/policy.

In a broader sense, this means all youth as a social cohort marginalised due to age. Yet more specifically, considering how policies mostly affect **marginalised** youth groups, this could be young people in agriculture, those in blue collar labour, low-income urban migrants (both international and national), poor young girls and boys, ethnic, religious and sexual minorities, young people in locations of armed conflict and transition states, and so on. These young people would also represent other members of their group.

Enlightenment relevance: 'The person's perspective and the reasons behind it bring important insights and discernments into an evaluation, and there is a case for listening to that assessment, whether or not the person is a directly involved part'.

Representation is best when it is self-representation. However, this does not prevent visionary/enlightened individuals, often youth leaders or adults from more privileged backgrounds, who themselves are not affected by the issue/issues, but have a particularly unique, transformational point of view, from participating as leaders/lobbyists. This would mark solidarity with marginalised groups.

Figure 7.2 Youth groups and distance from policy spaces

Young politicians (see Section 10.3.3), youth political wings and state-led or state-endorsed youth groups such as national youth services councils, youth club federations and youth parliaments might have the greatest levels of access to, and acceptance in, policy-making domains (even though there is a clear possibility of youth–adult tensions *among* politicians or mainstream institutions). Youth social movements/coalitions may have a more tenuous, and strained, access to and a greater distance from policy domains. Yet access to planning meetings/community hearings etc. is still possible through dialogue and negotiation.

The most marginalised group in this context becomes unaffiliated youth who are not organised, such as migrants, refugees, poor youth in informal employment and so on. So, while greater efforts must be made to bring youth social movements into decision-making processes compared with the incorporation of state-supported groups, even greater efforts need to be made to involve unaffiliated youth.

Of course, policy distance does not necessarily correlate with levels of acceptance of social groups. For example, it is likely that unaffiliated youth groups will be more readily accepted within policy domains than organised youth movements whose lobbies may significantly challenge the status quo. Box 7.4 explores ways in which governments can engage with young people on policy-making.

Box 7.4 How can governments seek to engage youth social movements and self-organised marginalised youth?

Youth social movements fall outside the agency-led forms of youth participation that this section mostly addresses. Many young people that join movements do so because they don't believe in the efficacy of mainstream processes and/or they fear that their agendas will be co-opted and led by adults. In some instances, they may view the formal structures for youth engagement (parliaments, councils) as spaces for elite youth. In this regard, it is important that departments strive to reach out by:

a. Ensuring that public consultation spaces visibly call for young people to participate via civil society groups and targeted media outlets.

b. Considering using digital ways of connecting with young people; for example, see the UN Children's Fund (UNICEF) U-report: a social messaging tool,[18] which allows young women and men to respond to polls and report issues. In Uganda, this tool has proved to be a promising way to monitor education and child protection efforts, as well as be a catalyst for more responsible and responsive governance.

During the World Conference on Youth held in Colombo, Sri Lanka, in 2014, ministers pledged to support youth organisations and NYCs 'to reach out to self-organised groups of marginalized young people'.[19] In practice, however, the evidence worldwide is that the links between independent groups and the state are widening, rather than narrowing.

7.8 Building capacity for participation[20]

Capacity building for participation involves building the capacity of young people for informed participation, and building the capacity of institutions to be able to attitudinally and structurally integrate youth participation into their structures (see Box 7.5).

7.9 Reporting the impact of youth participation

The interagency document *Critical Agents of Change in the 2030 Agenda: Youth-Inclusive Governance Indicators for National Level Monitoring*[21] sets out indicator development and monitoring guidance for Targets 16.6 (institutions), 16.7 (responsive, inclusive, participatory and representative decision-making) and 16.10 (public access to information and fundamental freedoms) with a specific focus on youth, which enables the monitoring of youth participation processes and their impact. It proposes three types of indicators: structural (the existence of institutions and policies), process (activities, resources or initiatives; actions

---

Box 7.5 Enhancing youth participation capacity

1. **Information provision and youth-led information creation:** Informed participation is not possible without access to relevant and reliable information (UNCRC Article 17, UDHR Article 19, SDG Target 16.10). This, of course, includes supporting young people to create their own information and knowledge through youth-led research processes, which is an often overlooked component of information and knowledge creation (Chapters 9, 17, 22).

2. **Skills, confidence and influence:** Participation is essentially an interplay of power – that between adults and youth. The more marginalised the youth groups, the greater the power distance. Therefore, ensuring that marginalised groups are adequately capacitated to participate in policy domains is a fundamental role of a functioning democracy. Skills for evidence gathering and advocacy often need to be advanced to contend with different interests that are brought to the table, including the confidence to engage in the formal spaces where many young people feel uncomfortable. Issues of language and translation are also critical factors to consider in enabling the participation of the most marginalised.

3. **Organisational capacity:** How do institutions reflect on their own capacity to support youth participation and enhance such capacity where required, including building attitudes, knowledge and skills, building safe spaces for participation, and implementing facilitative participation mechanisms (see Box 7.1 above and the Commonwealth's Youth Participation Practice Standards,[22] Annex 3).

4. **Managing 'positive disruptions':** Genuine youth participation also means potential positive disruptions to adult–youth power relations and the questioning of received wisdom around development planning. Organisational capacities should be enhanced to respond to these 'disruptions' in constructive ways, whereby the best interests of young people[23] are at the core of decision-making.

---

taken to achieve change) and outcome (change in the lived experience of the target) indicators. Box 7.6 elaborates on this.

7.10 Conclusion and reflections

Youth participation is a prerequisite for youth mainstreaming. Meaningful, transformational youth participation requires setting up criteria that acknowledge youth participation as an outcome in itself in enhancing young people's self-esteem, confidence and meeting their developmental rights, but also as a means to attain social equality between youth and adults. In our case, this is particularly for young people, with a focus on marginalised groups.

Deep, reflective processes must occur, and clear criteria should be set for how youth participation is defined and implemented

Box 7.6 Youth-Inclusive Indicators process for Targets 16.7 and 16.10

Proposed process indicators:

- Target 16.7 example: Existence of national, subnational and local-level policy that requires public bodies to consult with citizens in decision-making (include youth);
- Target 16.10: Existence and implementation of constitutional and structural guarantees for public access to information available in accessible formats (including for youth).

Proposed outcome indicator:

- Target 16.7 example: 'The number of cases where public policy has been developed, changed or revised based on civil society/youth feedback'.

within international and national agencies in all sectors. Otherwise, we all face the danger of implementing heavy, expensive and elite participation structures that reinforce the very inequality we are trying to combat.

Box 7.7 Reflections on Chapter 7: Transformational Youth Participation for Youth Mainstreaming

- Are the institutions you work with open to youth participation in decision-making?
- Do they have formal mechanisms to enable this participation?
- Even when we are working with young people, are we only working with those young people whose views we are 'comfortable' listening to?
- Do we allow youth voices that are legitimate and often challenge our assumptions of development planning?
- Are youth social movements and young politicians able to significantly influence the realisation of youth interests? If so, how?
- How do we enable ourselves to exert such influence in healthy and constructive ways?
- What needs to be done to strengthen youth participation in institutional and planning contexts?

Notes

1 Crowley 2014.
2 Refer also to Sen 2008, Capabilities Framework, in Chapter 1.4.
3 Commonwealth Youth Programme, Asia Centre, 2012.

4   The Youth-Inclusive Indicators document (Plan et al. 2016) suggests indicators that measure the influence of youth groups on policy and practice change throughout processes for selected targets of SDG 16.

5   See also DFID-CSO Youth Working Group 2010.

6   Commonwealth Youth Programme and UNICEF 2005.

7   This is adapted from the Australian Youth Affairs Coalition (AYAC) document *Youth Participation and AYAC's Work* (N.D.).

8   AYAC 2010.

9   AYAC N.D., 4.

10   White 1996, 6–15.

11   Several Commonwealth-supported tools for youth workers and young people have modules that facilitate youth-led research: India, *Co-Creating Youth Spaces* (Commonwealth Youth Programme 2014); Sri Lanka, *Ocean in a Drop Youth Workers' Training Manual* (Patel et al. 2013).

12   DFID-CSO Youth Working Group 2010, 3.

13   Channels Television 2013.

14   A marginality mapping tool is available from the Commonwealth Secretariat et al. 2013.

15   White 1996, 9.

16   Nuggehalli 2014.

17   Sen 2009.

18   UNICEF N.D.

19   World Conference on Youth 2014, 8.

20   The Sustainable Governance Index indicator on 'citizen participatory competence' is instrumental in assessing this.

21   Plan et al. 2016.

22   Commonwealth Youth Programme and UNICEF 2005.

23   The best interest principle is at the core of the Convention on the Rights of the Child, and is a critical concept for planning with and for all young people, not just those below 18.

References

Australian Youth Affairs Coalition (AYAC) (2010), *Where Are You Going with That? Maximising Young People's Impact on Organisational and Public Policy*, available at: http://www.yacwa.org.au/wp-content/uploads/2016/09/Where-are-you-going-with-that-Australian-Youth-Affairs-Coalition.pdf.

Australian Youth Affairs Coalition (AYAC) (N.D.), *Youth Participation and AYAC's Work*, available at: http://www.ayac.org.au/uploads/AYAC%20and%20its%20work%20with%20young%20people.pdf.

Channels Television (2013), *#NigeriaAt53: Youth Participation In Leadership, Governance*. [Online Video]. 5 October 2013. available at: http://www.youtube.com/watch?v=osSAUNkI5Xk (accessed September 2016)

Commonwealth Youth Programme, Asia Centre (2012), *Professional Youth Work: A Concept and Strategies*, Commonwealth Secretariat, London.

Commonwealth Youth Programme and UNICEF (2005), *Adolescent and Youth Participation: Adults Get Ready!*, Commonwealth Secretariat, London.

Commonwealth Youth Programme, Nehru Yuva Kendra Sangathan (NYKS) and Pravah (2014), *Co-Creating Youth Spaces: A Practice-Based Guide for Youth Facilitators*, Commonwealth Secretariat, London, available at: http://thecommonwealth.org/sites/default/files/inline/Co-Creating_Youth_Spaces_web.pdf. Accessed April 2017

Crowley, A (2014), 'Children's Participation in Public Decision-Making', in Westwood J, et al., *Participation, Citizenship and Inter-Generational*

Relations in Children and Young People's Lives, Palgrave Macmillan, Hampshire.

DFID CSO Youth Working Group (2010), *Youth Participation in Development: A Guide for Development Agencies and Policy Makers,* London.

Nuggehalli, R (2014), 'Children and Young People as Protagonists, and Adults as Partners', in Westwood J, et al., *Participation, Citizenship and Inter-Generational Relations in Children and Young People's Lives*, Palgrave Macmillan, Hampshire.

Patel, A M Venkateswaran, K Prakash, and A Shekar (2013), *Ocean in a Drop*, Sage, New Delhi.

Plan, Restless Development, Children's Environments Research Group, Queen's University and UNDP (2016), *Critical Agents of Change in the 2030 Agenda: Youth-Inclusive Governance Indicators for National-Level Monitoring.*

Sen, A (2008), *Civil Paths to Peace: Report of the Commonwealth Commission on Respect and Understanding,* Commonwealth Secretariat, London.

Sen, A (2009), The Idea of Justice, Allen Lane, London.

White, S (1996), 'Depoliticising Development: The Uses and Abuses of Participation', Development in Practice, 6.1, 6–15.

World Conference on Youth (2014), Colombo Declaration on Youth. Youth Mainstreaming in the Post-2015 Agenda. Colombo. Web. Available at http://www.cfa-international.org/userfiles/files/colombo-declaration-on-youthfinal. pdf (accessed Sep 2016).

Chapter 8
Stakeholder Engagement

This chapter examines:

- the critical role that collaborative, multistakeholder development planning plays in delivering with, and for, youth

- the need to make explicit the tensions and conflict among stakeholders in concrete planning.

8.1 Strengthening accountability and transparency between civil society, the private sector and government

The need for the acknowledgement of, and collaboration between, state and civil society/extra-governmental actors is a prerequisite of successful youth mainstreaming. No one party can do this alone.

Collaboration is critical because:

- government roles are increasingly complemented by non-governmental and private sector players, and technical knowledge is dispersed, and

- this helps accountability across stakeholders, particularly accountability to youth stakeholders.

The acknowledgement of this diversity is important because:

- It helps see a specific sector, i.e. the health sector, as a combination of players (just as we discussed in the case of the youth sector) – involving state, non-state and private sector players, including unions, professional associations and youth groups – and ensures co-ordinated planning.

- It helps understand the complexity of the relationship between stakeholders. Stakeholder interests are sometimes common, but sometimes conflict with each other. For example, while youth movements and academic groups around the world are working to protect education by demonstrating the benefits of public education for reaching the broader goals of education set out in SDG 4, other forces may lobby to deregulate education, which some feel threatens our ability to provide Education for All.

- It allows us to understand that conflicts are not necessarily divided according to 'stakeholder groups' such as youth, government, the private sector and so on; there can be conflicts among youth groups or professional associations themselves. The gay rights movement and the anti-gay movement, both represented through youth collectives, is one such example.

This approach to analysing extra-governmental players led to the relative success of gender mainstreaming, because it acknowledged the complexity of stakeholder roles and also enabled an adequate assessment of risks and advantages in development approaches that brought in a wide variety of players outside the state.[1] In this context, it is also worth examining the role of civil society in your context, and the extent of freedom of expression it has, considering shrinking spaces for the civil society voice and influence in many parts of the globe.[2] An environment that enables diversity and dissent is critical to youth mainstreaming. See Box 8.1 for an insight from gender mainstreaming that has implications for youth mainstreaming.

Figure 8.1 attempts to highlight main stakeholder groups, their functions and their interests.

Box 8.1 Sustaining effective civil society engagement

In relation to civil society and youth networks, once again a key learning from gender mainstreaming is that: 'It is important to note that women's groups that have organised outside state boundaries are critical to the continued strength and accountability of national machineries'. While the youth sector strengthens national youth councils and youth networking within state machineries, it must acknowledge the existence and concerns of independent young groups, which exist through 'proposing, pressuring, negotiating, overseeing, criticising, demanding explanations'[3] in alternative ways.

8.2 Stakeholder groups, functions and interests

Figure 8.1 Stakeholder groups, functions and interests[4]

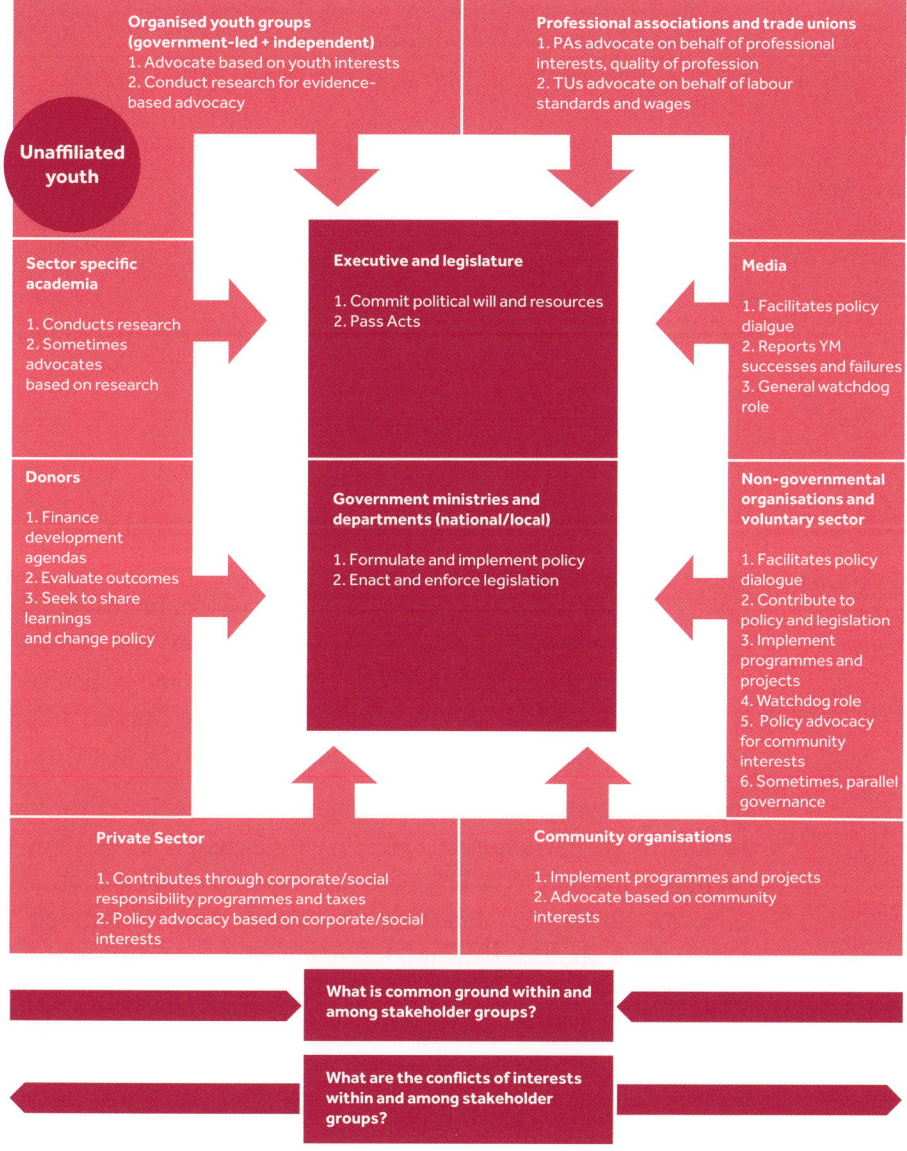

This figure:

- Helps identify potential commonalities and conflicts of interest among and within stakeholders.

- Highlights that youth mainstreaming needs to enhance the visibility of unorganised/unaffiliated youth (the red circle), who will most often be among the most

Box 8.2 Reflections on Chapter 8: Stakeholder Engagement

- Does all-of-government planning in your context involve all stakeholders we have outlined in Figure 8.1 for each sector?

- Are some stakeholders left out? If so, why, and how can they be involved?

- What are the main conflicts of interest among stakeholders in your context? How are these resolved? Through consensus or by rejecting certain ideas? Which ideas get rejected? Would these ideas have benefited youth?

- In general, are all stakeholders able to freely express themselves, irrespective of their viewpoint?

- How, in your opinion, does the power of stakeholders determine policy outcomes? Does this provide good outcomes for young people?

- Are youth stakeholders considered critical in national/subnational planning?

marginalised. For example, young people in post-conflict countries living in refugee camps may not have the tools or motivation for organisation and articulation of interests. How will they be reached, listened to and planned for through processes co-created by them?

Stakeholder engagement will of course be considered through paradigms of participation, which we discussed in relation to youth in Chapter 7. The ability to participate in policy consensus relies on power and interests. The Power Cube (outlined in Annex 6), a multidimensional concept that helps us ascertain the position of each player in relation to power centres, is once again a useful tool here, just as it is for youth participation advocates and policy-makers to analyse whose interests are strong and why. The Power Cube addresses participation in terms of levels of participation, spaces for participation and forms of participation (see Annex 6).

Notes

1   Rai 2003, 32.
2   CIVICUS 2017.
3   Ugalde 2003, 125.
4   This helps an analysis of stakeholder groups at the national/subnational, sectoral and other levels, as relevant to your planning context.

References

CIVICUS (2017), *Contested and under Pressure: A Snapshot of the Enabling Environment of Civil Society in 22 Countries*, available at: http://www.civicus.org/images/EENA_Report_English.pdf

Rai, SM (2003), *Mainstreaming Gender, Democratising the State*, Manchester University Press.

Ugalde, V (2003), 'The Role of the Women's Movement in Institutionalizing a Gender Focus in Public Policy: The Ecuadorian Experience', in Rai, S 2003 *Mainstreaming Gender, Democratising the State*, Manchester University Press.

Chapter 9
Youth-centric Evidence and Data Disaggregation

This chapter discusses:

- the role of research and evidence in informing youth mainstreaming

- the centrality of youth-led research in bringing youth-centric knowledge to the table

- the importance of data disaggregation for youth in articulating youth cohort involvement and outputs and outcomes for youth.

9.1 Research and youth-led research[1] and analysis provides the evidence base

Evidence tells us what works, and what does not work, for young people and society. It is the bedrock of objective planning.

For development research perspectives to legitimately represent young people's interests:

- All research needs to take on a youth lens.

- Young people must be involved as partners in the development research process.[2] This involves young people partnering and/or leading the identification of research topics as relevant to the sector, and leading the design, implementation, data interpretation and report writing of the research.

This can have a formidable influence on research outputs by virtue of the lived experiences young people bring into research. Part of the value, but also a positive challenge, of youth-led research is also that findings and recommendation have a great likelihood of challenging orthodox knowledge and assumptions about research, and putting forth transformational recommendations for change. This in turn requires readiness on the part of stakeholders to rethink and reconfigure development planning.

These processes require either in-house research capacity or strong links with collaborative research institutes, including youth research institutes. Box 9.1 describes an experimental research process undertaken by the Commonwealth Youth Programme.

Box 9.1 Young people research urban relocation[3]

In a Commonwealth-led youth research pilot in Punjab, India, members of a youth club run by India's Nehru Yuva Kendra Sangathan (NYKS) engaged in a co-created, small-scale research with adults on the issue of the relocation of their communities to government-assigned accommodation. The youth club members came from one of the lowest-income, provincial migratory communities in India, who lived in informal settlements and engaged primarily in employment in the informal sector. While the relocation afforded them better-quality housing, it had nevertheless lacked the necessary youth and community consultation that would have supported better planning to address transition challenges.

Implemented a few months after relocation, the research was designed in collaboration with the Commonwealth Secretariat's then-active Asia Regional Centre, NYKS and Pravah, a leading youth worker-training institution in India. It was designed to address the challenges faced by young people and communities due to the transition, which affected their social interactions, education and employment.

The young people were supported to identify their own research topic, design information-gathering tools, and analyse and present data. The research not only enhanced the young people's sense of agency in decision-making at a particularly significant transition in their lives, but also helped promote solidarity among youth, communities and the three participating development agencies.

As one youth researcher, Sandeep, said:

> 'One of the reasons we felt the need to conduct more research on the issues affecting our community was because earlier, we thought we were the only ones who felt that we faced problems. For example, I lost my job when we were relocated to Dhanas. We knew other people who were in the same situation. But when we got people to fill out the survey, we realised exactly how widespread the problem was. Eighty per cent of the people surveyed agreed that unemployment was the biggest problem arising out of the relocation. We were able to identify the impact of these problems on the community through research. Earlier, it was all abstract'.

During this process, the youth club also engaged with several stakeholders, including community leaders and government officials. They used the data collected through the research to advocate with the local authorities for effective resolutions. For example, the youth club shared the data on the impact of the relocation on employment with the Municipal Corporation of Chandigarh. The municipal corporation worked to address these issues, at least in part, by engaging the young people in cost-free skills development courses to increase their employability.

(Continued)

Box 9.1   Young people research urban relocation (*cont.*)

This research process had several implications for the young researchers, and the organisations that supported the youth-led research.

For these marginalised young people:

- It demystified the research process. They had no previous exposure to processes of inquiry, or indeed agency in decisions that affected their lives.
- It enhanced their confidence and skills in leading research implementation, analysing findings, and formulating and acting on research recommendations.
- It changed their level of agency in local government decision-making, even minimally.
- It changed their relationship to one of greater agency with the collaborating agencies.

For the collaborating organisations:

- It strengthened organisational capacity for working with young people, and allowing young people to lead inquiry.
- It enabled the organisations to restructure and re-prioritise capacity building for skills in working on youth-led research.
- It created the significant learning that organisations need to develop their own accountability to young people by supporting them **throughout the process of implementing research recommendations**, not just implementing the research, as this is the key goal of development research.

For service delivery organisations:

- required the opening up of spaces (in this case, local municipality spaces) to young people's voice and listening to youth on their issues, and
- influenced municipality decisions, at least in minimal ways.

These forms of youth engagement can change power relationships between adult research staff and youth.

9.2   Data disaggregation helps provide young people with visibility in planning

Assessing differential impacts of development for youth (pre-YM) and assessing outcomes for youth (post-YM) require systematic efforts to disaggregate data for youth and to harmonise methods of disaggregation across data sources, so that young people are made quantitatively visible in planning.

There are several forms of data that can inform the design of youth mainstreaming initiatives and help evaluate the impact of youth mainstreaming (these will be elaborated on in Part 2, Chapter 15):

1. data to measure youth cohort involvement in a sector in relation to other cohorts;

2. data to measure access for youth to resources, including for subgroups (youth age subgroups and other social categories), (comparative outputs for youth); and

3. data to measure equality and equity for youth, including for subgroups (youth age subgroups and other social categories), in relation to other cohorts (comparative outcomes for youth).

Box 9.2 contains an elaboration for explanation of equality data versus equity data.

As the youth inclusive indicators document points out, quoting the *2030 Agenda for Sustainable Development*, Target 17.18, states have committed to improve measurements to ensure that data are disaggregated 'by income, gender, age, race, ethnicity, migratory status, disability, geographic location and other characteristics relevant in national contexts'. It also points out how some existing measures overlook children and young people, and highlights the importance of harmonising disaggregation across data sources, which has specific implications for multi-sectoral approaches to youth development.[4]

In data disaggregation, it is also important to ensure that youth data are disaggregated for different youth age groups and for

---

Box 9.2 Social equality/equity data

There are quantitative measures for both equity and equality. Formulating both forms of data is important to demonstrate existing and projected outcomes for young people through youth mainstreaming.

For example, if we say that the youth unemployment rates is three times those of the adult unemployment rate in Country X, this is clearly an **inequality** measure – because it is measuring the same variable (employment), but comparing the youth in the job market against the youth unemployed cohort, and the adults in the job market with the adults unemployed cohort.

There can be quantitative measures for equity too. For example, if youth are 30 per cent the total adults + youth in the job market in Country Y, but they make up only 12 per cent of those employed, then this is an expression of **inequity**.

Box 9.3 The Youth Development Index and aboriginal youth, Australia

In the National YDI for Australia, the index is being used with aboriginal youth groups to ensure that educational, economic and empowerment data are specifically gathered for this group of historically marginalised people to demonstrate the disparities *among* youth groups in the country.

---

socially, politically, economically and geographically vulnerable groups, depending on the context, to ensure that there is not just equality for youth, but equality for all youth groups irrespective of difference. This will also harmonise planning with the SDG agenda of 'leaving no one behind'. An example of data disaggregation for a marginalised youth cohort in Australia, aboriginal youth, is indicated in Box 9.3.

9.3 Conclusions and reflections

Without the right kinds of evidence, and evidence that young people have participated in creating, youth mainstreaming will not become a reality. Organisations should ensure that there is adequate attention to research within the organisation's priorities, including building research partnerships; that young people are active agents in evidence creation; and that

---

Box 9.4 Reflections on Chapter 9: Youth-centric Evidence and Data Disaggregation

- Is evidence considered an important part of planning in your context?
- Is there a youth perspective in the research that is relevant to your work, including data disaggregation for youth where the focus is on quantitative data?
- Are young people involved as researchers? If so, which young people?
- If so, how does this involvement help provide a youth lens to planning?
- Where tensions exist between organisational assumptions and the findings of youth-centric research, how is this dealt with? Is the process of decision-making fair and open?
- How can youth-centric approaches be strengthened in research and evidence gathering?

evidence is used meaningfully and impartially in the design of policies and programmes for youth. Where evidence challenges predominant assumptions of organisations, these need to be dealt with fairly and openly.

Notes

1 Simple tools for small-scale, youth-led research are available in the Commonwealth joint publication with India's Nehru Yuva Kendra Sangathan and Pravah, New Delhi (Commonwealth Youth Programme et al. 2014).

2 Development research, as opposed to academic research, focuses on evidence to inform development policy and practice, and is often more participatory than academic research.

3 This youth-led research initiative was part of a youth club pilot conducted by the Commonwealth Youth Programme in collaboration with Pravah, an Indian youth work training institute, and the Punjab offices of Nehru Yuva Kendra Sangathan (NYKS), the largest youth club network in the world. This case study appears in Commonwealth Youth Programme et al. 2014.

4 Plan et al. 2016, 7. The elaboration says: 'Disaggregation by age should move towards greater consistency between data sources (e.g. standardisation of 5- or 10-year age brackets), and reporting of results within each source should be consistent (e.g. avoid combining or splitting age brackets, such as 1–18, 19–35, 36–65, 65+).'

References

Commonwealth Youth Programme, Nehru Yuva Kendra Sangathan (NYKS) and Pravah (2014), *Co-Creating Youth Spaces: A Practice-Based Guide for Youth Facilitators*, Commonwealth Secretariat, London, available at: http://thecommonwealth.org/sites/default/files/inline/Co-Creating_Youth_Spaces_web.pdf.

Plan, Restless Development, Children's Environments Research Group, Queen's University and UNDP (2016), *Critical Agents of Change in the 2030 Agenda: Youth-Inclusive Governance Indicators for National-Level Monitoring*.

Chapter 10
Structural Enablers

This chapter provides:

- a discussion of structural considerations outlined in the Enablers Framework
- reflections on the need to engage with the big picture in youth mainstreaming.

10.1 The big picture

This chapter looks at the higher levels in the Enablers Framework: structural enablers – the broader policy contexts that shape youth mainstreaming. Strategies and innovations will depend on how macro-policy enablers are appropriated in planning or where macro-policy limitations are mitigated. How do broader economic and social policy prescriptions determine the way a local government, nation or region is able to invest in, and deliver for, youth through every sector? How does this awareness matter for our planning?

Some enabling macro- and meso-policy factors decision-makers will need to examine are discussed below.

10.2 Assessing structures 1: Pre-planning environment

These factors are influenced by larger structural policy contexts, but are immediately relevant to youth mainstreaming in terms of national-to-subnational and organisational commitments to youth mainstreaming processes.

10.2.1 Political will determines policy direction and commitments

'Political will' refers distinctly to the political commitment of a leader to a specific process, in this case, to youth mainstreaming. Obtaining political will requires the adequate framing of youth mainstreaming in relation to political incentives and disincentives, including an analysis of what might support and detract from political will towards youth mainstreaming. Interest groups may lobby either for or against youth mainstreaming, given contexts, and the way to generate and sustain political will rests on the ability to assess and negotiate these conditions.

10.2.2 Public spending and donor commitments help translate political will into practice

Public spending and donor commitments will not result automatically from the mere existence of political will, and will be determined by a multitude of factors – including government commitments to youth development (percentage of budget allocated for youth development and the allocation of budget across sectors in order to integrate a youth lens) or the directions and priorities of the policies of financial institutions and donors.

Both may require different forms of systematic evidence-based advocacy to enhance state investment and investments of donors, including an analysis of funding trends and providing reliable evidence for the need for investment in youth (Box 10.1). It is also important to keep in mind

---

Box 10.1 Investing in young people

The ODI project briefing *Youth and International Development Policy: The Case for Investing in Young People* (2013) identifies six key areas of youth development in which enhancing investment for the most marginalised young people would 'expand the reach of development assistance and support poverty reduction through equitable growth'.

These are:

1. **Post-primary education**, which builds resilience and enables the enhancement of life skills and employment skills;
2. **Work**, which fosters social inclusion not just through wages, but by forging identity and social networks;
3. **Health**, where good health influences access to education and work;
4. **Sustainability**, where young people are among the most seriously affected by climate change;
5. **Conflict and crime**, where young people are deeply affected, including their education and development, even as they contribute to peaceful societies; and
6. **Civic engagement**, where adult civic engagement is influenced by habits of participation development during youth.

that youth-centric elements of planning, if not adequately mainstreamed and made an integral part of planning across sectors, may be the first casualties of defunding public services, as is evident across the world.

10.3 Assessing structures 2: The macro-policy environment

This section looks at policy environments, which could be at the global, national, subnational or sectoral level and which can determine positive outcomes for youth.

10.3.1 Non-discrimination/equality conventions and legislation strengthen young people's equality aspirations

Legislative enactment of aspirational goals set by human rights conventions makes the case stronger for youth mainstreaming. Legal initiatives such as a right to information and affirmative action programmes (quotas for young people's meaningful participation as party candidates etc.) can dramatically enhance youth-mainstreamed approaches. Similarly, there can be legal initiatives – such as anti-gay laws or laws that impinge on women's reproductive health rights – that can be detrimental to young people's freedom and dignity.

While the youth mainstreaming endeavour does not yet have a specific set of human rights instruments, such as the Convention on the Elimination of Discrimination against Women (CEDAW) which is a powerful tool for the gender mainstreaming movement, a convention on youth rights[1] becomes an important subject for deliberation in this context. Sectors planning for youth mainstreaming will need to assess their own legislative environment to buttress the rationale for youth mainstreaming. An example of young people seizing opportunities created through legislation is the use of the Right to Information Act (RTI) by young people in India (Box 10.2).

10.3.2 Policy commitments to social equality and peace sets the foundations

Youth mainstreaming has a greater chance of succeeding in contexts where macro-policy environments commit

Box 10.2 Young people exercise information rights in India

India's Right to Information (RTI) Act, 2005, is an Act that came into being to realise government commitments of transparency and accountability and to encourage public participation in governance. According to The YP Foundation (TYPF), a youth-led organisation in India, 'the Act recognises that for a democracy, having both informed citizens and transparency of information in government functioning is key.' The Act grants citizens the right to request and receive information on processes, spending and outcomes of any government programme or process. The Supreme Court of India has recognised the right to information as an integral part of the right to freedom of speech and expression, as well as the right to life. The Act was campaigned for by the National Campaign for People's Right to Information (NCPRI), and campaigning continues to disseminate information about the Act itself and to ensure that it is implemented in its intended spirit.

The YP Foundation has been at the forefront of disseminating information about the RTI Act among young people and training young people on its use. TYPF is encouraging dialogue both on the relevance of the RTI Act and on its application to young people's daily lives, in areas of civic governance as well as human rights. Because of many such initiatives, young people across India have been active in exercising their rights as established by the RTI Act, in seeking and obtaining information around services and processes within government, and also in using the Act for the larger public interest. RTI, in one estimation, has been 'taken over by young people'. As an NCPRI member himself has stated, 'It is heartening to see the youth using the RTI Act in larger public interest. And the phenomenon is not restricted to the cities. It is happening at the village level too...'[2]

meaningfully to social equality, public goods[3] such as health and education, and peaceful, rather than militarised, resolution of social and political conflict.

In Scandinavia, successes in mainstreaming gender and attaining relative equality for women were linked to the welfare state,[4] where the participation of women in the economy, in political movements and in political parties was tied to ideologies of care and social security. From a youth development perspective, recognising services such as education, healthcare, housing for the economically disadvantaged, social safety nets for young people who 'fall through the cracks' and so on is an invaluable consideration. Adequately financed public services will be a great facilitator in integrating a youth lens to social policy planning, and has indeed proved possible – even in contexts of global pressure for structural reform.[5] Box 10.3 provides a further example of the relationship between tax cultures and equality.

Box 10.3 Tax evasion and inequality

Reducing inequalities means redistributive economic policies and adequate public investment in social services and infrastructure. This, in turn, is reliant on progressive taxation and fiscal responsibility.

Tax evasion, for example, removes investment from multiple sectors. Save the Children found that US$15 billion is lost in tax revenue from trade mis-invoicing in sub-Saharan Africa alone. In some countries, the scale of tax losses is greater than the average health spend.[6] Going beyond tax evasion to other illicit financial flows that negatively affect Africa's governance and development agenda, some estimates indicate that 'illicit flows from Africa could be as much as US$50 billion per annum. This is approximately double the official development assistance (ODA) that Africa receives'.[7]

Similarly, promoting peace-building and prioritising dialogue and understanding initiatives over militarised conflict resolution ensure a cohesive and content society and also ensure the investment of valuable public funds for the benefit of society and youth.

By contrast, modern paradigms of development based on austerity, small government, increasing cuts to the social sector and a trend of militarised conflict resolution attempts require extra effort to prioritise social safety nets, to enhance youth welfare and youth participation, and to ensure access to healthcare, education, peaceful societies and so on.

Working to mainstream youth, therefore, also requires working to strengthen public services and public service financing, enhancing dialogue and social cohesion, as well as institutionalising care economies, which facilitate the participation of marginalised groups and can cede power to them. Box 10.4 describes the link between military conflict and poverty.

10.3.3 Democratic politics, accountability and transparency ensure youth-centric party politics

The level of democratisation of political institutions plays a critical role in the success of youth mainstreaming, in that politics define in whose interests policy directions are set. Democratic political spaces allow the opening up of policy debates to broader, diverse audiences including youth, and to truly representative and inclusive government and governance

Box 10.4 Military conflict, public expenditure and poverty

The World Bank's 2011 *World Development Report* found that no low-income country classified as 'fragile' or 'conflict-affected' had yet achieved a single one of the Millennium Development Goals. People in fragile and conflict-affected states were found to be more than twice as likely to be undernourished as those in other developing countries, more than three times as likely to be unable to send their children to school, twice as likely to see their children die before age five, and more than twice as likely to lack clean water.[8]

On average, a country that experienced major violence during the period from 1981 to 2005 has a poverty rate 21 percentage points higher than a country that saw no violence. The average cost of civil war was found to be equivalent to more than 30 years of gross domestic product (GDP) growth for a medium-sized developing country.

In the same year's *Global Monitoring Report* data (2011),[9] UNESCO found that:

- Education accounted for just 2 per cent of humanitarian aid and no sector had a smaller share of humanitarian appeals funded than education (38 per cent).

- Armed conflict was diverting public funds from education into military spending,[10] while 21 developing countries were spending more on arms than on primary schools.

- Military spending was also diverting aid resources. It would have taken just six days of military spending by rich countries to close the US$16 billion Education for All (EFA) external financing gap.

represented by youth-friendly political mandates. Political structures can be assessed at the local government, national or global level. We discuss government democratisation here through five prisms:[11]

1. **Devolution and decentralisation**

   This refers to the extent of power sharing a) geographically and b) among stakeholders, including the privatisation of formerly public services, as analysed in gender mainstreaming. Member countries taking up youth mainstreaming will benefit from an analysis of how social sectors function, to what extent local governments have autonomy over decision-making, and to what extent control of decisions is influenced by civil society or private sector players for respective sectors. In the gender mainstreaming experience, local government decentralisation facilitated building diversity into programmes, while the feminist movement could lobby for equitable services through private sector services provision where privatisation was replacing public services.

2. **Party political cultures and genuine multiparty politics**

The political stances of dominant political parties, and their openness to youth participation in party politics, can either promote or hinder youth mainstreaming. Are party discourses aligned to youth rights? Are governments, both the executive and the administration, genuinely listening to young people? Is it truly democratic, shared leadership, or centralised leadership? Is there genuine multiparty politics that facilitates diversity of opinion and the consideration of different policy options? This would facilitate youth mainstreaming.

3. **Youth participation in party politics**

While young people may reject the present political status quo in some contexts, they are yet ready to create more enabling and transparent party political structures. Are there mechanisms to encourage young people's participation in party politics, such as affirmative action programmes? What are the push factors that encourage, and pull factors that discourage, young people contending as political party candidates? Are there affirmative action programmes to redress imbalances in youth participation in party politics?

Also, and more importantly, is youth participation in party politics seen as a distinctive means of representing legitimate youth interests and interests of other marginalised groups in political decision-making, and of bringing new forms of youth-centric, democratic, co-shared political leadership cultures into party political spaces? Or is such participation nominal?

4. **Monitoring and auditing mechanisms**

State mechanisms that are accountable, transparent and fair will lend themselves well to prioritising youth issues in policy and practice. Democratic elections that are transparent, capacitated and participatory, including youth-participatory monitoring and evaluation mechanisms, open, learning relationships between state and civil society, and openness to legitimate, evidence-based scrutiny and critique by all parties in the policy process, all facilitate youth mainstreaming. The freedom of the media, and exposure of local youth groups and concerns in global contexts, would further add to the transparency of the process.

5. **Global governance**

In an increasingly globalised world, where the obligations of Commonwealth member countries are tied to international agreements and conventions, it is critical that legitimate, representative youth voices of the most marginalised groups in society, who are most affected by policy decisions, be heard in framing global policy and conventions. How open is global governance to the participation of diverse global communities in deliberations? How are international forums set up to facilitate the articulation of diversity, which comes with issues of language, translation, consultation cultures and so on? Are we, in many ways, reinforcing elitism in global participatory structures, or can international conventions and agreements and global policy directions truly represent the most local voices, which are affected the most by policy decisions?

Box 10.5 illustrates a young person's perspectives on youth participation in party politics.

Box 10.5 Do young people want to participate in party politics?

Youth participation [in party politics] has been a dwindling [sic] issue both in the West and the global South. That is partly because young people find the democratic structures quite frustrating, and we have seen activism as a trend with young people, when you look at the Arab Spring, or riots in Europe, it is about young people who care about issues ... but maybe aren't that interested in political structures. In my country, 70 per cent are under 35, but we have limited numbers in governance ... we need to think about how we engage with [the] young in [party] politics generally.[12]

– Young woman from a Commonwealth member country, Africa

10.4 Connected government serves young people more effectively

'Connected', or 'joined-up', government refers to the increasingly co-ordinated ways in which government and governance (government involving multiple stakeholders) operate to provide services, including for young people. This helps different sectors work together beyond their sectoral silos, for more efficient and responsive outcomes for service seekers, and is a critical part of youth mainstreaming which recognises the cross-sectoral implications of policy and practice. Table 10.1 helps look at some ways in which joined-up government can support youth mainstreaming.[13]

In beginning a youth mainstreaming process, it would be useful to map the extent of joined up government in your country/sector etc., in order to understand the implications of youth mainstreaming for your sector. Box 10.6 provides an example from the United Kingdom of joined-up government for delivering services to youth.

Table 10.1 Joined-up government and youth mainstreaming

Ways joined-up government works	Youth mainstreaming example
Joining organisations – Intra-departmental, interdepartmental, national to local	Youth mainstreaming within a national development framework requires all sectors to work in co-ordination horizontally (government and other stakeholders) and vertically (national to local government) to deliver optimally for young people.
For social groups – Joined up services for a specific social group	Joined-up services for young people in conflict with the law may include education, rehabilitation, restorative justice, youth services and social services coming together to provide integrated services.
Joining a policy/issue/sector	Joined-up government delivers more effectively if, for example, the education and employment sectors work more closely to look at education meeting employment needs, to ensure a smooth transition for young people from education to employment.
Joining up in a geographical area	Particularly disadvantaged youth groups in geographical locations, such as a conflict region or a remote rural region, may need urgent joined-up services to ensure that education, psychosocial care, employment services etc. work hand in hand.
Mode of service delivery	The mode of service delivery for young people can deliver all the above if different sector services are located in a 'one-stop-shop', such as a local government office with offices for all sectors.

Box 10.6 Youth Connexions One Stop Shops and Centres, UK

A 'Youth Connexions One Stop Shop', through the Connexions Youth Services in the UK, is a venue where local partners come together to deliver a wide range of services for young people. These services include the provision of youth work, information, advice, guidance and support on education, work, training and volunteering, advice on drugs, finance, health, including sexual health, housing and much more. A Youth Connexions 'Centre' will offer or signpost to all the above, but less services may be available directly at the site.[14]

This is also a means of multiple sectors working together to provide co-ordinated services for youth, which not only co-ordinates the services, but also co-ordinates each young person's holistic needs in terms of health, employment, recreation and empowerment. This also helps sectors focus more on the youth dimension of their services.

10.5 Free and responsible media facilitate transparency and accountability

Free and responsible media are the cornerstone of a democracy and ensure transparency and justice in social decisions. Other than being an indicator of good governance and social responsibility, free and responsible media are a critical structural enabler for youth mainstreaming. They can be a strong partner in sharing media material on the need for and the successes of youth mainstreaming, while also functioning, along with professional associations and sectors, as a watchdog on the process of working towards reducing inequality for young people.

10.6 Responsible business help investment for development

Responsible business practices that go beyond corporate social responsibility (CSR) projects to broader environmental, fiscal and other forms of accountability to governments and citizens, including positive tax behaviours, help boost sustainable development and contribute to sustainable public revenue and socio-economic development.[15]

The role of civil society was discussed in Chapter 8, Stakeholder Engagement.

10.7 Conclusions and reflections

These broader enabling attributes can be considered at the global, regional, national or local level in planning for youth mainstreaming, and advocating for better contexts for YM. At the global level, macro-policy contexts have not been enabling of youth mainstreaming in instances where governments have been forced to reduce public spending, service debt and deregulate services at the cost of serving all citizens, particularly the most marginalised. Yet there are creative means of addressing the broader challenges to achieving equality for young people.

Box 10.7 Reflections on Chapter 10: Structural Enablers

- In considering the Enablers Framework, what aspects of the macro- and meso-policy environment in your context support youth mainstreaming?
- What aspects of this environment are less conducive to youth mainstreaming?
- Are there initiatives that are challenging the less conducive aspects of macro-policy in your context?

Notes

1 The Ibero American Convention on Youth Rights (2009) was the first regional framework. Yet, despite calls from UN bodies and the European Youth Forum, there is no International youth convention at present.

2 *Governance Now*, 2010.

3 A public good is an item or service that is provided free at the point of supply to all citizens. It can be provided by the state or another sector. In the case of the state, public goods are usually financed by taxation. Examples are free healthcare and education, public parks, government postal services etc. Citizens pay indirectly for these goods through taxation, but all citizens have equal access to public goods irrespective of taxes paid. This is considered a step towards creating equality and the redistribution of wealth. See also Koo 2013.

4 Rai 2003, 8.

5 Gaventa and Martorano 2016, 18.

6 Save the Children 2015.

7 United Nations Economic Commission for Africa N.D.

8 In 2013, a new World Bank analysis revealed that some 'fragile' countries – including Commonwealth members Kiribati and Tuvalu – had met the target on gender parity in school enrolment. Tuvalu had also met the target on improved access to water, while Sierra Leone was on track to do so. Eight countries had met the goal to halve extreme poverty (defined as the number of people living on less than US$1.25 a day); however, this represented only about 20 per cent of countries so defined.

9 UNESCO 2011.

10 In the years leading up to 2008, the average duration of violent conflict episodes in low-income countries was 12 years. This clearly shows how catch-up education during and after armed conflict is a matter of the youth cohort, as well as of children.

11 Rai 2003, 26–37

12 Channels Television 2013.

13 These categories are adapted from Central Government Office 2009.

14 Youth Connexions N.D.

15 Includes observations from ActionAid 2015.

References

ActionAid (2015), *Responsible Tax Practices by Companies: A Mapping and Review of Current Proposals,* ActionAid.

Central Government Office (2009), *Joined-Up Government*, Efficiency Unit, Hong Kong.

Channels Television (2013), *#NigeriaAt53: Youth Participation In Leadership, Governance* [Online Video], 5 October, available at: https://www.youtube.com/watch?v=osSAUNkI5Xk

Gaventa, J and B Martorano (2016), 'Inequality, Power and Participation: Revisiting the Links', *IDS Bulletin Transforming Development Knowledge, Power, Poverty and Inequality*, Vol. 47 No. 5, November.

Governance Now (2010), 'RTI and the Power of Youth', available at: http://www.governancenow.com/gov-next/rti/rti-and-power-youth.

Koo, S (2013), 'Public Goods: From Market Efficiency to Democratic Effectiveness', in *Commonwealth Governance Handbook, 2013/14,* Nexus Strategic Partnerships, Cambridge, 97–100.

Rai, SM (2003), *Mainstreaming Gender, Democratising the State,* Manchester University Press.

Save the Children (2015), *Making a Killing*, available at: https://www.savethechildren.org.uk/sites/default/files/images/Making_a_Killing_NCBTD.pdf.

ODI (2013), 'Youth and international development policy: the case for investing in young people', *Project Briefing* No. 80, May 2013. Available at: http://www.youthpolicy.org/library/wp-content/uploads/library/2013_ODI_Project_Briefing_Youth_International_Development_Policy_Eng.pdf (accessed April 2017).

UN Educational, Scientific and Cultural Organization (UNESCO) (2011), *Global Monitoring Report,* UNESCO, Paris.

United Nations Economic Commission for Africa (UNECA) (N.D.), 'IFF Background', available at: http://www.uneca.org/pages/iff-background.

World Bank (2011), *World Development Report*, World Bank, Washington, DC.

Youth Connexions (N.D.), *Youth Connexions One-Shop-Stops and Centres, Youth Connexions, Herfordshire*, available at: http://www.youthconnexions-hertfordshire.org/advice-and-support/youth-connexions-one-stop-shops-and-centres-1

Part 2

Implementation

This part helps us translate discussions in Part 1 into practical steps in youth mainstreaming in our organisations, sectors and national planning processes. It looks at how youth mainstreaming is implemented as results-oriented processes, rather than youth activities, and focuses on harmonising aspirational, legal, strategic and operational interventions to ensure accountability to young people.

Chapter 17 takes implementers through steps in planning, implementation, and monitoring and evaluation. Chapter 18, on mobilising financial commitments for youth mainstreaming, begins a discussion on enhancing donor and fiscal support.

Cross-referencing is done wherever possible to link practical steps to concept and practice discussions in Part 1 and Part 3.

Chapter 11
Implications for Development Planning

This chapter looks at:

- integrating a youth lens into planning, including drawing in key players and expertise
- the importance of planning beyond 'youth activities'.

11.1 Integrating youth mainstreaming

How do the discussions in Part 1 influence our approach to development planning? How is a youth lens 'integrated' into the way we plan? This is the focus of Part 2.

Youth mainstreaming 'connects the dots' between legislation and policy, finance and political commitment, organisations and programmes within the context of a comprehensive sociodemographic lens in all planning. Youth mainstreaming is not random youth initiatives, but integrated, co-ordinated planning. It intentionally incorporates youth capacities and rights in analysis, planning, implementation and the measurement of outcomes at all levels of the development process.

What we are looking for as results, then, is changes in resource distribution of all kinds (human and natural resources, financial and political power) in ways that better serve both youth and non-youth populations. As discussed in Part 1, the work of youth mainstreaming manifests itself as improved access to education, public health, improved incomes, improved civic and political participation, and so on.

To achieve this, several youth mainstreaming (YM) considerations and expertise requirements have to be factored in (Table 11.1) and a youth lens should be integrated at all levels and spaces of planning, so that they ensure equity and justice for young people (Figure 11.1). This harmonisation ensures co-shared youth-adult guarantees of accountability of the process to youth.

Table 11.1 Youth mainstreaming planning considerations and principal expertise

YM considerations	Cross-sectoral expertise
1. A full comprehension of the implications for youth in planning, including their developmental rights.	**Youth empowerment/psychosocial** Youth development/empowerment specialisation
2. Systematic and meaningful youth participation structures for decisions across the programme cycle, including incorporating the skills and expertise of the youth sector in building in youth empowerment strategies.	**Participation and democracy** Youth development specialisation Youth participation expertise Expertise in democracy Initiatives
3. Ensuring an evidence base and data disaggregation to measure a) youth cohort involvement, b) outputs and c) outcomes for youth, including for youth age and social subgroups and including global harmonisation of data disaggregation.	**Data** Census and data specialisation Quantitative and qualitative research specialisation Expertise of young researchers' collectives
4. Integrating youth safeguarding within the planning process and in programmes where young people are safe and secure within participation and programme implementation processes.	**Safeguarding** Child and youth safeguarding specialisation
5. Ensuring financing and budgets for youth at the global, national and subnational levels.	**Finance** Youth budgeting expertise Youth-centric financing and planning specialisation

Figure 11.1 Integrating youth mainstreaming into development planning

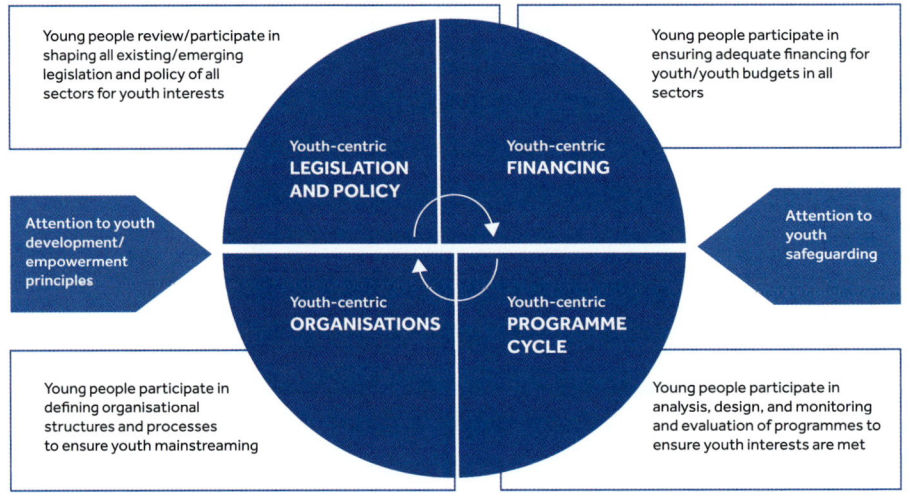

11.2 What does this mean for planning?

Our discussions in Part 1 have several implications for integrating a youth lens into planning in all sectors and organisations, including in inter-sectoral co-ordination and drawing in relevant expertise. Some of these are set out in Table 11.1.

YM policy, tools and accountability mechanisms (designed and implemented with young people) need to be in place to ensure that this collaborative planning occurs.

In this cycle, which aligns cross-sectoral policy, financing, programming and connected planning, how do we perceive youth mainstreaming that goes beyond youth programmes and projects within sectoral silos to holistic, cross-sectoral planning? The case study in Box 11.1 examines such broad strategic implications.

Box 11.1 Youth-centric employment strategies in development planning

Youth mainstreaming would mean perceiving all strategies as being cross-sectoral and multipronged, with a youth-centric paradigm at the heart of planning. Youth employment strategies, for example, are not just youth employment projects. It would mean holistically examining global, national and subnational policy contexts and strategies through a youth lens that considers young people's social, political and economic aspirations.

Young people's historic aspirations in employment have included full participation in numbers in employment, job security, education that meets employment needs, pay commensurate with contributions, work with dignity and the right to participate in labour associations. These aspirations are strongly aligned to the economic and social rights articulated in human rights conventions and SDG Target 8, which relates to employment. How then do national employment strategies ensure that consolidated initiatives bring together public, private and other sectors to ensure these aspirations are met?

Research conducted in Country X (left unidentified here for reasons of political sensitivity and the need to retain anonymity) is indicative of how some forms of employment strategy may not necessarily support the employment stability, commensurate pay and decent work that a youth-mainstreamed employment approach might suggest. What the research highlights in the context of Country X may be a lesson for countries where a better relationship needs to be built between youth aspirations and employment strategies that serve national development goals and the economic, social and political rights of the most marginalised.

(Continued)

Box 11.1 Youth-centric employment strategies in development planning (*cont.*)

The analysis of this subnational employment strategy, which targets youth as a significant cohort of 'beneficiaries', points out how focusing predominantly on self-employment, which indeed had good outcomes for some, and would have been an integral part of a holistic employment strategy, did not have the desired outcomes for the large numbers of youth and adults that were reached by the programme. This initiative, in which evidence shows millions of dollars have been invested, has resulted in high levels of indebtedness on the part of expected beneficiaries. In general, documentation from across the Commonwealth also shows that strategies that focus primarily on self-employment also leave large groups of young people, especially poor young people, and others, isolated in an informal sector, which may not be adequately organised for support or benefits in the event of failure. This is particularly so for marginalised groups.

These trends also come in the face of a failure to adequately invest in larger and disappearing strategic industries that could generate secure and dignified employment, catalyse investment and meet strategic economic and social objectives. This, in more formal employment contexts, has resulted in limited opportunities for secure employment options, low-paid work, where many youth, particularly young women, are employed in often adverse working conditions, pay barely able to support a decent quality of life, significant pay inequality across organisational hierarchies, and often restrictions on the right to association and the formation of labour unions.

From the perspectives of youth mainstreaming and organisational planning, this implies a multipronged approach by all stakeholders in delivering on youth-centric employment strategies. This is not possible without long-term, transformative, collaborative efforts where all organisations involved reflect youth-mainstreamed planning paradigms, listen to young people about their priorities, and examine ways of working creatively within existing policy and financial contexts for young people's economic and social empowerment. This would include collaborative partnerships with the private sector, national industrial sector and so on.

11.3 Conclusions

Youth mainstreaming has specific planning implications across a range of policy, legislative and institutional processes, underpinned by principles of youth development and safeguarding. For this to become a reality, planning processes should be holistic, and need to be self-reflective and open to self-critique and innovation. This requires long-term vertical and horizontal accountability to young people.

Box 11.2 Reflections on Chapter 11: Implications for Development Planning

- Which of the above planning elements for YM exist in your planning context?
- Is relevant expertise drawn in?
- Is there a holistic, strategic approach to planning in general that goes beyond random activities for youth?
- If not, how can more strategic approaches be integrated, and what would be the challenges of this integration?

Chapter 12
Youth Mainstreaming Spaces and Accountability

This chapter examines:

- the spaces/places of national planning and implications for youth mainstreaming

- the importance of horizontal linkages (across finance, planning, the youth sector and all other sectors) and vertical linkages (from aspirational frameworks, legislation, policy, planning, implementation, and monitoring and evaluation) in ensuring accountability to young people

- the role of independent accountability mechanisms.

12.1 Harmonising planning: Finding the linkages

How does a process/strategy approach translate into real-life planning? Figure 12.1 provides the different domains in the scenario of all-of-government youth mainstreaming. This diagram helps us 'connect the dots' in planning in the state sector (working collaboratively with all other players, private, non-governmental and voluntary associations etc. [=stakeholders]). This is a useful tool to understand the integration of YM mechanisms into national development plans for each component part and level:

- horizontal linkages of all sectors to harmonise YM across sectors, with the finance and planning sectors, and the youth sector;

- vertical linkages in aligning planning at all levels (global, national, subnational) to endorsed global/national/local human rights and development frameworks to enhance accountability to young people;

- mechanisms/processes in place to facilitate youth mainstreaming.

Figure 12.1 Youth mainstreaming spaces

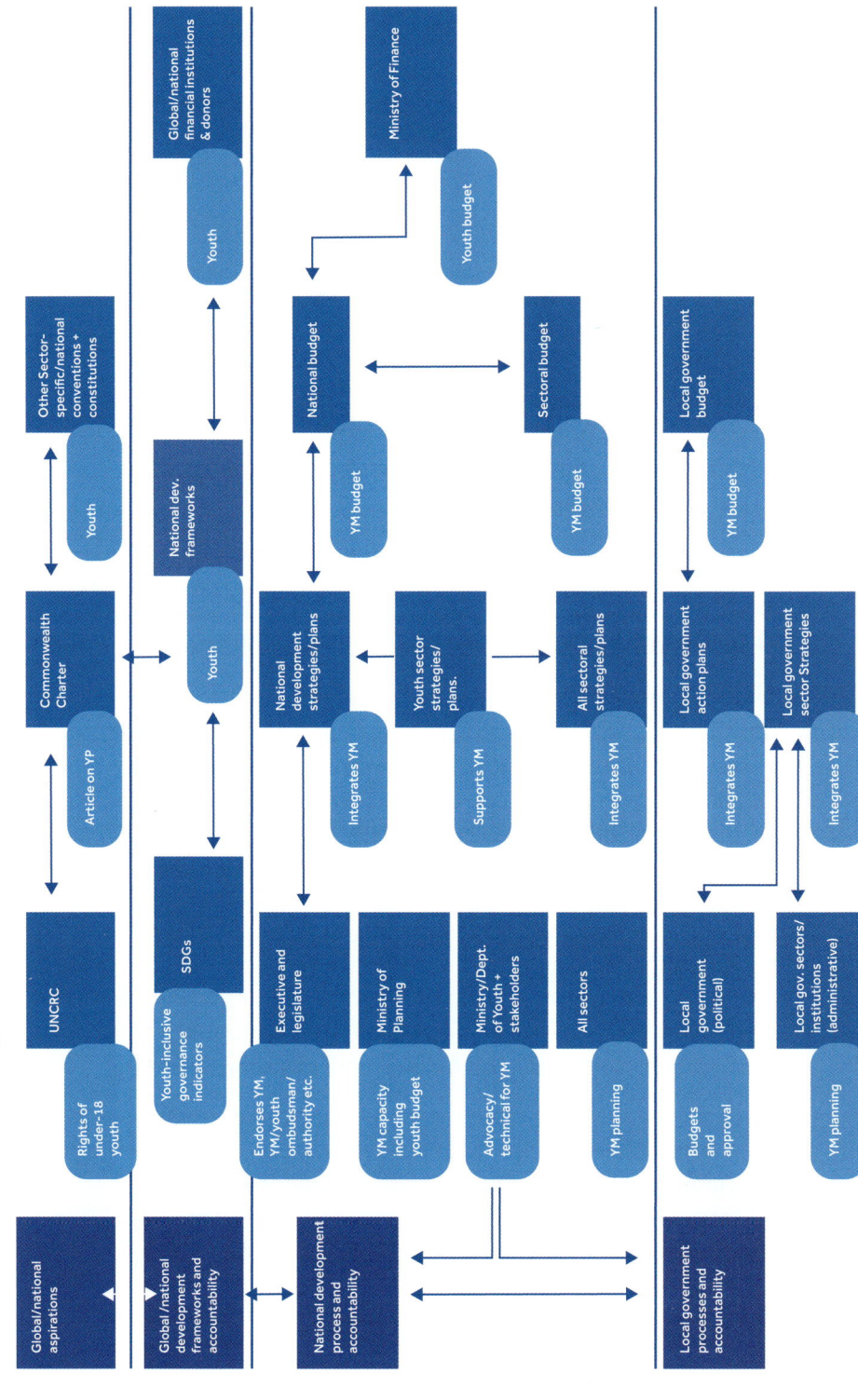

12.1.1 Aligning implementation to human rights and development aspirations

Other than the global conventions and frameworks already discussed in Part 1, each sector may have its own thematic guidance that needs to be assessed for its focus on young people as a specific social category, and the nature of the articulation of their rights and needs.[1] If such recognition exists, it should be used to the optimum in designing political briefs and in policy planning.

While the SDGs have already been recognised as being at the heart of YM planning for the purposes of this publication, efforts to align national planning to the SDGs may differ in each country and perhaps across sectors. However, using the SDGs and other benchmarks set in the Equality Matrix for Youth (Table 3.1) will only strengthen YM efforts.

This will be complemented by mechanisms at all levels that ensure youth mainstreaming, as discussed below.

12.1.2 National mechanisms and accountability

National mechanisms and accountability would include:

- the executive and the legislature's commitments to youth mainstreaming in terms of legislation and policy;

- youth priorities in administrative bodies – in programmes and planning, and in youth budgeting;

- the youth sector, including all its stakeholders, in functioning as the nodal point in advocating for, and providing technical support to, youth mainstreaming; and

- an independent accountability mechanism that ensures the faithfulness of YM implementation to YM policy.

Box 12.1 contains an example of a national accountability mechanism.

12.1.3 Subnational mechanisms and accountability

The autonomy of whole-of-government approaches at the subnational level will be determined by the extent of devolution

Box 12.1 An accountability mechanism: The Children and Young People's Commissioner Scotland

The Children and Young People's Commissioner Scotland is a post that promotes and safeguards the rights of children and young people. The position, equivalent to the children's ombudsman agencies of many other countries, was established by the Commissioner for Children and Young People (Scotland) Act of 2003.

Children and young people from all over the country helped choose the current commissioner in Scotland. Children were part of the interview process that helped select the commissioner, ensuring child and youth participation from the onset.

The commissioner has the responsibility to:

- promote awareness and understanding of the rights of children and young people;
- review law, policy and practice to examine their effectiveness in respecting the rights of children and young people;
- promote best practice by service providers;
- promote and commission research on matters relating to the rights of children and young people; and
- encourage the involvement of children and young people in his/her work and – in particular – consult with them on the work that he/she should be doing to improve the rights of children and young people.[2]

The commissioner represents the interests of collectives of children and youth, and not individual children.

The remit of the Children and Young People's Commissioner is to act on behalf of those under the age of 18. However, such legislated positions/structures for the youth category, if effectively functioning, can play a vital role in recognised youth mainstreaming and ensuring that all stakeholders deliver effectively for youth.

Children's authorities and youth councils etc. often perform the same independent regulatory function in many Commonwealth countries.

of powers, the extent to which local governments recognise youth mainstreaming as leading to more equitable and sustainable development, and their ability to plan and procure funds for YM. Box 12.2 describes two notable examples of accountability mechanisms for children, youth and women set up in two states in India.

Box 12.2 A local government mechanism: Children's and young people's councils

Children are not only discussing and trying to solve their problems through the Makkala Panchayats, but they are also showing the adults how to run the government in harmony.

> *– CM Udaasi, Minister, Department of Rural Government of Karnataka, India*

The two stories below are from Karnataka, a state in southern India, where children and young people have been able to co-create mechanisms that feed into local government planning. Concerned for Working Children (CWC), a child rights organisation in India which also works with young people, played a key role in both processes.

Children's local government: *Makkala Panchayats* (children's local governments) are designed as a children's and young people's equivalent to *Grama Panchayats*, the elected adult councils at the most local level, which manage day-to-day life in rural India under the 'Panchayati Raj' scheme of decentralised government. Elected by all the children of a Panchayat, the Makkala Panchayat monitors the work of the adult Panchayat, identifies problems facing children and young people, works to create solutions and, where necessary, demands action from adult representatives.

Within a few years of being set up, Makkala Panchayats proved highly effective at enabling children and young people to organise and demand solutions to their problems. In one village named Alur, the Makkala Panchayat helped children and young people convince adult elected representatives of the need for a high school in the village, enabling many youth, especially girls, who would otherwise have dropped out, to go to school. In Keradi Panchayat, members of the Makkala Panchayat persuaded the Grama Panchayat to close illegal alcohol shops in their community.

Children and youth in areas where Makkala Panchayats exist informed CWC that they had altered the whole attitude of adults to youth. Often dismissive before, elected adult representatives are now attentive to children's and young people's concerns. Makkala Panchayats have identified and helped resolve many issues which affect not just children and youth, but entire communities, and helped invigorate local democracy at the adult level. In 2004, for example, Makkala Panchayats were central to CWC's work facilitating 20,000 children of the Taluk of Kundapur to participate in their village's contributions to the national five-year planning process. State officials were so impressed with their work that they recruited Makkala Panchayat members to provide training to 82,000 adult Panchayat members state-wide. This is documented in detail in *A Unique Revolution*, published by CWC.[3]

In 2006, CWC published a *Protocol of Makkala Panchayats*, a publication designed to help local councils set up these children's and young people's councils.[4]

Mandating children's village councils: In a recent, even more far-reaching development in Karnataka, Children's Grama Sabhas (village councils) have been mandated as part of the Grama Swaraj and Panchayat Raj Act, in the drafting of which CWC's campaign for political decentralisation was a key

(Continued)

Box 12.2 A local government mechanism: Children's and young people's councils (*cont.*)

factor. This Act is radical in the way it empowers citizens and encourages their participation, including that of children, youth and women. Going forward, children's councils are to be held each year in all 6,020 Panchayats (India's lowest level of local government administration) of Karnataka, where local governments **must** listen to issues raised by children and report back to them on action taken.[5]

– Adapted from material on the Concerned for Working Children website

Notes

1   For example, the health sector in many Commonwealth member countries has guidance on reproductive health delivery, which focuses on young men and women.
2   Children and Young People's Commissioner Scotland N.D.
3   Concerned for Working Children N.D.
4   Mentioned in Concerned for Working Children N.D.
5   Direct information from Concerned for Working Children, March 2017.

References

Children and Young People's Commissioner Scotland (N.D.), 'The Commissioner's Role', available at: https://www.cypcs.org.uk/about/commissioner/role

Concerned for Working Children (N.D.), *A Unique Revolution,* available at: http://www.concernedforworkingchildren.org/wp-content/uploads/6.A-UNIQUE-REVOLUTION.pdf

Chapter 13
Planning Levels and Preliminary Assessments

This chapter looks at:

- the implications for youth mainstreaming at different levels of planning

- the opportunities for influence across these levels

- guidance for preliminary assessments to help initiate youth mainstreaming.

13.1 Levels of youth mainstreaming

We acknowledge four levels at which youth mainstreaming can focus. These are:

1. whole-of-government at national/subnational levels

2. sectoral level (single/multiple)

3. institutional level

4. project level.

Equality for youth can be reached only through systemic, co-ordinated efforts at all four levels. However, there is nothing to preclude sectoral, institutional or project youth mainstreaming where national mechanisms are absent, and indeed these approaches can catalyse broad-based change informed by local experience (Figure 13.1).

13.2 Preliminary assessments and feasibility

Before we begin systematic planning for youth mainstreaming, it is important to conduct a preliminary assessment at the relevant level (Box 13.1).

Here, we will look at suggested preliminary planning/feasibility questions at the national/local, sectoral, institutional and project planning levels to get you started. These questions should ideally be developed into more relevant assessment questions in your respective contexts. Sections and chapters of this publication that will support this survey preparation process are indicated in the right-hand column of the matrix at each level.

Figure 13.1 Governance levels and cross-fertilisation in youth mainstreaming

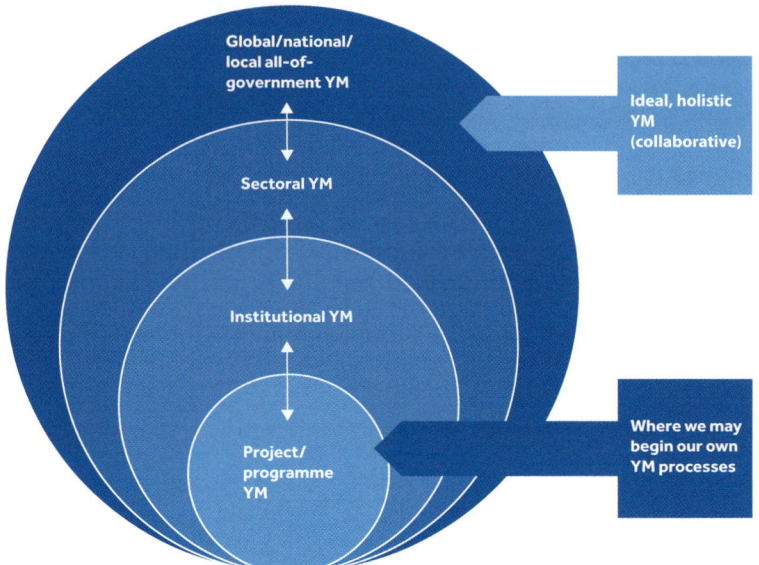

13.2.1 National planning (national development framework) level

Youth mainstreaming in its best form will be integrated at the level of formulating and implementing national development plans (NDPs) as they apply in your country context. This may include Poverty Reduction Strategy Papers (PRSPs), medium-term development plans (MTDPs) and other national development frameworks.

Here, ideally, the principal youth sector representative (ministry, department, youth peak body etc.) is usually the nodal point for steering the YM process in national planning. This is the most far-reaching form of YM. Table 13.1 helps you conduct a preliminary assessment at this level.

Box 13.1 Participatory assessment

This preliminary assessment process itself should be independent and accountable to all young people. Who is involved in the assessment will determine the accuracy and representativeness of the preliminary assessment outcomes. All stakeholders in the process, particularly young people affected by the work of your sector, or most affected by policy decisions, should be involved.

How can this independence be managed? Who, other than youth themselves, will participate in identifying critical stakeholders and marginalised stakeholders?

Table 13.1 Preliminary assessment questions for YM at national level

Category	Assessment questions for national planning	Sections to support survey questions
Governance and planning	1: What are the key national planning processes and documents?	Context-specific
	2: Are there existing commitments to youth mainstreaming in these processes/documents? If so, how are they articulated? How can YM be strengthened?	
	3: Which national legal frameworks facilitate/suppress youth mainstreaming? Are there constitutional commitments to young people?	Part 1: Chapter 4 – Enablers Framework
	4: When does the national government planning process begin?	Context-specific
	5: What is the process for negotiating with departments/ministries of planning and finance and how can the youth sector engage?	Context-specific
Political	7: What national political mandates facilitate/suppress proposals for youth mainstreaming?	Part 1: Chapter 4 – Enablers Framework
	8: Whose political will would be the most conducive to establishing YM? How would this be obtained?	Part 1: Chapter 10
Organisational	9: How does general institutional make-up in government and in non-governmental/private sector players facilitate/work against youth mainstreaming?	Part 1: Chapter 4 – Enablers Framework
Youth sector	10: How are youth sector players organised at the national level to support youth mainstreaming?	Part 1: Chapter 6
Participating sectors	11: Who are the strongest youth-serving stakeholders that are potential allies?	Part 1: Chapters 6, 8, 11, 17
	12: Has a capacity assessment been done of all sectoral institutions for youth mainstreaming? If not, how do we plan for this?	
	14: Are there enough time and resources to fill capacity gaps in youth empowerment and youth mainstreaming prior to the next planning cycle? How can this be managed?	
	15: Are there stakeholders/youth groups that are traditionally left out of planning processes and should be involved? Who are they?	
	16: Are there stakeholders who may resist meaningful youth mainstreaming?	
Lessons learnt	16: What are the lessons of the multiple sectors' work on programmes for youth?	Part 3: Case studies

13.2.2 Subnational/local level

At the subnational/local level, sectors and partners will be structured the same way as for national planning, but at a different governance level. Local government contexts are a potentially vibrant level at which to pilot cost-effective and impactful youth mainstreaming, because it can:

- contribute to approaches for subsequent scaling up, as proved in the case of gender mainstreaming;

- provide evidence to form a rationale for scaling up and a rationale for financing youth mainstreaming;

- ensure a bottom-up approach, where national initiatives are informed by the needs of diverse youth groups located in different contexts countrywide; and

- empower local government.

This could be spearheaded by local youth sector players. Some preliminary questions to initiate a local government youth mainstreaming process are outlined in Table 13.2.

13.2.3 Sectoral level

Youth mainstreaming within individual sectors (national or local) is still possible where there are no national youth mainstreaming programmes to link with sectoral work. In fact, this can have spill-over effects:

- to other sectors immediately relevant to that specific sector; and

- potentially, to influence a whole-of-government approach.

For example, a youth restorative justice initiative in the justice sector could have an immediate influence in the finance sector to consider financing not only for youth justice but for youth mainstreaming in other sectors if the justice sector is able to demonstrate evidence/benefits. Table 13.3 sets out some preliminary sectoral considerations.

13.2.4 Institutional/project level

Where none of the above trends exist, it is always possible for youth mainstreaming to be undertaken at an institutional,

Table 13.2 Preliminary assessment questions for YM at subnational level

Category	Assessment questions for subnational planning	Sections to support survey questions
Governance and planning	1: To what extent are powers devolved to the specific subnational level under consideration (social, economic, legal, defence etc.)?	Context-specific
	2: When does the local government planning process in your province/state etc. begin?	Context-specific
	3: What is the process for negotiating with departments/ministries of planning and finance?	Context-specific
	4: Are there national and local donor, fiscal and policy documents that explicitly mention planning for and with, and investing in, youth?	Part 1: Chapter 4 – Enablers Framework
Political	5: What national and local political mandates facilitate/suppress proposals for youth mainstreaming?	Part 1: Chapters 4, 10
	6: Whose political will would be the most conducive to establishing YM?	Part 1: Chapter 10
Organisational	7: How does general institutional make-up in government and in non-governmental/private sector players facilitate/work against youth mainstreaming? Are there any specific commitments in these sectors to planning for and with, and investing in, youth?	Part 1: Chapters 4, 11, 17
Youth sector	8: How are youth sector players organised at the subnational level to support youth mainstreaming?	Part 1: Chapter 6
Participating sectors: Capacity	9: Who are the strong youth-serving organisations at the subnational level?	Part 1, Chapters 6, 8
	10: Has a capacity assessment been done of local institutions for youth mainstreaming? If not, how do we plan for this? If so, what are the capacity gaps?	Part 2: Chapters 11, 17
	11: Is there time and resources to fill capacity gaps in youth empowerment and youth mainstreaming?	
	12: Are there stakeholders/youth groups that are traditionally left out of planning processes and should be involved?	Part 1: Chapters 6, 8
	13: Are there any stakeholders who will resist meaningful youth mainstreaming?	
Participating sectors: Lessons learnt	14: What are the lessons of the multiple sectors' work on programmes for youth?	Part 3: Case studies

Table 13.3 Preliminary assessment questions for YM for sectoral level

Category	Assessment questions for sectors (needs to include broader national/local questions above where relevant)	Sections to support survey questions
Governance and planning	1: How organised is the sector? Is there already a sector network nationally/locally? That is, a health network, a justice network etc.?	Part 1: Chapter 6
	2: Is there a sector-wide planning process? What are the timelines?	
Structure/policy	3: Does the sector have specific global/national/subnational conventions/frameworks that direct its work? If so, what are they? Do they incorporate youth issues/rights?	Part 1: Chapters 1, 12
	4: Are there sectoral policies/guidelines for working with youth?	Annex 3
	5: How strong is the sector's existing work with young people? Which players in the sector have initiated these?	Part 1: Chapters 6, 8
	6: What are the lessons of the sector's work with young people?	
Political	7: Whose political will matters? How can this be obtained?	Part 1: Chapter 10
	8: Who are the strong youth-serving players in the sector?	Part 1: Chapter 10
Sector capacity	9: Has a capacity assessment been done of institutions for youth mainstreaming? If not, how do we plan for this? If so, what are the gaps and how are they to be filled?	Part 2: Chapters 11, 17
	10. Are there stakeholders who are left out of planning processes generally? Who are they? 11. Are there stakeholders who would resist youth mainstreaming? Who are they?	Part 1: Chapters 6, 8
	10: Are there enough time and resources to build youth mainstreaming and youth empowerment knowledge among stakeholders in collaboration with youth sector stakeholders?	Context-specific

Table 13.4   Assessment questions for YM at institutional/project level

Category	Assessment questions for institutional/project planning	Sections for guidance on survey questions
Governance and planning	1: Are there institutional policies/guidelines for programming for youth/youth mainstreaming?	Context-specific
	2: When does institutional/project planning begin?	Context-specific
	3: How likely is buy-in and how would you persuade on the need for YM?	Context-specific
	4: What are the existing organisational policies that can facilitate or work against youth mainstreaming?	Part 1: Chapters 4, 17
	5: What are the mechanisms/processes that might facilitate budgeting/financing for youth mainstreaming?	Part 1: Chapter 18
Capacity	6: Are there existing programmes/projects serving youth from which lessons can be learnt?	Part 3
	5: What are the institutional capacity gaps and how can these be filled?	Part 2: Chapters 11, 17
	10: What level of youth rights and youth development knowledge exists in the organisation?	Part 1: Chapters 1, 6
	11: Are there enough time and resources to build capacity at your institution/among project staff for YM, and to build the necessary institutional structures?	Context-specific
Programmes and partnerships	6: What existing programmes focus on youth and what have been the outcomes? How can these be made systematic?	Context-specific
	7: Who are the youth-focused partners with whom you work? 8: Are there partners who will resist youth mainstreaming?	Part 1: Chapters 6, 8
	9: How can these lessons from existing contextual negotiations, programmes and partnerships be used to formulate comprehensive institutional plans for youth mainstreaming?	Part 3: Case studies
	12: How can collaborations be developed with stakeholders in the youth sector to inform youth mainstreaming?	Part 1: Chapter 6
	13: Who within your organisational structure would give the greatest support for YM? Is this person influential over the extra budget allocations required for implementing YM?	Part 1: Chapters 10, 17

and if not project, level. Again, this can have a positive influence on upward replication to the sector and beyond. There is a high likelihood that youth mainstreaming at the institutional or project level will operate with a minimum of the enablers discussed in Part 1, and should be the beginning of an incremental approach. Preliminary questions for this level are in Table 13.4.

Chapter 14
Establishing Principles

This chapter looks at:

- the establishment of principles before embarking on youth mainstreaming processes based on the human rights foundations expressed in Part 1

- tools for monitoring and evaluating principles.

14.1 Principles set the foundation

Principles[1] are the bedrock of ethical and responsive youth mainstreaming, which respect ownership, participation, youth safeguarding and so on. They also shape the way we develop a shared vision for youth mainstreaming and help institutionalise quality standards to the process.

Box 14.1 sets down the principles that form the basis of discussions in this document. This can be adapted to suit your context. Again, it is important that young people are involved in the shaping of these principles.

Box 14.1 Example: rights-based principles for youth mainstreaming

Principle 1: Human rights foundations

Youth mainstreaming must be explicitly linked to human rights aspirations and the principles set out in the Commonwealth Charter, including its commitment to promoting **development, democracy and diversity.**

Youth mainstreaming spearheaded by the Commonwealth is driven by all aspirations set out in the Universal Declaration of Human Rights (UDHR), the UN Convention on the Rights of the Child (UNCRC) and all other human rights frameworks articulating the economic, social and political rights of all citizens. These aspirations are strengthened by the *Commonwealth Charter*, the foundational document that underpins all work at the Commonwealth.[2] All policies and programmes need to reflect these aspirations.

Principle 2: Outcomes for youth

Youth mainstreaming should leverage **sustainable, quality programmes** *for young men and women with clear beneficial outcomes.*

(Continued)

Systematic youth mainstreaming should be undertaken by participating agencies to ensure that youth mainstreaming brings added value to programmes. The fact that youth mainstreaming makes cross-sectoral programmes more viable and sustainable for young people needs to be demonstrable through monitoring and evaluation (M&E) and impact assessment.

Principle 3: Youth participation

Youth participation should play an integral role in youth mainstreaming. YM processes should recognise young people as assets in the entire process and draw on their experiences and knowledge to formulate relevant, responsive programmes for them.

Young people are not merely beneficiaries of programmes and projects, but participants in the entire youth mainstreaming process and should be recognised for their capacity to contribute; they are active planners and decision-makers.

Principle 4: Recognising heterogeneity

*Youth mainstreaming should recognise the multiple dimensions of social exclusion and the **heterogeneity of young men and women** when planning projects and programmes.*

Young people are not homogeneous. All programmes and projects should embrace modes of analysis and delivery that account for the social, cultural, political, economic and geographical heterogeneity of young people. They should address context-specific concerns of young people and adapt programmes and projects to the diverse needs of all young people.

Principle 5: Policy harmonisation

*Youth mainstreaming should be integrated into, and support, **global, regional, national and local development priorities**.*

The most successful youth mainstreaming initiatives will be those that are linked to global, regional, national or local commitments to, and investments in, development strategies. This will help harmonise initiatives and bring young people into the mainstream of broader development agendas.

Principle 6: Youth safeguarding

*Youth mainstreaming should ensure that participants in programmes and projects are **safeguarded** at all times.*

While development programmes are meant to support positive outcomes for youth, such programmes may sometimes, unintentionally, expose young people to situations that compromise their safety and security. This is particularly likely in contexts of regions affected by conflict, violent neighbourhoods, countries in transition, and places where young people are exercising political voice and freedom of expression. All sectors must guarantee that engagement with, and initiatives for, young people always ensure safe spaces for them, and provide psychosocial support where necessary.

(Continued)

Box 14.1 Example: rights-based principles for youth mainstreaming (*cont.*)

Principle 7: Decentralisation

*Youth mainstreaming should ensure **decentralisation of programmes** and the **participation** of young men and women and other key stakeholders in all stages of planning and assessment.*

Decentralisation is the cornerstone of true participation, and the greatest impact of participation occurs at the local government level. Decentralised, bottom-up programmes where young people are seen as the experts on their own lives most clearly help evolve into responsive programmes for young people. Programme decentralisation is further strengthened where there is a general culture of participation and ability to listen to stakeholders, especially youth, and where there is devolution of powers. This is key in the Commonwealth, which believes that, even though administrative efficiency may not happen as fast as we would wish, 'democratic values such as accountability, transparency, representation and diversity, among others, promoted through decentralisation are worth the cost'.[3]

Principle 8: An evidence base

*Youth mainstreaming initiatives should be founded on **evidence-based models** and should be followed up with systematic monitoring and evaluation based on jointly determined output, outcome and impact indicators.*

All YM decisions should be based on evidence, particularly evidence created by independent youth groups. Pre-planning participatory research and post-implementation participatory M&E and impact assessment should be in-built into the planning process to ensure programme learning and the continuing relevance of youth-mainstreamed programmes for young people.

As with any aspect of programming, it is important to ensure throughout the planning and implementation process that our work is upholding the principles we established at the outset. The above framework is preliminary and may be adapted to your needs. Table 14.1 helps identify measures for successful implementation of youth mainstreaming principles.

Table 14.1 Indicators of success for implementing youth mainstreaming principles

Principles	Indicators of success
Principle 1: Human rights foundations	1.1 Explicit commitments are articulated towards human rights principles 1.2 Policy frameworks exist for YM 1.3 Guidelines exist for value-based youth mainstreaming
Principle 2: Outcomes for youth	1.1 Resources are budgeted and allocated for YM 1.2 YM planning, risk management, and monitoring and evaluation systems are established 1.3 YM capacity-building offers exist 1.4 YM messaging for all sectors exists 1.5 YM networks, forums and symposiums exist
Principle 3: Youth participation	1.1 Guidelines exist for principles and practices of youth participation 1.2 Young people are accepted as equal partners in development planning 1.3 Induction on guidelines is conducted 1.4 Guidelines are translated into practice and show outputs and outcomes for youth
Principle 4: Recognising heterogeneity	4.1 Heterogeneity of youth is explicitly recognised and mandates are articulated that provide targeted approaches for marginalised youth 4.2 Tools and methodologies are developed and used for understanding multiple marginality and developing responsive programmes
Principle 5: Policy harmonisation	5.1 YM strategies are linked to broader development strategies, particularly SDGs (see Table 3.1, the Equality Matrix for Youth) 5.2 Advocacy for YM takes place in international, regional, national and local development agendas 5.3 Resources are invested in YM in all sectors 5.4 All sectors are aligned to the values of asset-based youth development
Principle 6: Youth safeguarding	6.1 Youth safeguarding is written into broader legislation and policy and recognised in programme implementation 6.2 Guidelines are available for nodal and participating agencies for youth safeguarding during programmes 6.3 Designated youth safeguarding officers are available 6.4 Mechanisms are in place for monitoring and evaluating youth safeguarding guidelines
Principle 7: Decentralisation	7.1 Decentralised co-ordination strategies and funding mechanisms exist for increasing youth mainstreaming potential 7.2 Opportunities exist for young people, youth networks and all stakeholders to develop co-ordinated YM strategies at all levels 7.3 Formal structures are in place for youth participation at the sectoral/institutional level 7.4 Platforms exist for vertical YM networking
Principle 8: An evidence base	8.1 High value is placed within organisations on learning and knowledge creation 8.2 YM research projects are initiated, with the backing of higher education and youth development think tanks 8.3 Monitoring and evaluation mechanisms are in place to track progress and impact of YM

Notes

1 These principles have been adapted from *The Commonwealth Guide to Advancing Development through Sport* (Kay and Dudfield 2013).
2 Out of the total 16 values/principles of the Commonwealth Charter, the more relevant principles to youth mainstreaming are democracy, human rights, tolerance, respect and understanding, freedom of expression, sustainable development, protecting the environment, access to health, education, food and shelter, gender equality, the importance of young people in the Commonwealth, and the role of civil society.
3 Kobia and Bagaka 2013, 17.

References

Kay, T and O Dudfield (2013), *The Commonwealth Guide to Advancing Development through Sport,* Commonwealth Secretariat, London.

Kobia, M and O Bagaka (2013), 'Separation of Powers in Kenya's Devolved Administration System: Opportunities and Challenges', in *Commonwealth Governance Handbook: Democracy Development and Public Administration 2013/14*, Nexus Strategic Partnerships, Cambridge. 14–18.

Chapter 15
Conducting a Youth-centric Analysis

This chapter elaborates on:

- detailed steps and examples in conducting a youth-centric analysis

- implications for quantitative and qualitative analysis.

15.1 What is youth-centric analysis?

Youth-centric analysis involves assessing legislation, policy and national/sectoral development frameworks from a youth perspective. It helps define the implications for young people of a specific policy and related programmes in ways that enable and empower young people. This analysis would ideally be integrated into a fuller age/demographic cohort analysis for children, youth, adults and senior citizens within a national/ local development framework, or within your specific sector.

A youth analysis should occur during the stages of formulation, review and revision for policies and programmes at all levels.

15.2 What are 'youth interests'?

What, then, are 'youth interests?' Which youth define this term? And how do some interests gain precedence over others in policy processes? In gender mainstreaming, 'interests' have been defined as the 'shared understandings and articulations of concern of an individual or group'.[1] They constitute both:

1. the objectives of the individual or group; and

2. the power of the individual or group to attract attention to those objectives.[2]

In the recent past, the focus has shifted towards increasing collectivisation of advocacy efforts. Refer to Part 1: Chapter 7 for points to consider with youth representation. Good YM approaches will always recognise diversity within the collective group, including in assessing interests.

15.3 Components of a youth analysis

The following factors[3] are necessary to ensure that a youth lens is applied in all analysis:

youth-centric analysis (qualitative)

+

data disaggregated for youth (quantitative)

=

a youth lens

A youth-centric analysis is not possible without the involvement of young men and women themselves.

15.3.1 Youth-centric qualitative analysis

Let's look at different forms of analysis that may be either more or less empowering for young people. This discussion will reflect the deficit and asset-based approaches to youth development that we discussed in Part 1: Chapter 1 (Box 15.1). See also Annex 7 for other analytical frameworks.

Table 15.1 looks at two different forms of analysis for the same issue: unwanted teenage pregnancy.

The analytical option in the second column is often considered more enabling for young women facing early, unplanned pregnancies. Such an approach will help develop more responsive programmes, leading to reduction in unwanted teenage pregnancies and attendant problems. Consultations with young mothers facing unwanted pregnancy has often, in fact, resulted in informed policy interventions of this nature.

The second analysis sees young people as 'assets' rather than 'problems': it perceives the importance of external structures in determining young people's realities, and young people as

Box 15.1 An asset-based approach and structural/environmental factors

An asset-based approach includes a focus on the structural and environmental factors that can lift up or push down young people's rights and capabilities. By contrast, a 'deficit' approach only focuses on the individual and places sole responsibility for life circumstances on that individual.

Table 15.1 Analysis issue: Unwanted teenage pregnancy

Analysis 1 – Deficit	Analysis 2 – Asset-based
Young, unmarried women face unwanted pregnancies because: • they are permissive and do not respect social decorum around sexual practice; • they are stubborn and do not listen to adults' advice.	Young, unmarried women faced unwanted pregnancies because: • they did not have access to information and affordable, accessible services on reproductive health; • the unequal power relations between young women and both young men/adult men hampered young women's decision-making around sexual activity.
Perceived policy solution for Analysis 1	**Perceived policy solution for Analysis 2**
There should be education programmes to highlight the ill effects of permissive sexual behaviour and the positive role of sexual abstinence before marriage. Young women need programmes that influence their attitudes on, and abstinence from, sexual activity.	Young women need to be better consulted on their reproductive health needs in programme development, with higher levels of information provision and better access to healthcare needs to be provided. There should be programmes that highlight the gender perspective of decision-making around sexual activity between young men and women.
Analytical framework	**Analytical framework**
This analysis would relate mostly to a deficit and functionalist model, where youth are required to conform to a specific, predetermined social order with its own codes of sexual practice. In many cases, these assumptions can also have detrimental impacts on youth people's right to information and services, and exacerbate the issue they set out to resolve.	This analysis would relate predominantly to asset- and rights-based frameworks, where unequal power relations between men and women are analysed, and the rights of young women as rights-holders are acknowledged to information and services from duty-bearers.

rights-holders who can claim entitlements from duty-bearers (including for information and services, primarily from the state, but also from other duty-bearers).

15.4 Data disaggregation for youth and quantitative analysis[4]

Data disaggregation for youth is an indication that youth are explicitly recognised as a specific cohort, with specific programme considerations, receiving the benefits of services. Data disaggregation facilitates both a) planning for young people and b) monitoring and evaluating the outputs and outcomes of sectoral programmes and national development planning. The Youth Development Index (YDI) is a good example of how measuring development outcomes for youth has been possible thanks to data disaggregation.

Data disaggregation/data analysis for youth occurs in several typical ways:

- **youth cohort involvement** in a specific sector that enables a comparative analysis across all generational/ social cohorts;

- **outputs for young people**, disaggregated also for different youth age subgroups and marginalised youth groups: for example, access to services such as health and credit, which enables a comparative analysis of outputs across all generational/social cohorts; and

- **outcomes for young people**, disaggregated also for different youth age subgroups and marginalised youth groups: for example, health and employment outcomes such as lack of disease, the employment rate etc., which allow comparative analysis across all generational/social cohorts.

It is important to note that vulnerabilities for younger youth (those below 21, or 24, as relevant) are *generally* far greater than for older youth within all social categories, just as they are greater for other marginalised groups.

15.4.1 Youth cohort: who is active/inactive in a sector

A critical step in integrating a youth lens would be to assess how important the youth cohort is, compared with other age cohorts in the sector; for example, youth involved in employment, in agriculture, in conflict with the law, in drug use etc. If we take the example of youth unemployment, this would typically involve the employment sector asking: How significant is youth cohort involvement in relation to other groups in employment/ seeking employment (i.e. the unemployed)?[5] Table 15.2 is an illustrative example.

15.4.2 Data to measure young people's access to resources (outputs)

Agencies also need to assess differences pertaining to young people's *access to* resources, time, space, information and money, political and economic power, qualifications, transport, use of public services etc. How far are young people's resource needs,

Table 15.2 Youth cohort data: Illustrative example

General data	Data disaggregated for youth cohort
A recent study demonstrated that there was an 8 per cent unemployment rate in Country X.	A recent study demonstrated that, of a total of 8 per cent unemployed in Country X, 5 per cent were young people between the ages of 15 and 29; and of that 5 per cent, 55 per cent were youth between 15 and 24.

and an analysis of access to needs in health, education and social welfare, incorporated into planning processes in relevant departments? Table 15.3 provides an illustrative example.

Table 15.3 Illustrative general data and data disaggregated for youth

General data for access to resources	Data disaggregated for youth access
The Employment Bureau of Country X recently released a report indicating that 60 per cent of small business owners did not have access to micro-credit programmes.	The Employment Bureau of Country X recently released a report indicating that, out of a total of 60 per cent reporting lack of access to micro-credit programmes, 40 per cent were young people below the age of 29; of these, 70 per cent (of the 40 per cent) were below 24; and of the 40 per cent, 75 per cent were youth from ethnic minority group x (i.e. disaggregation for youth age and ethnicity).

15.4.3 Data disaggregation to measure inequality and inequity for youth (outcomes)

We also need to be able to express equality/equity for youth through data (see Table 15.4).

Table 15.4 Data disaggregation for inequality and inequity

General data	Inequality for youth
In Country X, the unemployment rate is 8 per cent.	In Country X, the unemployment rate for young people under 29 is three times the rate for adults, four times the rate for adults for youth under 24, and four times the rate of adults for youth living with a physical disability (i.e. disaggregation for youth age and social groups).
	Inequity for youth
	In Country X, young people constitute 30 per cent of those in the job market, but only 12 per cent of those who are employed. Out of the 70 per cent adults in the job market, 60 per cent are employed.

The budget consideration here is the way in which social sector allocations and spending reflect resourcing programmes and projects for young people, considering the rate of their involvement in the sector and the gravity of issues for youth in the sector. In Part 3 of this document, Case Study 4 examines youth budgeting and Case Study 6 examines youth participation in urban planning – both entry points for YM into different types of resources.

15.4.4 Assessing data availability

Prior to beginning data disaggregation processes, it is important to assess what disaggregated data are available with census departments, governments ministries and departments, and other research and data agencies, including practical possibilities of expanding the scope of existing disaggregation (see Box 15.2).

Box 15.2 Data disaggregation

- Do national census departments/sectors/organisations disaggregate data for youth?
- What type of data for youth already exist?
- Which statistics and other data institutions can support this process?
- How can data disaggregation be globally co-ordinated as far as possible to report effectively for youth at an international level?
- How do we harmonise data categorisation across sectors and organisations by:
    - harmonising age subgroups within the youth cohort[6] (adolescents, older youth etc.) across sectors, including harmonising for global youth categories, and
    - harmonising disaggregation for marginalised youth (as relevant) across sectors, so that data from all organisations/sectors are disaggregated in such a way that they can serve national/sectoral planning and reporting?
- Do we have sufficient data on youth to report on:
    - youth cohort involvement in a sector?
    - outputs for youth, including in relation to other generational groups?
    - outcomes for youth, including in relation to other generational groups?
- If not, can we do this? What are the resource and financial implications?

Box 15.3 Data disaggregation initiatives – Barbados

Barbados, at the time of writing, was in the process of assessing existing youth data and developing improved youth data mechanisms. Initial assessments in the country found that:

- primary data sources had inadequate information for disaggregation for youth;
- there was a lack of human resource capacity for data disaggregation;
- data sources were outdated;
- there systematic reporting cultures were lacking; and
- there was a lack of linkages between national strategies and data collection.

Interventions proposed have included identifying and filling data gaps, mapping training needs and training delivery, including training on appropriate software, and establishing data collecting agencies and end-users. A national youth survey has also been proposed to collect data. Additionally, proposed interventions include mainstreaming the YDI framework to monitoring and evaluation design.[7]

Box 15.3 contains analysis from Barbados that provides an example of an initiative taken in the Commonwealth for data disaggregation.

Notes

1 Rai 2003, 23.
2 Ibid.
3 Much of this analysis section is based on the gender analysis section in *Gender Mainstreaming in Practice: A Toolkit* (Niemanis 2007), 88–90.
4 See also Chapter 9.
5 Tools such as the one used in the Mexico Youth Participation Index are in fact youth cohort analysis indices, which help determine the number of young people in each institutional setting. From a Commonwealth perspective, this can be considered a youth cohort involvement index.
6 Marshall 2016. This youth-inclusive indicators document points out the complexity of this exercise in terms of ensuring the reporting on harmonised and globally agreed-on age ranges.
7 Information on data disaggregation in Barbados has been derived from a presentation at a symposium on data disaggregation organised by the Commonwealth in Kingston, Jamaica, in 2016. The Barbados experience was presented by Cleviston Hunte, Director of Youth, Government of Barbados.

References

Marshall, C (2016), *Critical Agents of Change in the 2030 Agenda: Youth-Inclusive Governance Indicators for National-Level Monitoring*, Plan International, available at: http://restlessdevelopment.org/file/critical-agents-of-change-youth-inclusive-governance-indicators-for-national-level-sdg-monitoring-pdf

Niemanis, A (2007), *Gender Mainstreaming in Practice: A Toolkit*, Regional Bureau for Europe and the CIS, United Nations Development Programme (UNDP), Bratislava.

Rai, SM (2003), *Mainstreaming Gender, Democratising the State*, Manchester University Press.

Chapter 16
The Programme Cycle

This chapter:

- builds on the preliminary assessment questions outlined in Chapter 13
- helps us analyse youth mainstreaming at different levels of the development process.

16.1 Youth analysis and stages of the programme cycle[1]

Now, we move on to look in detail at youth mainstreaming in policy frameworks and programming elements (programming being the translation of policy into practice), and how we integrate a youth lens into their analysis, whether it is a whole-of-government or sectoral approach. This analysis is more detailed than the initial assessment questions in Chapter 13, and should be undertaken when the process has moved further forward, with greater participation of stakeholders. Figure 16.1 indicates the key stages of analysis in planning.

Figure 16.1 Stages of the youth analysis cycle

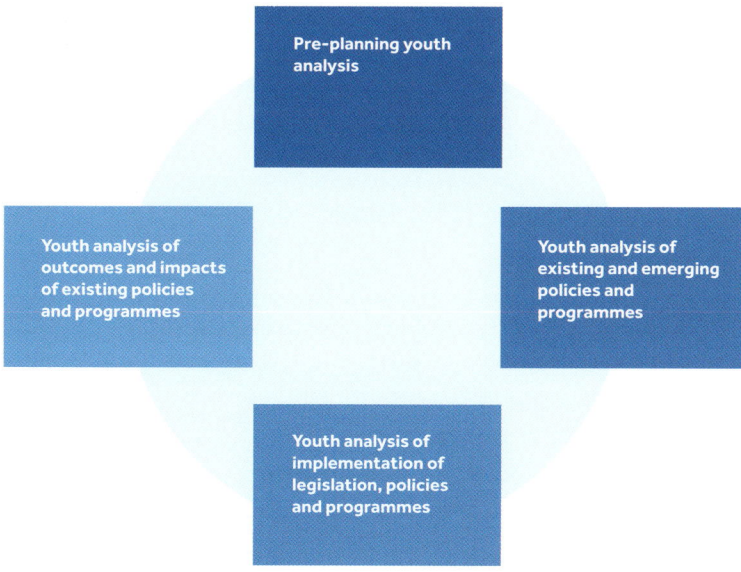

Box 16.1 An owned analysis

Again, it is important to remember that this analysis is to be undertaken by all stakeholders, particularly young people who are affected by the respective planning process, policies and programmes, or those with a youth-serving voice on issues.

16.1.1 Analysis questions

What is the nature of existing youth mainstreaming in policy, legislation, institutions and programmes? What needs to be strengthened?

Addressing these questions will help agencies identify work that is in fact youth mainstreaming, but which is not necessarily identified as such. The levels of analysis are described in Table 16.1.

Table 16.1 Policy, programme and organisational analysis

Level of analysis (global, regional, national, local, sectoral)	Some analysis questions
Legislation and policy analysis Analysis of policy, legislation and legal systems to assess a youth lens	• What are the broader enablers and disablers that inform legislative and policy directions? • Is there a comprehensive sociodemographic lens integrated into legislation and policy? • To what extent is youth-related policy strengthened through legislation? • Are young people's rights written into legislation and policy? If so, at what levels or in what sectors? • If so, has this affected, or can it affect, youth mainstreaming? • Are accountability mechanisms for youth written into legislation and policy? • Is there any legislation/policy that explicitly discriminates against youth? • What needs to be done to strengthen legislation/policy for young people's rights? • Which sectors have a critical role to play in this? • If you are conducting YM planning for a sector, what role does your sector play in strengthening legislation/policy for young people? • Are young people participating in formulating and assessing legislation/policy nationally or in your sector? If so, which young people? • Are some professional and youth groups excluded in the legislative/policy decision-making process? If so, why? And how can this affect drafting? How can the process be made more inclusive? • Are young people's developmental and safeguarding rights written into legislation/policy?

Table 16.1 Policy, programme and organisational analysis (*cont.*)

Level of analysis (global, regional, national, local, sectoral)	Some analysis questions
Planning/sector analysis Analysis of national and subnational planning, including all sectors – education, employment etc. – as a general network of institutions to see overall commitments and action on youth mainstreaming	• Into which development planning opportunities can YM be integrated? For example, is it possible to advocate for YM in poverty reduction strategy papers, national development plans and other holistic national development plans? • What are the national and subnational planning or sectoral enablers/disablers for youth mainstreaming from a macro- legal/policy perspective? • Is planning/your sector committed to addressing issues determined by sociodemographic variables in general? • Is planning/your sector committed to youth mainstreaming? If so, which sorts of agencies demonstrate this commitment? State sector agencies, civil society, academia? • Is youth mainstreaming written into policy in national/subnational planning or the work of the sector? If so, how? And where? At the ministry/organisational level? • Does planning support and recognise the implementation of accountability mechanisms for youth? • Is adequate specialist expertise (Table 11.1) drawn in? • Is there a youth perspective at the level of analysis? Are data disaggregated for young men and women? • Which programmes best exemplify youth mainstreaming? • Is meaningful youth participation factored into planning? • What needs to be done to strengthen youth mainstreaming? • Are young people's developmental and safeguarding rights built into planning/sectoral policy?

(*Continued*)

Table 16.1 Policy, programme and organisational analysis (*cont.*)

Level of analysis (global, regional, national, local, sectoral)	Some analysis questions
Organisational analysis Analysis of each individual participating agency's institutional mechanisms and processes, including youth sector agencies, to assess conduciveness to youth mainstreaming	• Do organisational policies generally reflect the significance of sociodemographic variables in development planning? • Are there organisational policies that support youth mainstreaming? • Are there accountability mechanisms with youth participation, to ensure that implementation is aligned to policy? • Are staff aware of the youth dimension of the specific sector's programmes? • Is specific specialism brought in? • Is there staff capacity building on youth empowerment/development, youth participation and youth mainstreaming? • What are the attitudes of staff to youth, youth participation and youth mainstreaming? Is there consensus on the broader rationale for youth mainstreaming? • Are planning structures open to youth participation? Are the right kinds of young people genuinely representative of youth groups involved in planning through formal structures? Are the young people involved those who are the most affected by the sector's/organisation's policies? • Do institutions have meaningful youth participation on their boards? Are these young people able to represent the diversity of youth voices, as applying to the work of your organisation, and contribute to institutional strengthening? • Does youth research and data disaggregation capacity exist in the organisation? • Are stakeholders involved? Are diversity and inclusion principles adopted in stakeholder involvement? • Are young people participating in this specific organisational analysis? • Are young people's developmental and safeguarding rights built into organisational policies?

Table 16.1 Policy, programme and organisational analysis (*cont.*)

Level of analysis (global, regional, national, local, sectoral)	Some analysis questions
Programme analysis Analysis of programmes of individual participating agencies to assess youth mainstreaming in the planning process	• To what extent do programmes reflect aspirations/legal commitments to youth rights and support the implementation of policy? • Do programmes generally reflect sensitivity to sociodemographic variables such as age, gender, disability, ethnicity etc., social formations, values etc.? • What are the youth dimensions of programmes in the thematic areas of participating agencies? • Do programme goals/objectives refer to impact on young people or for different age cohorts? • In a more transformative sense, do the goals/objectives include a broader commitment to changing institutions, attitudes or other factors that discriminate against young people? • Does the programme have sufficient tools to analyse youth-specific concerns in the sector? • Is there sufficient information on young people affected by this programme area? If not, where can such information be found? • Are the young people affected by the programme area addressed sufficiently in programme planning? • Are programme data disaggregated for youth, including for young men and women, and youth age subgroups? • Are all required specialisations and young men and women brought into the planning process? • Are some professional and social groups, including youth groups, excluded from planning? If so, who and why? How will this affect programme design? • How is youth mainstreaming reflected in analysis, planning, implementation, and M&E and impact assessment? Is there a youth lens integrated to analysis and planning? Are young people participating in the programme cycle? Are data segregated for youth at the M&E level? • Are young people participating in programme analysis? • Is the organisation providing sufficient investment/finance to mainstream youth into programming, such as for training, implementation, monitoring and evaluation, and so on? • Are young people's developmental and safeguarding rights built into programme development?

Box 16.2 contains some examples of how this analysis has been conducted in Commonwealth member countries.

Box 16.2 Policy, institution and programme analysis

Jamaica

The *2012 Quality Survey of Youth in Jamaica* (the 'Quality Survey') reviewed a comprehensive range of youth development plans, policies and programmes. It subsequently unearthed substantial gaps in processes, providing a useful insight into the key challenges facing young people:

- *The macroeconomic context:* In a context of low growth and inequity, 'youth are particularly affected by the attending structural constraints'. The data showed low labour force participation and high levels of unemployment, with attendant social consequences.

- *Poverty, urban and rural:* Poverty is often transmitted across generations, compromising the life chances of children and young people, through to adults and the elderly. However, there was concern that youth who consider themselves to be excluded from national production plans and who are frustrated by poverty may opt to find alternative – including underground – avenues to survive, with serious social and economic consequences.

Following the Quality Survey and its recommendations, the Government of Jamaica recalibrated the National Youth Policy (NYP) 2015–2030 to make it more responsive and relevant to the current challenges facing the nation's youth. Tabled in parliament in May 2015, the NYP reasserted the YM concept[2] and its implications, committed itself to the active participation of young people in areas integral to their own development, and set out its vision for young people thus:

All young people in Jamaica to achieve holistic development and optimal potential, empowered to innovate and compete globally, being respectful of diversity and the rights of self and others, while contributing to the national development and growth.

(Ministry of Youth and Culture 2015)

Solomon Islands

Given the content and profiling of the Commonwealth Plan of Action for Youth Empowerment (PAYE),[3] its impact on youth policy and programme analysis is irrefutable. This has been established in one form or another at six Commonwealth Youth Ministers' Meetings (CYMMs) since 1998, and received some profile at the 2000 World Conference of Youth Ministers in Portugal. The deep roots of the Commonwealth Secretariat's long-term mandates and action on national youth policy, and its rights-based paradigm, were bolstered by this strategic and practical publication. It responded affirmatively to ministerial mandates for YM, driving conscientisation and providing a springboard.

(Continued)

Box 16.2 Policy, institution and programme analysis (*cont.*)

The Pacific Youth Development Framework (PYDF): A co-ordinated approach to youth-centred development in the Pacific 2014–2023 and YM

The quest for a PYDF featured highly on the Commonwealth Youth Programme South Pacific Regional Centre's (CYPSPRC) YM agenda in 2008–10, as it actively pursued engagement and collaboration with all Pacific regional stakeholders to a) highlight the Commonwealth Secretariat's work in the region, b) minimise duplication and c) increase resource sharing and goodwill among all youth agency stakeholders.

In September–October 2011, the CYPSPRC convened a meeting of ten Pacific regional organisations in Brisbane, Australia, in the wings of the Commonwealth Youth Forum (CYF) youth leadership conference, where delegates met to prepare for the 2011 Commonwealth Heads of Government Meeting (CHOGM) in Perth. South Pacific region UN agencies, the Duke of Edinburgh's Award, the Oceania Football Confederation and the Pacific Community (SPC) attended the consultation. After the 2011 Brisbane meeting, the SPC took the lead for the National Youth Development Framework (NYDF), assimilating the inputs garnered from the Secretariat and other regional stakeholders. The CYPSPRC seized the PYDF momentum as a critical opportunity to advance the YM agenda in the region. The SPC and the Pacific Youth Council (PYC) presented the draft PYDF at the 8CYMM in Papua New Guinea. The PYDF was endorsed by the Pacific Ministers for Youth and Sports in December 2013 in Noumea, New Caledonia, during the Pacific Youth and Sports Ministers Conference.

This was the first time that regional organisations had worked together in a collaborative yet structured manner to ensure that their programmes and interventions were co-ordinated and their resources shared, combining their collective energies to reach more young people in a meaningful way. The PYDF 2014–2023 is the blue print for youth development in the region.

Notes

1   Adapted from the Gender Mainstreaming Toolkit (Niemanis 2007).
2   The NYP drew on a range of national research and policy documents, treaties and obligations, viz. a) the World Programme of Action on Youth (WPAY) 2010, UNDESA; b) the CARICOM Youth Development Action Plan (CYDAP) 2012; c) the Plan of Action for Youth Empowerment (PAYE) 2007–2015 (Commonwealth Youth Programme 2007); d) the UN Convention on the Rights of the Child (CRC); e) the Millennium Development Goals (MDGs); f) the UNFPA Programme of Action of the 1994 International Conference on Population and Development.
3   Commonwealth Youth Programme 2007.

References

Commonwealth Youth Programme (2007), *The Commonwealth Plan of Action for Youth Empowerment 2007–2015*, Commonwealth Secretariat, London.

Ministry of Youth and Culture, Government of Jamaica (2015), *National Youth Policy 2015–2030*, available online at: http://jis.gov.jm/media/Final-Green-Paper-2015_April-9.pdf

Niemanis, A (2007), *Gender Mainstreaming in Practice: A Toolkit,* Regional Bureau for Europe and the CIS, United Nations Development Programme (UNDP), Bratislava.

Chapter 17
The Process

This chapter will look at:

- specific stages of youth mainstreaming in its political and technical forms

- challenges and solutions for working within and across these stages.

Box 17.1 YM is not linear, it is adaptive and responsive

It is not possible to outline a linear process for mainstreaming. Each element will be relevant to different parts of the process in different ways, while the nature of each element will change and adapt according to changing structural and institutional contexts through time, and depending on the stage of the process. For example, stakeholders will join, or leave, a process depending on interest and changing political contexts, at which point a reconfiguration of collaboration may be called for. So each of these components will be iterative, not static or linear.

Box 17.2 Process stages

For each process element, we identify three steps in the evolution towards a fully formed element; initiated, developing and established. This indicates that, while each stage of development contributes to youth mainstreaming, the fullest impact of YM will be achieved only when the established stage is reached. Processes where one element is at the 'initiated' or 'developing' stage will have only limited outcomes for young people.

In your discussion of each of the process elements, it would be useful to examine the challenges in moving from one level to the next. What are the challenges, for example, in working with stakeholders (Stage 1) to move from initiation (mapping and acknowledgement of stakeholders), to allowing them formal access to decision-making (developing), to fully formed engagement that genuinely influences changes for youth through stakeholder engagement (established)? This analysis should be done for each stage of each process element.

The following diagram helps us see parts of the process (though it is not as linear as indicated in Figure 17.1).

Figure 17.1 The youth mainstreaming process

17.1 Stakeholder engagement[1]

The first step in YM is broadening the ownership of the process from the outset to all stakeholders in planning. In sectoral planning, this requires broadening the scope of 'what' that sector is to enable drawing everyone in – including research bodies, civil society organisations, professional associations, unaffiliated but affected groups[2] etc. This also involves working with the diverse bodies in the youth sector (Chapter 6) to obtain technical support for youth mainstreaming.

It is important here to develop tools for your context that help you answer questions such as:

- Are all stakeholders involved in planning? (See Figure 8.1 – Stakeholder groups, functions and interests.)

- Are we involving the youth sector in incorporating youth development/empowerment expertise to our planning?

- Is the diversity and inclusion principle applied to stakeholder engagement?

- What strategies should be used to involve all stakeholders?

Table 17.1 Stakeholder engagement

Initiated	Developing	Established
Stakeholders mapped and engaged in forums on youth mainstreaming in informal ways.	Stakeholders have formal access to provide inputs to youth mainstreaming planning across other sectors.	Stakeholder engagement is sustained, transforms planning and establishes youth-centric policy, planning and implementation.

17.2 Political buy-in and financial commitments

Obtaining political will and policy/financial commitments requires framing youth mainstreaming in the context of dominant political priorities and advocating in cases where YM does not fit existing priorities.

In this case, a policy brief usually begins this process. The task of a policy brief is to articulate the value of youth mainstreaming in achieving development outcomes, and particularly in reaching the SDGs. While there are technical elements in this, it is largely a political task that involves:

- framing the issue of youth mainstreaming in terms of already articulated national development priorities and well-articulated political priorities; and

Table 17.2 Political buy-in and financial commitments

Initiated	Developing	Established
Policy brief designed and presented to cabinet.	Circulars and government directives prioritising youth mainstreaming.	Circulars and government directives implemented with adequate resourcing.
	Policy and legislative commitments to youth mainstreaming.	Policy and legislative commitments translated into programmes with adequate resourcing.

- anticipating possible objections and framing responses to these.

Depending on the context of YM, whether project, sectoral or all-of-government at the national or local government level, the policy brief might be a good rallying point for stakeholder engagement around creating a common message and purpose for advocating for YM. We should typically work with universities and research institutes to ensure a robust policy paper. Box 17.3 provides brief guidance on formulating a policy brief.

Box 17.3 Preparing an effective policy brief[3]

Process – young people and all stakeholders enabling youth rights have to be at the centre of the preparation of the policy brief.

Content (suggested headings)

Background

- Rationale for the policy brief and who is involved: the need to promote intergenerational justice; youth voice on youth rights.

Why invest?

- Data on status of youth inequality with age- and gender-disaggregated data, and youth participation in governance.
- How mechanisms and processes are delivering; current levels of investment.
- Implications for government expenditure targets.
- Sector papers should highlight sector issues.

Connecting YM to national development agendas

- Present alternative scenarios for national development agendas and sectors through integrating youth mainstreaming.
- In addition, present alternative scenarios to direct public expenditure for youth in national/subnational/sectoral development.

Conclusions and recommendations

- Concise, practical conclusions and recommendations indicating who would be responsible, and what is to be achieved through the process/mechanism in the recommendation.

TIPS

Keep it brief – no longer than eight A4 pages, and nothing beyond 3,000 words usually. Of course, the length will ultimately be determined by specific contextual requirements.

Keep it promotional – make it attractive, professionally formatted and well designed yet understated. The design should not take away from the message.

17

Box 17.4 sets out some examples of YM policy advocacy in Commonwealth member countries.

Box 17.4 Developing a policy brief

Jamaica

In 2006, the Ministry of Youth and Culture (MoYC) spearheaded Jamaica's YM initiatives, stepping up efforts following the explicit mandates that emanated from the 7CYMM in Sri Lanka in 2008. In 2009/2010, the Government of Jamaica, through the MoYC's National Youth Development Centre, contracted the Centre for Leadership and Governance (CLG) at the University of the West Indies to develop a National Youth Mainstreaming Strategy and Manual, as part of a wider youth development initiative sponsored by the Inter-American Development Bank (IDB). The CLG's remit was to provide technical expertise for the national strategy and to mainstream the issues and concerns of young people and their contributions within and across the efforts of the public, private and non-governmental organisation (NGO) sectors. The CLG's processes included co-ordinating stakeholder consultations; developing YM definitions; drafting the scope and contents of YM tools; and sensitising the public and private sectors on YM.

A policy brief was published after the June 2011 National Youth Mainstreaming Strategy Workshop. The brief contained seven elements: 1) context of the YM study; 2) key YM terms; 3) data collection for strategy and action plan; 4) situation analysis; 5) proposed YM framework; 6) strategies (thematic areas and goals); and 7) overview of the YM process.

Malaysia

Between 2012 and 2015, the Institute for Youth Research (IYRES) and the Ministry of Youth and Sports, Malaysia, instituted extensive consultations with a range of stakeholders on the proposed modifications required for Malaysia Youth Policy (MYP) 2018–2035, researching and reviewing key studies under the rubric of the country's Vision 2020 strategy. IYRES submitted 16 resolutions to Cabinet. Two major resolutions were accepted: the embedding of a youth mainstreaming approach to youth development and an amendment to the youth-age definition, bringing Malaysia into line with Commonwealth and international standards.

The policy brief outlined three goals: 1) increase the involvement of young people as responsible citizens; 2) highlight the potential of each individual young person by celebrating everyone's diversity and differences; and 3) expand access to priority areas and youth development initiatives for the benefit of all target groups.

Solomon Islands

The Commonwealth's Plan of Action for Youth Empowerment (PAYE) was the critical foundation document for guiding youth development in Solomon Islands. Benefiting from immediate accessibility to and expertise of the staff at the CYP South Pacific Regional Centre (CYPSPRC), as well as the PAYE and YM anchors, the Ministry of Women, Youth, Children and Family Affairs

(Continued)

Box 17.4 Developing a policy brief (*cont.*)

(MWYCFA) optimised the technical support available for the development of the Solomon Islands National Youth Policy (SINYP) 2010–2015, its plan of action and its monitoring framework. Endorsed by Cabinet in 2010, the SINYP set the stage for projects to be implemented, monitored and evaluated through a youth lens and mobilised through a multi-sectoral approach to youth development. In accordance with the mandate emanating from 7CYMM in Sri Lanka in 2008, the Solomon Islands Government intensified its YM initiatives at the national level.

In 2011, through the driving force of the MWYCFA Permanent Secretary, Ethel Sigimanu, and in partnership with CYPSPRC, the Solomon Islands Government intensified youth mainstreaming efforts at the provincial level. In partnership with the provincial government and non-government stakeholders, and with support from the Pacific Leadership Programme and the CYPSPRC, Provincial Youth Mainstreaming Summits in all nine provinces and another in the city of Honiara resulted in ten Provincial Youth Policies, aligned to SINYP 2010–2015.

High-level endorsements resulting in YM initiatives are elaborated in Box 17.5.

Political endorsement comprises public political support to the agendas of youth mainstreaming and is supported by political will. This may, or may not, include financial commitments at this stage, but is an initial step to buttress further advocacy if need be. Political endorsement might be indicated at the highest level through an Act of Parliament, or administrative tools such as circulars endorsed by the highest political office. The best forms of political endorsement would be evidence-based and have considered significant objections and responses to these, including through parliamentary/cabinet debate. These endorsements may be actualised at the highest level through legal stipulations, or otherwise, through parliamentary/cabinet directives, institutional guidelines or general circulars.

Policy commitments will also include:

- increased commitments to public expenditure for youth; or

- attracting donor commitments to youth mainstreaming initiatives, including affecting transformations in donor/lending policies to inform investment in youth-centric planning.

Box 17.5 High-level endorsement and stakeholder engagement

Malaysia

The prime minister's commendation for the MYP 2018–2035 exhorted all ministries to embrace a paradigm which valued all young people as positive assets, in keeping with the policy's intention to maximise young people's agency. The Minister of Youth and Sports/Kementarian Belia & Sukan (KBS), Minister Khairy Jamaluddin Abu Bakar, has ultimate responsibility for delivering the MYP. A strong advocate of holistic learning and a champion for young people's involvement and participation in politics, Minister Khairy was selected as Young Global Leader in 2006 by the World Economic Forum, Davos, and was president of the youth wing of the United Malays National Organisation at the time of this research. As the highest government authority responsible for youth policy and youth development targets, Minister Khairy is one of the most important protagonists for advancing YM. Together with KBS's research arm, the IYRES and the Malaysia Youth Council (MBM), the three central organisations have used their combined platforms of influence, skills, education, passion, values and a human-rights orientation to affect the landscape of youth development in Malaysia.

Solomon Islands

The MWYCFA, under the stewardship of the Permanent Secretary, directs youth and gender mainstreaming efforts and YM implementation in Solomon Islands. Recognising that the needs and concerns of women, youth and children – and other marginalised groups – are cross-cutting, the MWYCFA articulated a method of working that placed young people's, children's and women's concerns at the centre of planning and resource distribution. Cognisant of the fact that partnerships between government, NGOs/civil society organisations (CSOs) and donor partners can facilitate holistic development, state and non-state actors present at the 2010 National Youth Summit on Mainstreaming – *The SINYP: Youth at the Centre of our Work* – committed themselves to implement the SINYP 2010–2015 within the framework of YM.

An implementation matrix served as a practical mechanism for the co-ordination of stakeholder programmes and targets. The matrix ensured that better-resourced agencies, e.g. the UN Development Programme (UNDP) and other multilateral organisations, could easily link their own key outcomes to SINYP Priority Policy Outcomes (PPOs). Agencies assessed best use of their expertise and resources to reinforce practical tools for young people to understand and get involved in SINYP targets and outcomes. This was an efficient mechanism for all youth-serving providers to map their youth offer in a manner that ensured that they could retain their core business, yet align their work to a policy document and plan of action collectively agreed by multi-sectoral stakeholders. Apart from providing a basis for a more collaborative approach to human and financial resources, the matrix was also used a tool to identify and plug gaps.

Young people were integrally involved in the National and Regional Youth Summits on YM in 2010, as contributors, as active implementers and as critical stakeholders in the evaluation and monitoring system. Twenty-four organisations, including members of the Provincial Assembly, the

(Continued)

Box 17.5 High-level endorsement and stakeholder engagement (*cont.*)

provincial government executive, all heads of divisions, church and youth representatives, NGOs, CSOs and other stakeholders on the Central Island and in the province attended and signed up to the SINYP 2010–2015. The summits formalised and gave structure to the ongoing efforts of different youth stakeholders in each province and at the centre, enabling partners to buy in to the YM approach; and align their activities and implement their plans according to the six PPOs of the SINYP, while still remaining true to their core business.

The process systematically brought youth development activities and programmes into the core of government, private sector and civil society business. Recommendations and follow-up actions were agreed to and were captured in communiqués, signed by all participants, pledging their commitment to implement programmes using a YM methodology and progressing targets which aligned to SINYP priorities and desired outcomes. Stakeholders linked their obligations by signing the Panatina Communiqué.

17.3 Establishing YM guidelines and principles[4]

Guidelines, such as this broader set of Commonwealth guidelines for YM, should address the specific contexts of youth as they relate to the country/sector/geographical region/organisation etc., and address the specific institutional dynamics and cultures relevant to your country/sector or geographical region.

This need not be fully in place for youth mainstreaming to begin, but the process itself could be an ideal starting point for discussions around formalised, standard-setting national/sectoral/institutional or geographical criteria for youth mainstreaming that are set firmly in the political and institutional contexts under discussion. Guidelines could potentially set out a structure, establishing training frameworks, roles and responsibilities, implementation, and monitoring and evaluation arrangements. This structure could be framed with the support of the youth sector/youth development specialists.

Table 17.3 Establishing YM guidelines and principles

Initiated	Developing	Established
Youth mainstreaming guidelines developed collectively, prepared and published.	Inductions on youth mainstreaming guidelines begun.	Youth mainstreaming guidelines implemented and effecting youth mainstreaming structural and programme changes.

Similar guidelines should exist for organisational guidance for youth participation (see Annex 3).

Box 17.6 indicates the commitments of the African Union Commission to institutional mainstreaming.

Box 17.6 African Union Commission's framework for institutional youth mainstreaming

The African Union Commission (AUC) launched a youth mainstreaming framework to inform the practices of the commission in 2016. It is meant to position the AUC to 'coordinate youth mainstreaming in order to leverage resources and respond to the call on youth investment'. The AUC youth mainstreaming initiative aims to fast-track ongoing youth activities at the commission in a strategic and co-ordinated manner, as a pathway to realising the sixth aspiration of the African Development Framework – Agenda 2063.

The framework has resulted in discussions around bolstering interdepartmental collaboration within the AUC and has accelerated youth policies and programmes in the commission to implement the youth mainstreaming framework. It will apply to all departments of the commission.

This framework is buttressed by the African Youth Decade Plan of Action, which calls for a continental youth mainstreaming agenda as part of development objectives and for the development of programmes for youth empowerment. Mainstreaming the participation of youth and women in Africa's development is an essential part in delivering the rapid, but balanced, economic and social development of Africa.[5]

17.4 Establishing/strengthening structures and organisations

No general prescription is possible for defining youth mainstreaming structures. This will depend on the context and level of YM. The central tenet of structures that drive YM should be that they are able to drive political interests, incorporate technical skills and sustain YM processes in multiple sectors through collaboration, dialogue and constructive M&E.

Table 17.4 Establishing/strengthening structures and organisations

Initiated	Developing	Established
Youth mainstreaming co-ordination structures defined and agreed.	Co-ordination structures active and sustained.	Co-ordination structures provide results for YM, in terms of the planning process from analysis to monitoring and evaluation.

Although civil society and even government may begin with a degree of informality and experimentation, in due course having determinate responses is critical for accountability. 'Where' structures sit is also integral to the resources available and the authority the process wields.

Figure 17.2 proposes a three-tier option where:

- the top tier represents a) a national task force that steers the process, b) an independent regulatory body that ensures coherence and accountability to young people of YM aspirations, strategic goals and plans, and c) a multiparty parliamentary committee that ensures sustainability of the process irrespective of party in power;

- the middle tier represents thematic focal points for each principal sector that will represent the interests and strategies of respective sectors participating in the process; and

- the bottom tier represents agency focal points that will link to sectoral focal points.

What is most important, as in any structure, is that there is good communication across and between tiers, and that thematic focal points do not prevent agency-level focal points interacting with top tiers, but are simply a mechanism for effective co-ordination where necessary.

Figure 17.2 Example structure for an all-of-government youth mainstreaming process

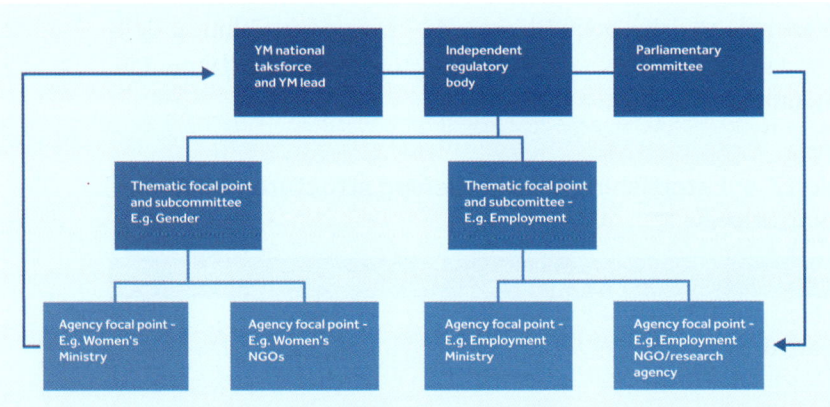

The establishment of 'focal points' for youth mainstreaming has been a much-advocated model for effective mainstreaming, and is often evident in youth justice systems (see Case Study Theme 5 in Part 3). This concept is given further scrutiny in Box 17.7.

Box 17.7 What do we mean by focal points?

Mainstreaming mechanisms will often designate individuals as 'focal points' to co-ordinate and assess progress within each given department/agency. It may be that they have many other responsibilities (including as focal points for other processes); this model can fail where practicalities of resources and support have not been adequately considered. Some aspects to consider:

- The focal point role could be given to **senior rather than middle management**, to maintain the profile of YM in participating agencies. Whether or not the manager devotes most of their time to this portfolio, they will bring to bear the human resources working for them (subordinates), along with sufficient authority and influencing ability.

- Focal points do not just play a co-ordination role, but have a **critical substantive role**. They must convey to other stakeholders the importance of grasping their respective responsibilities, and this means continuously advocating, brokering and catalysing strategic-level actions. It also involves using 'weak ties', as well as compliance-based 'strong ties'.

- The focal point's role must be seen in the context of the **commitment of entire institutions** (tiers, thematic areas of government) to the SDGs as a whole. Youth mainstreaming can then gain traction, with adequate commitment to resources and processes.

- Acting as a focal point does not mean that it must come into the job title; however, it does mean that relevant managers meet regularly as mainstreaming focal points (i.e. as a peer-level network) to update one another and achieve second-order co-ordination. Like leadership, this role is **a function rather than a person**. (At the highest levels, ministers in effect act as focal points during cabinet meetings.)

Box 17.8 is a list of questions that will help you determine possibilities for a whole-of-government structure.

Box 17.8 Establishing structures – sample questions

1. What is the highest level of influence that the issue network contains? How is parliamentary/cabinet-level representation to be achieved?

2. How co-ordinated is the taskforce in advocating for youth mainstreaming? Which other agendas is it perceived to be linked to – correctly/incorrectly?

Box 17.8 Establishing structures – sample questions (*cont.*)

3. For any given department/agency, at what level of seniority are those who best understand YM?

4. Does the structure facilitate sufficient ownership of the youth mainstreaming process within organisations and within sectors?

5. Are young people participating in the structure? What norms should govern youth structures' access to the ministerial level, and vice versa?

6. What would happen if a given department/agency (or designated lead team/person within it) were to leave the network? Which processes might be delayed or disabled?

7. How are handovers ensured within the institutions when individuals leave the youth mainstreaming structure?

8. Is a co-ordinating office function (adequately resourced) to be hosted within one of the existing structures, or is it better set up afresh, outside such structures?

Examples of structures established through the influence of the Commonwealth's former work on YM are described in Box 17.9.

Box 17.10 is an example of the implications for strong organisations that facilitate sustainable structures.

Box 17.9 Establishing structures

Malaysia

The KBS, the IYRES, and the National Youth Consultative Council (NYCC)/ Cabinet Committee on Youth, Malaysia Youth Council (MBM) and Malaysia Youth Parliament (PBM) form the main structures co-ordinating YM. The KBS works in close partnership and consultation with a range of youth organisations, but MBM is the major stakeholder. With strong links to the KBS, the IYRES and others, MBM has huge potential to hold policy-makers and politicians to account, particularly because of its pivotal role in the Association of South east Asian Nations (ASEAN). Leading and empowering youth through 1) advocacy, 2) youth-led programmes and 3) national and international partnerships, MBM represents Malaysian youth's opinion to the government through the PBM; NYCC; federal consultative councils and state government; national budget dialogue; committees at different levels in government; position papers on selected issues; and regular media statements, which express the younger generation's views and aspirations. As the major stakeholders in advancing the youth development agenda, the KBS and MBM's catalytic roles will require ongoing operational adaptation to YM concepts and practice. The IYRES becomes a critical facilitator in this regard.

Box 17.9 Establishing structures (*cont.*)

Solomon Islands

The MWYCFA embraced a mainstreaming approach to implement all policies and commitments affecting women, youth, children and families, and YM's suitability and adaptation to local needs and situations. MWYCFA worked with partners on issues of common interest, e.g. HIIV/AIDS, disaster management, environmental sustainability and research on related subjects, and provided capacity building for support to its stakeholders. YM policy and programmes were implemented through its four directorates – Human Resources; Women; Youth; and Research, Policy, Planning and Information – and co-ordinated by the National Sports Council (NSC) and Solomon Islands National Youth Council (SINYC). Because of the Provincial Youth Mainstreaming and Provincial Youth Policy summits, provincial governments increased budget allocations for youth development and/or established new positions for youth development staff.

National and Regional Youth Parliament programmes provided excellent mechanisms for young people to understand how to lobby and participate in political processes. They not only educated young people on parliamentary democracy and governance, but provided an avenue whereby young people came together to learn about and discuss pertinent issues affecting the countries in the region, using the parliamentary programmes to identify ways to contribute and positively address pressing issues.

Box 17.10 Strengthening organisations for youth mainstreaming – a lesson from gender

Strengthening structures also requires strengthening organisations that make up these national/local structures. The following excerpt looked at how organisations were strengthened to facilitate gender mainstreaming:

In response to the call for gender mainstreaming many development organisations, private donors and NGOs took steps to implement mainstreaming policies. They set up gender units, hired gender specialists and adopted gender training. Some organisations also made budget allocations. On the operational side, they required gender analysis at various stages of development assistance and some started working with other organisations, such as civil society or country governments and other donors.

At the country level, governments established national women's machineries (ministry, department or office), charging them with responsibility for gender mainstreaming throughout government institutions and operations. In practice, women's machineries played multiple roles as policy co-ordinating units, knowledge and support providers and advocates and catalysts. Like development organisations, they also appointed gender specialists and focal points and launched training programs for all staff. A few countries also established accountability mechanisms to assess progress.

Gender Mainstreaming: Making It Happen[6]

17.5 Capacity building

Capacity building[7] covers institutional and individual attributes such as structures and mechanisms, attitudes, skills and competencies to support the implementation of successful youth mainstreaming. Capacity building is about more than just training. It involves:

- A holistic governance/institutional approach in the case of youth mainstreaming that not only builds capacities of institutions, but also capacities of relationships and sustainability across institutions. This includes the ability of institutions to 'respond to the demands'[8] of multiple stakeholders.

- Strengthening accountability, transparency, legitimacy, pluralism and participation.

- Enriching information sharing and trust between players. It may include changes to structures themselves.

- Arranging the structures to get more capacity out of the same resources. This involves capacity to engage with policy, processes, procedures, mechanisms, rules, regulations, values and so on.

- Building the institutional capacity of players, including capacities to integrate formal youth participation

Table 17.5 Capacity building

Initiated	Developing	Established
Staff: Youth mainstreaming symposia and workshops conducted for staff to inform attitudes and practice.	Targeted youth mainstreaming training programmes delivered to participating agencies/ sectors.	Capacity-built staff contribute effectively to youth mainstreaming, and demonstrate youth-friendly attitudes and act as mentors.
	Degree/MA programmes in development and youth development integrate youth mainstreaming modules.	
Organisation: Institutional capacity-building processes exist for youth mainstreaming.	Organisational capacity strengthened.	Organisational capacity reflected in YM implementation.

17

structures, as well as building thematic capacities in youth development, human rights, equity and justice.

- Linking youth mainstreaming to results-based programming and outputs that integrate youth mainstreaming and clearly measure outcomes for youth.

Skills training usually needs to be preceded by orientation, which means a chance for individuals and groups to self-organise and achieve internal consensus. This makes it possible to then get players 'facing the same direction', without revisiting unresolved interpersonal or personal issues.[9]

Some YM capacity-building examples from Commonwealth member countries are set out in Box 17.12.

Box 17.11 Checklist for integrating youth participation capacity into organisations

- The organisation articulates youth mainstreaming in organisational policy
- The organisation has accountability mechanisms to ensure faithfulness of implementation to policy
- Staff have a clear understanding of the implications of the organisation's work for young people
- The organisation has minimum standards for youth participation[10]
- Staff are trained for working with youth as partners in development
- The institution's boards and programme decision-making forums include young people
- Young people are involved in the entire programme cycle from situation analysis, planning, implementation (in practical ways), and monitoring and evaluation
- There is ethical and accountable stakeholder participation
- The organisation has co-created tools and techniques for evaluating the effects of youth mainstreaming and youth participation

See also Annex 3.

Box 17.12 Capacity building

Malaysia

Capacity building of youth workers: The Commonwealth Diploma in Youth Development Work (DYDW) – ASEAN

What opportunities exist for augmenting YM initiatives through youth workers and youth work officials? Increases in the national development allocation for youth

(Continued)

Box 17.12   Capacity building (*cont.*)

work and related programmes, and its discrete place in the Malaysia Youth Policy (MYP) 2018–2035, testify to a national commitment to the nation's youth work agenda. The Commonwealth's Diploma in Youth Development Work (DYDW) was launched by the KBS at the CYMM in May 1998, and was approved for delivery at the Universiti Putra Malaysia (UPM) by the Ministry of Education in June 1999. The UPM was a critical voice and influencer of policy and good practice pertaining to the delivery of the DYDW in the Asia region of the Commonwealth, particularly with respect to quality assurance, tutorials, assessment, professionalisation etc.

In 2005, local scholars and UPM advocates agitated for the creation of a code of ethics for youth workers and the development of standards of practice as integral steps toward raising the level and quality of youth work in the country.

Capacity building of KBS youth officials: The Youth in Executive Development Work Diploma

The UPM delivers the Youth in Executive Development Work Diploma (DBKB) programme, in partnership with the Selangor State Government. The DBKB provides assistant youth officers, youth officers, training officers/executive managers for youth development, human resource planning officers, administrative officers and youth development researchers with skills in proactive planning, implementation and evaluation of youth development programmes at the community level.

Capacity building through the Perdana Fellows Programme

The Perdana Fellows Programme caters to youth leaders who have a strong interest in public policy and current affairs. It provides exceptionally talented young Malaysians with first-hand experience in matters of national governance. Serving as executive interns to cabinet ministers, fellows work at the highest levels of the federal government, assisting ministers in substantiating the national agenda.

The programme is designed to add value to cabinet ministers as well as to the fellows. The ministers gain fresh perspectives from young, idealistic, energetic and assertive interns. Fellows in turn are exposed to substantial policy work at the highest levels of government. Fellows assist their mentor and his/her senior officials in planning and executing government policy and complement existing efforts to communicate government programmes via social media and other strategic communication platforms. As leaders of their generation, fellows are expected to contribute new and bold ideas to their respective ministries, to act as a bridge between their generation and the government, and to have opportunities to serve the national agenda and the prime minister's Government Transformation Programmes.

17.6   Youth analysis – for context, institutions and programmes

The youth analysis section (Chapter 15) adequately unpacked elements of youth analysis of legislation, policy, programmes and institutions and should be referred to here. Chapter 9 covered evidence and data.

Table 17.6 Youth analysis – for context, institutions and programmes

Initiated	Developing	Established
Commitments made to youth research, including training and investment in youth-led research.	Youth research and youth-led research conducted and completed.	Youth research and youth-led research influence policy and programme planning, implementation, and monitoring and evaluation in all sectors.
Commitments made to monitoring and evaluation that integrates youth mainstreaming.	YM monitoring and evaluation plans are part of the official planning process.	YM monitoring and evaluation creates learning and improvement for YM processes.
Commitments made to institutional analysis for capacities to deliver youth mainstreaming.	Organisations assessed for ability to plan and deliver for youth.	Evidence of organisational capacity to deliver on YM demonstrated.

The best, grounded analysis/research is almost always achieved when junior colleagues and young people/young service receivers are involved in informing design through their lived experiences.[11]

Box 17.13 Questions around youth-led research

When bringing young people to the centre of a planning process, this raises several questions for policy-makers and youth work professionals:[12]

- How do we determine the relative validity of social research data in relation to the stated positions of youth participants and representatives?

- How do we reconcile the necessarily restricted domain of public service (open to specified professionals and elected politicians) with the open domain of social dialogue? In particular, what gives legitimacy to non-formal or semi-formal processes?

- At the same time, how do we build formal structures within government for youth dialogue?

- How do we manage the physical and political risks to which both young people and decision-makers may be exposed? For young people, there may be safeguarding issues involved where their safety and security may be challenged by the consultation/research process itself. For decision-makers, there may be issues of political sensitivity involved if young people challenge orthodox positions in development planning.

Box 17.14 Participatory analysis, research validity and information sharing

Situation analysis does not happen just once – it needs to happen with each group of young people.

While some professional analyses take place away from young people on the ground, the task is therefore to share findings between levels and sectors, as far as possible, to the benefit of each.[13]

How broad participation needs to be is a civic/political question, related to whose involvement is sought and why. It is also a theoretical question to do with research validity. The important things to ensure are that, while representation is wide, the findings are analysed by young people; if not, then that they are fed back to young people; and also that the way quantitative and qualitative data are brought in is within the standards and parameters of reliability and validity of research.

Possible means of involving youth in planning include:

- collaborative action and consultation in youth-friendly spaces;

- dialogue through online and broadcast media; and

- involving youth in formal decision-making spaces.

17.7 Strategic and operational planning and budgeting

The programme cycle includes the translation of legislation and policy into strategic plans and, thereafter, programmes and projects, and monitoring and evaluation that facilitate youth mainstreaming. Table 17.8 will help planners assess to what extent the cycle incorporates youth mainstreaming, and what more needs to be done. It is vital at this stage to ensure that all strategies are adequately budgeted in consultation with young people.

Table 17.7 Strategic and operational planning and budgeting

Initiated	Developing	Established
Training and capacity building on integrating youth mainstreaming into all levels of the programme cycle in all sectors.	All sectors integrate youth mainstreaming into all levels of the planning cycle in harmony with existing conventions, legislation and policy.	All sectors demonstrate improved outcomes and impacts for young people because of youth-mainstreamed planning.

Table 17.8 Indicators of success for YM monitoring and evaluation

Phase	Indicators of success
1: Stakeholder engagement	• Organisational mapping to identify nodal agency and participating agencies based on Figure 8.1 is completed • All stakeholders committed to youth empowerment are mapped and engaged • Participating agencies show interest • Preliminary advocacy and dialogue are conducted on mainstreaming an asset-based youth lens to implementing-agency research, planning, implementation, and monitoring and evaluation • Young men and women participate in partner identification process and are identified as stakeholders
2: Political endorsement and financial commitments	• Political and fiscal environment scanned for enablers, disablers and dominant political interests that may align with youth mainstreaming (Chapters 4–10) • Policy brief prepared • Policy brief influences high-level decision-makers • Written commitments exist at national government or youth ministry level for YM, including legislative enactments, guidelines, circulars etc. • National/local institutional financial planning aligned for youth mainstreaming
3: YM guidelines and principles formulated	• YM guideline consultations held with all stakeholders, especially young people • YM guidelines reviewed and finalised • YM guidelines endorsed and utilised to inform planning in sectors
4: Establishing structures	• Structure consulted and finalised • Functions of structure clearly articulated and written down • Terms of reference written for focal points and committee members • Structures reviewed and reorganised for relevance and effectiveness

5: Capacity building	• Institutional and Individual capacity building completed for:
	  • individual skills
	  • effective organisations and entities
	  • building interrelationships between entities
	  • an enabling environment
	• Subject-specific capacity building completed for:
	  • youth dimensions of planning and asset-based youth development
	  • human rights conventions and their relationship to youth rights
	  • the Sustainable Development Goals and their relationship to attaining development outcomes for youth
	  • the YDI
	  • institutionalising youth participation and creating formal youth participation structures
	  • research, planning, implementation, and monitoring and evaluation with youth participation and a youth lens
	  • information sharing on youth policy where relevant
	  • an understanding of and access to relevant global/national/local data on key youth issues in health, welfare, education, employment, finance and all other sectoral areas, as relevant to implementing agencies

(Continued)

Table 17.8 Indicators of success for YM monitoring and evaluation (*cont.*)

Phase	Indicators of Success

6a: Youth analysis of existing policy/ legislation, institutions and programmes (Chapter 15)	• Policy and legislation analysis:
	  • tools available for policy and legislation analysis for youth mainstreaming
	  • right stakeholders brought in for analysis
	  • gaps in policy and legislation identified
	  • young people participate in analysis
	
	• Institutional analysis:
	  • assessment tools for institutional analysis in YM developed, including for youth participation at all levels
	  • young men and women participate in the process
	  • tools implemented
	  • report written and shared with youth mainstreaming taskforce
	  • analysis informs institutional change
	
	• Programme and sectoral analysis:
	  • programme/sectoral analysis tool agreed on
	  • tool administered
	  • report written and shared with the taskforce
	  • young men and women participate in the process

6b: Cross-sectoral situation analysis with a youth lens or by integrating a youth lens into existing research frameworks of participating agencies	• Tools developed and piloted in each sector for integration of a youth lens • Research conducted, especially youth-led/youth participatory research • Young men and women participate in research design and implementation • Research findings utilised in strategic planning
7: Strategic and operational planning and budgeting	• Young people and other youth sector stakeholders participate in strategic planning • Youth are an integral part of developed strategies and are mentioned explicitly in specific objectives • Inter-organisational planning on integrating a youth lens to all levels of the planning process, including budgeting that demonstrates expenditure on youth services/youth work • Young men and women participate in planning and budgeting • Official written commitment to youth mainstreaming ensured by participating agencies • The nodal youth agency has an action plan to ensure a youth lens and youth participation in planning • Budgeting at the national/sector/institutional or project level ensures adequate consideration of the youth elements of the programme and allocate adequate resources
8: Implementation	• Timely and effective implementation in partnership with youth sector, including young people • Sectoral collaboration during implementation ensured through co-ordination mechanisms, processes and guidelines • Participation of young people in implementation

(Continued)

Table 17.8 Indicators of success for YM monitoring and evaluation (*cont.*)

Phase	Indicators of Success
9: Participatory monitoring evaluation (short- and medium-term change – outputs and outcomes)	• M&E plans prepared against output, process and outcome indicators, with a clear focus on young people reached and impacts of programmes on young people • Participatory M&E tools are used • Training conducted on the principles of results-based participatory monitoring and evaluation and disaggregation of data for youth • Youth-friendly M&E systems in place to ensure meaningful youth participation in M&E • Collaborative monitoring of progress with young people • Young men and women participate in monitoring and evaluation • Stakeholders participating in M&E represent the diversity of identities and interests of those benefiting from programmes • M&E experts brought in are sensitive to youth issues • M&E becomes part of an institutional learning process • M&E results disseminated to all key stakeholders, including youth • Clear, practical recommendations for cross-sectoral action formulated based on M&E findings • Impact assessment tools prepared against impact indicators • Young people participate in impact assessment • Data demonstrate long-term sustainable impact of youth mainstreaming strategies
10: Sustainability and risk management (see Section 17.10)	• Sustainability strategies developed and implemented • Risk assessment tools developed and implemented

Depending on your sector, Table 3.1, The Equality Matrix for Youth, may help integrate relevant strategic planning questions.

17.8 Implementation

Implementation requires ensuring that it is faithful to the strategic intent of youth mainstreaming throughout the process, including ensuring redirection where real-life limitations are diverting programmes and projects from their original intent. Monitoring is a key process (see Section 17.9) that will ensure this sense of timely direction.

17.9 Participatory monitoring and evaluation

Monitoring and evaluation is a process of ensuring that implementation of programmes and projects is indeed moving towards reaching the youth mainstreaming objectives of the sector, and will apply to each of the youth mainstreaming process elements.

Effective monitoring and evaluation involves young people and communities in the design, implementation, data interpretation and data presentation of M&E. This particularly pertains to young people who are directly affected by a policy/programme. Table 17.8 helps with some initial indicators for measuring success of the YM process.

17.10 Sustainability and risk management

The incentives facing politicians in a multiparty democracy are at best medium term (linked to electoral cycles) and often very short term. Once in office, the need to focus on day-to-day crisis management ('fire-fighting') can crowd out time for long-term strategy.

Therefore, it is important that:

- All three branches of government – legislative (makes the law), executive (carries out the law) and judicial (enforces the law) – are involved in the youth mainstreaming endeavour (see Figure 17.2).

- We focus on *the best possible integration* with the *best-funded* and *most long-lived* policy instruments. In the SDGs, we have an international policy framework that will remain valid to 2030 and which, crucially, gives renewed emphasis to sustainable development.

- Risk management processes are built into planning.

Country contexts differ; so do departmental structures. Accordingly, central governments will take differing approaches to clustering SDGs and selecting lead agencies and social partners. Dealing with forecasts and estimates, as well as facts, government will also take different economic approaches to reaching their goals. The consequential trade-offs between different options are highly complex. However, youth

Table 17.9 Sustainability and risk management

Initiated	Developing	Established
Sustainability and risk identification developed by all stakeholders, including youth.	Inductions take place on sustainability and risk identification and management in partnership with youth.	Sustainability plans are implemented, risks are assessed and adequate action taken.

mainstreaming policy design succeeds if it manages to place on the table some simple questions:

1. What are the actions that will take us forward more quickly across a broader range of interlinked goals?

2. Of the policy options before us, which (even if evidence-based and laudable in their own terms) are likely to exacerbate youth poverty as a 'necessary cost'?

3. Of the policy options before us, which constitute an unambiguous investment in poverty reduction among the youth cohort?

Having in place a proper risk management plan helps mitigate adverse conditions, and optimise positive ones. Table 17.10 represents an example risk management matrix.

Table 17.10 Risk management approaches

YM context/process	Implications	Managing risk
Structural		
1. Global, national, subnational and sectoral legislation and policies that are not youth-friendly	• Discrimination against youth, lack of security and safety for youth	• Research to demonstrate impact of policy on youth • Support to review policy with young people
2. Organisational structures with orthodox cultures that refuse to change	• Will not involve young people in planning • Will not enable multiple stakeholder participation or diversity of thought • Will not deliver optimal results for young people	• Ensure capacity building for inclusive, non-discriminatory planning • Set in place accountability mechanisms, including accountability to young people • Assess attitudinal disposition in staff recruitment and commitments to social equality and justice
3. Not all stakeholders are integrated into planning, particularly marginalised youth groups, youth movements	• Will not be a youth-friendly planning process • Will not deliver optimal results for youth	• Develop comprehensive stakeholder-mapping tools and engagement strategies
4. Lack of data and capacity for youth mainstreaming advocacy	• Will not be able to convince decision-makers and donors of the need and relevance of youth mainstreaming as a youth right, and as a strategy that informs meeting development targets	• Develop and implement research • Engage research agencies with the capacity for rights-based research

(Continued)

Table 17.10 Risk management approaches (*cont.*)

YM context/process	Implications	Managing risk
5. Lack of political endorsement and financial commitments	• No systemic foundation for youth mainstreaming • Isolated youth mainstreaming initiatives will be disconnected and will not deliver co-ordinated results for equality for youth	• Revise policy briefs and strategies for more effective advocacy • Peg further linkages to existing political and financial priorities • Articulate, with evidence, the human and financial cost of failing to mainstream youth
6. Structures and process are not sustained, fail to deliver	• Co-ordination across sectors will be lost for interlinked programming • Impacts for young people will be low • Will not be able to report comprehensively on youth mainstreaming outcomes • Therefore, poor data for ongoing advocacy with political authorities and donors	• Seek support for structures • Keep structures simple, fit for purpose, low in bureaucracy • Work to link committed individuals for sustaining the work • Ensure comprehensive inductions for focal points and other co-ordinators
Organisational		
1. Capacity building is not sustained, is not rights-based, is not comprehensive and does not connect to implementation	• Capacity-building costs deliver no return on investment • Not translated into action • Does not result in transforming attitudes towards young people or working with young people	• Develop on-the-job capacity building • Develop coaching and mentoring schemes • Link with capacitated training institutes • Ensure building of institutional capacity, including in recruitment
2. Youth analysis/ situation analysis is not youth-centric	• Does not result in youth-enabling interpretations of data • Resulting programmes may violate youth rights and/or harm the safety and security of young people	• Train staff on youth-centric and youth-led analysis • Ensure analysis implementation guidelines are met • Bring in appropriate skills from youth sector stakeholders
3. Programme plan is not faithful to human rights aspirations and/or does not involve young people	• Does not result in transformative results for young people	• Review plans with multiple stakeholders • Set down planning principles • Ensure the implementation of planning principles • Revise plans
4. Implementation is not faithful to human rights aspirations and strategic and programme plans	• Does not result in transformative results for young people	• Ensure monitoring and evaluation to harmonise implementation with planning • Involve young people in monitoring and evaluation • Build partner skills in implementation and involve all partners in planning

(Continued)

Table 17.10 Risk management approaches (*cont*.)

YM context/process	Implications	Managing risk
5. Monitoring and evaluation is weak and/or does not involve young people	• Inability to learn from process and improve • Inability to provide evidence for further investment	• Build evaluation cultures in the organisation • Build research and learning units
6. There is no data disaggregation for youth	• The impact of sectoral/national programmes on young people cannot be assessed	• See **Chapters 9 and 17** for implementing data disaggregation strategies • Involve census departments and other research bodies
7. Programming is not values-based/ rights-based/ asset-based	• Does not deliver transformative results for young people	• Review with multiple stakeholders • Set down clear principles and goals in partnership with young people • Monitor the implementation of principles
8. Youth-safeguarding issues emerge during the YM process; the safety and security of young people are compromised	• Young people are at risk • Organisations' accountability and transparency is compromised	• Ensure youth-safeguarding guidelines for engaging with young people, particularly younger age groups

Notes

1   See also Chapter 8.
2   Unaffiliated but affected youth groups are the most difficult to reach because of their lack of collective strength, often because they are geographically dispersed or because mobility or freedom of organisation/ association is limited. Each sector should bear this in mind when designing stakeholder engagement strategies.
3   See, for instance, Overseas Development Institute 2013.
4   Institutional guidance for youth mainstreaming within the AU Secretariat developed by the African Union is available from the Secretariat on request.
5   African Union Commission N.D.
6   Mehra and Gupta 2006, 3.
7   See also Jasimuddin 2012 and Teskey 2011.
8   Bhagavan and Virgin 2004.
9   From a youth work perspective, social attitudes and identities/hierarchies (sexuality, disability, ethnicity, youth, gender etc.) are *always* present in the equation.
10 See Annex 3 of the Commonwealth Youth Participation Guidelines.
11 Some leading scientific journals (including the *British Medical Journal*) are now screening and revising research papers in accordance with feedback from persons with disabilities and other patient ('lived experience') reviewers.

12 By re-asserting the twin importance of age-related data (SDG 17) and of participatory institutions (SDG 16), the Sustainable Development Goals give these considerations fresh impetus. The UN and Commonwealth frameworks are now more united than ever before, in recognising governance and poverty reduction as issues in their own right (justice and dignity motivations), as well as being important instruments for other things (growth, stability).

13 In Solomon Islands, the MWYCFA works in close collaboration with the Ministry of Development Planning and Aid Co-ordination and the National Statistics Office in developing indicators.

References

African Union Commission (N.D.), 'African Union Commission Holds Youth Mainstreaming Workshop', available at: https://www.au.int/en/pressreleases/31593/african-union-commission-holds-youth-mainstreaming-workshop.

Bhagavan, MR and I Virgin (2004), *Generic Aspects of Institutional Capacity Development in Developing Countries*, Stockholm Environmental Institute, Stockholm.

Jasimuddin, M (2012), 'Institutional Capacity Development', in *Commonwealth Governance Handbook: Democracy Development and Public Administration 2012/13*, Nexus Strategic Partnerships, Cambridge, 77–80.

Mehra, R and GR Gupta (2006), *Gender Mainstreaming: Making It Happen*, The International Centre for Research on Women.

Overseas Development Institute (2013), 'Youth and International Development Policy: The Case for Investing in Young People', *Project Briefing Paper* No. 80, May.

Teskey, G (2011), 'State-Building and Development: Getting beyond Capacity', in *Commonwealth Governance Handbook: Democracy Development and Public Administration 2011/12*, Nexus Strategic Partnerships, Cambridge, 44–48.

Chapter 18
Financing Youth Mainstreaming

18.1 Introduction

This chapter begins a discussion, to be elaborated on in your contexts on:

- the importance of financing for youth mainstreaming
- leveraging the interest of donors and financial institutions to ensure sustained, impactful youth mainstreaming.

18.2 Long-term, strategic financing

To ensure strategic, long-term financing for youth mainstreaming, YM strategies must be integrated into financing for development (FFD) strategies. While youth mainstreaming involves integrating a youth lens into existing planning processes, the added requirements on policy and planning – in terms of youth-specific research, youth participation and so on – imply costs that may not otherwise have been accounted for.

A positive sign is the recognition, for the first time, of young people as a specific social category for financial investment in the resolutions of the Financing for Development Conference held in Addis Ababa in 2015. The resolution acknowledged the importance of:

- investing in children and youth as critical to achieving inclusive, equitable and sustainable development for present and future generations,[1]

and committed to:

- 'promote appropriate, affordable and stable access to credit to micro, small and medium-sized enterprises, as well as adequate skills development training for all, particularly for youth and entrepreneurs';

- 'promote national youth strategies as a key instrument for meeting the needs and aspirations of young people';

- develop and operationalise, by 2020, 'a global strategy for youth employment and implementing the International Labour Organization (ILO) global jobs pact';[2] and

- promote access to technology and science for women, youth and children.[3]

These commitments indicate a focus for specific thematic areas such as credit, employment, technology and science, but also for broader, cross-sectoral approaches – as implied through commitments to 'national youth strategies'. This creates an excellent opportunity to advocate for investment in youth mainstreaming as a specific strategy that development planners should be aware of.

Each subnational and sectoral planning strategy should also ensure this harmonising with financing, as discussed above.

These FFD commitments must be buttressed by:

- targeting all sources of finance, including the private sector;

- advocating for increased public spending on youth, based on evidence and as a foundation for all sustainable development; and

- ensuring an intergovernmental follow-up process for FFD financing and integrating youth mainstreaming into FFD processes.

For donors to be convinced that holistic youth mainstreaming is a strategy that both benefits youth and benefits reaching the Sustainable Development Goals, the youth sector and all sectors need to provide credible evidence of the relevance of a holistic approach to integrating youth capacities, participation and interests into global, national and subnational planning (see Figure 18.1). This can be done by:

- highlighting the nature of youth empowerment in relation to intergenerational equity, and the value of youth empowerment strategies and programmes across sectors in making programmes more relevant and responsive;

- highlighting the rationale behind working with youth as a specific, unique category, with their own unique needs and interests in all social, political and economic spheres; and

- demonstrating the impact of youth-mainstreamed work, both for youth and for larger society.

Figure 18.1 Youth mainstreaming stakeholders engaging finance and donors

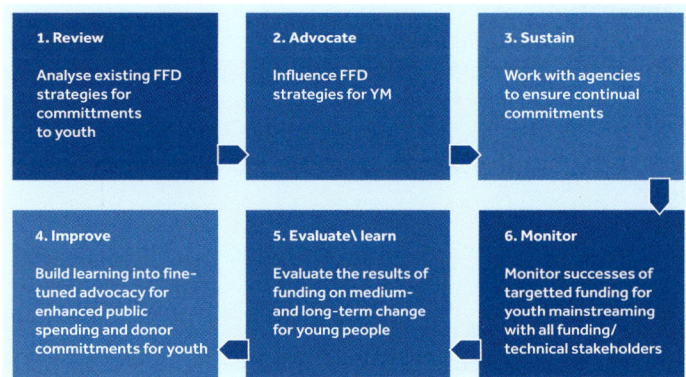

As much as youth mainstreaming stakeholders engage donors and development finance institutions, it is imperative that donors and finance institutions play a proactive role in supporting youth mainstreaming globally, nationally and at the subnational level. Box 18.1 shows possible ways in which donors can engage in the process.

> **Box 18.1 Donors engaging youth mainstreaming stakeholders**
>
> - Ensure that youth stakeholders and central planning processes talk to each other, particularly that alternative voices are heard in planning
> - Ensure that YM planning is viewed against trends of social exclusion, economic turbulence, military conflict and so on
> - Ensure long-term aid flows for youth mainstreaming
> - Support governments in integrating aid planning for YM and other mainstreaming processes
> - Promote and adhere to aid effectiveness principles in financing YM
> - Promote co-ordination with debt management and trade processes
> - Promote a long-term view: conflict prevention, decent work agendas
> - Facilitate knowledge management: input to the process, allowing reciprocal government input into donor planning, and refer back to sectors if youth analysis is missing
> - In building consolidated expenditure programmes, ensure that tools are built in at this stage to monitor and evaluate impact of programmes on youth
> - Promote and invest in data disaggregation methodologies and data gathering for youth across sectors and nations
> - Ensure that proposal writing guidance calls for integrating YM.

Ensuring budgeting and allocation for the processes and programmes of youth mainstreaming is critical to successful implementation.

Notes

1   UN General Assembly 2015, 5.
2   Ibid, 7.
3   Ibid, 31.

Reference

UN General Assembly (2015), Conference on Financing for Development, *Resolution adopted by the General Assembly on 27 July 2015 [without reference to a Main Committee (A/69/L.82)]*, 69/313, Addis Ababa Action Agenda of the Third International, Conference on Financing for Development, available at: http://www.un.org/ga/search/view_doc. asp?symbol=A/RES/69/313&Lang=E

Chapter 19
Towards Practical, Principled Youth Mainstreaming

Youth mainstreaming is a society- and sector-wide approach to ensuring social equality for youth, measured by gains in young people's social status, access to education, healthcare, and other services and resources. YM is not activities as ends in themselves, but fully assessed, co-ordinated and principled processes informed by positive, egalitarian social norms. Youth mainstreaming will be a success where there are solid partnerships among sectors and continuing dialogue with society on policy and planning for and with youth.

The seeds for youth mainstreaming (among institutions) were planted at the beginning of the twenty-first century via the Commonwealth, UNESCO and the World Bank. Since then, momentum has been building, including with the African Union Commission, UNDP, the US Agency for International Development (USAID) and other bilateral and multilateral agencies that recognise the need for youth mainstreaming within their institutions.

It is now time to bring youth mainstreaming into the spotlight, especially in the context of achieving and surpassing the SDGs.

The Commonwealth Secretariat and the Commonwealth Youth Council hope that member countries will make use of this publication to continue, and strengthen, youth mainstreaming in your countries.

We hope the three parts will help you analyse your own contexts and provide robust solutions for young people and with them.

Part 3

Full Case Studies

This part highlights examples of youth mainstreaming in practice in the sectors of poverty alleviation, health, employment, finance, justice and urban planning, with case studies from Commonwealth member countries and other countries. They attempt to link the conceptual and process/procedural discussions in Parts 1 and 2 to the way sectoral youth mainstreaming strategies have been designed, applied and evaluated in the real world.

Chapter 20
Introduction to Full Case Studies

20.1 Introduction

This section helps demonstrate practical steps taken to implement youth mainstreaming. It includes six sectoral case studies from across the Commonwealth and elsewhere that look at how the sectors of poverty alleviation, health, employment, finance, justice and urban planning have taken on youth mainstreaming in their respective domains, how this work feeds into the SDGs' targets, and the implications for institutions and structures in realising such initiatives. It is these kinds of sectoral initiatives that will be part of the process of holistic national youth mainstreaming.

The SDGs are the development targets to which governments have agreed. Many governments may align new national and local development frameworks to the goals. This chapter responds to the questions: Why is working with young people critical to achieving these targets? How does work with and for young people help achieve these targets and help ensure equitable outcomes for young people? and Why is it that *not* working with young people will lead to shortfalls in reaching the targets?

20.2 Case studies and the SDGs

This section looks at sectoral case studies through the lens of selected SDGs to explore the opportunities they generate for youth mainstreaming. Working towards the SDGs for young people does not mean that we need to always find entirely novel ways of working, even though this too is important. But often, youth mainstreaming is about ways of replicating existing good practices across sectors and expanding these visions and strategies.

Most of the examples below demonstrate that providing a youth lens for the SDGs involves the meaningful and sustained participation of young people in research, legislation, policy and programming related to the goal in question; achieving the SDGs is not possible without their participation. It also demonstrates the importance of working with the youth sector.

The case studies have several features. They:

- represent both national and subnational initiatives and highlight links between them – e.g. Ghana's youth budget example, where local efforts ultimately influenced national outcomes as well;

- are drawn from civil society and government programmes and show how different players within a single sector can influence each other – e.g. civil society influencing broader state adoption of good practice, as in the case of South Africa's Youth-Friendly Health Centres; and

- demonstrate government, civil society and other stakeholders' accountability to young people, to human rights aspirations and legislation, and to global and national development frameworks.

These stories are not meant to be comprehensive in terms of the sectoral technical specificities or the details of their implementation, and are meant only to serve as guides for youth mainstreaming which should catalyse further dialogue with sectoral and youth specialists.

Chapter 21
Case Study Theme 1: Youth and Poverty Alleviation – India and South Africa

---

Box 21.1 SDG 1 No Poverty

Targets: All targets

SDG 10: Reduce inequality

Target: 10.2 includes social, economic and political inclusion of all, irrespective of age

Main sector: Poverty alleviation

Issue: Reducing youth poverty

Strategy: Youth and child poverty analysis, India, South Africa, United Kingdom

21.1 Introduction

This case study looks at how a youth analysis of poverty factors can help mainstream youth in poverty analysis and support evidence-based, youth-focused programmes and projects. It is framed by how a youth focus can be integrated into national targets to reach SDG 1 – No Poverty.

21.2 Youth and poverty

Combating poverty requires the elimination of poverty for all groups. Poverty dimensions for young people can be starkly different as entrants into employment, those straddling both education and employment, and those grappling with issues of entry into housing markets, access to credit, starting a family and so on.

To introduce a youth angle to the poverty goal, policy-makers in the youth sector and other sectors related to poverty alleviation must:

1. bring evidence to the table of the reality of youth poverty and its causes, markers and impacts;

2. be constantly vigilant about emerging legislation, policy and programming, and be able to assess their impact on youth poverty; and

3. ensure that the youth sector, young people and youth experts participate in the drafting of all new poverty alleviation programmes to ensure that young people's concerns are integrated in national poverty alleviation frameworks.

21.3 What helps us understand and assess youth poverty?

The analysis and case studies below are primarily focused on point (1) above, bringing evidence to the table on youth poverty. There is clear evidence from countries where systemic poverty studies have been conducted that young people are vulnerable to poverty due to the 'age-based discrimination and the uncertainties and dynamism surrounding the transition from childhood to adulthood'.[1] This of course comes with the caveat that youth are not always disproportionately poor, and that it is a combination of factors that leads to youth poverty.

In this case study, we bring together examples of analysis and implementation relating to research on youth poverty derived from the Chronic Poverty Research Centre (CPRC) of the University of Manchester[2] and its observations on analysing youth poverty and the implications of these findings on programming drawn from two countries: India and South Africa.

The CPRC proposes that, to assess youth poverty, specific concepts such as chronic poverty, life-course poverty and intergenerational poverty need to be understood, studied and integrated into policy-making frameworks. That is:

- An analysis of chronic poverty helps locate the relative position of different groups of the poor and facilitate policy prioritisation.

- Life-course events (leaving school, starting work, giving birth and raising children) play a significant role in shaping youth poverty. These events, though not always related to the stage of youth, are typically related to youth.

- An intergenerational perspective to poverty is also important, because youth poverty is often linked to parental poverty and childhood deprivation and can have implications for the rest of the young person's later life as an adult and senior citizen.

The CPRC also establishes, as do other development organisations such as the UK's Overseas Development Institute (ODI), that, even though youth may not always be the poorest or most vulnerable group, it is nevertheless the adolescent or young adulthood period where anti-poverty interventions have the most potential for long-term positive change and for ending cyclical poverty; poverty in one age cohort increases the likelihood of poverty in the next, so youth is one of the earlier stages at which poverty can be alleviated.

Intra-household to global factors affect chronic poverty. Some maintain poverty, such as the drawing back of social protection programmes, while others mitigate poverty, such as enhanced youth and stakeholder participation in creating poverty alleviation programmes, or the design of needs- and rights-based social protection programmes. What mitigates or maintains poverty in your context? What reinforces youth poverty systemically, and keeps poor people poor and poor youth poor?

Of course, gender politics, economic policy contexts, inheritance and other laws, attitudes towards youth etc. all influence these trends. Alleviating youth poverty, as observed above, is also linked to state provision of public services and social protection, programmes that support asset generation and retention,[3] and campaigns and legal action to prevent discrimination against age cohorts. Box 21.2 highlights an example of a campaign that creates solidarity between young people and adults.

The poverty research of the CPRC also highlights the need to 'take empowerment seriously' and the need to take a system-wide approach to youth poverty alleviation:

Policy must move beyond the cosy rhetoric of participatory approaches, decentralisation and theories about rights. It needs to address the difficult political process of challenging the layers of discrimination that keep people trapped in poverty. For many youth, age-based discrimination adds to the discrimination they face due to gender, ethnicity and

Box 21.2 Reducing intergenerational poverty and pensions

In the United Kingdom, the Work and Pensions Select Committee's inquiry into *Intergenerational Fairness* has been identified by the UK's Intergenerational Foundation (IF) as 'a pioneering exploration of how arguments about intergenerational fairness should be factored into contemporary welfare policy'. This is an example of how a state committee has undertaken the analysis of a non-youth-related policy and its impact on young people.

As the IF observes on the committee's report:

> [The Work and Pensions Select Committee] *came down heavily in favour of the view that young people are receiving a raw deal compared to older generations in modern Britain. The report characterises intergenerational unfairness as a problem of the British economy having become 'skewed towards baby boomers and against millennials'. The committee fully accepted the argument that today's young people face great difficulty in building up asset wealth because of rising house prices and changes to the pension system, while at the same time their taxes are being used to support the most successful members of the baby-boomer generation who have accumulated more wealth than they will ever be able to.*

The [committee's chair], MP Frank Field, explained the problem using the concept of the intergenerational social contract, which IF emphasised in [its] submission to the inquiry:

> *'The welfare state is underpinned by an implicit intergenerational contract. Each generation is supported in retirement by their in-work successors. This is supported by all age groups, but a combination of factors has sent the balance out of kilter. It is now the working young and their children who face the daunting challenge of getting on in an economy skewed against them.'*

From the Intergenerational Foundation website[4]

even poverty itself. But children and young people are able to be effective change agents within their communities. There is an urgent need to enhancing their capacity to influence institutions that affect their lives, through removing the political, legal and social barriers that work against them and other poor and chronically poor people.[5]

Some examples of projects where youth poverty analysis has been implemented are:

- **Young Lives, India (also Ethiopia, Peru and Vietnam):** This investigation of change in child poverty over 15 years can be easily adapted for youth poverty analysis programmes.[6]

- **Birth-to-Twenty, South Africa:** Initiated in 1990, this study explores the social, economic, political, demographic and nutrition transitions under way in urban South Africa and the impact on a cohort of children, adolescents and their families.[7]

- **The British Household Panel Survey:** This survey analysed life-course effects on income using ten waves of study. Here, the authors looked at how income was affected, through time, for specific age groups such as youth, adults and the elderly. This enabled the researchers to identify income dynamics in people's lives across the life cycle.

The two programmes from India and South Africa are highlighted in Boxes 21.3 and 21.4, respectively.

Box 21.3 Young Lives, former United Andhra Pradesh, India

Young Lives India, conducted in Andhra Pradesh, with 7 per cent of India's 1.2 billion population, was an attempt to understand the relationship between child and youth poverty through the study of the same cohort of children and youth across a period of 15 years.

Andhra Pradesh was one of the first Indian states to initiate the reform process for fiscal and institutional restructuring at the state level and was the model for several new poverty reduction initiatives during the 1990s. It is particularly interesting to see the shifts and changes in child and youth poverty where such initiatives have taken place. These types of longitudinal data on children and youth also help assess the impact of policies and programmes for them, and inform the formulation of new ones.

Four rounds of data collection were conducted for a group of 2,000 children, who were aged between 6 and 18 months at the beginning of the project, and 1,000 children between the ages of 7.5 and 8.5, with the first round conducted in 2002. The final round of data was collected between 2013 and 2014, with the same children then aged 11–12 in the younger cohort and 18–19 in the older cohort. Data were collected from communities with different economic status, but with oversampling for poor families spread across representative geographical units of Andhra Pradesh.

The study comprised a large-scale household survey of all the children and their primary caregivers, and qualitative data through focus groups and dialogue with sub-samples. Data included information about their material and social circumstances, their perception on their lives and their aspirations for the future, set against their environmental and social realities. This has become a unique, cross-country longitudinal dataset exploring the causes and consequences of child and youth poverty.

Data collected for the child and young adult groups were invariably different, with youth data including parent and caregiver updates, mobility, subjective wellbeing, education, employment, earnings, and time use. Data on feelings and attitudes, household decision-making, marital and living arrangements, fertility, body measurements (anthropometry), health and nutrition and cognitive tests[8] were also noted.

(Continued)

Box 21.3 Young Lives, former United Andhra Pradesh, India (*cont.*)

This kind of data enables the assessment of poverty and capability factors for young adults in relation to what their status was as children and helps study the relationship between child and youth poverty, and shifts in status across time given various factors.

The Young Lives report for round 4 for Andhra Pradesh reported on outcomes for the older cohort at age 19 in terms of education, employment and marriage, showing clearly how young people's opportunities in life are influenced by household wealth level, background circumstances and intergenerational factors assessed through earlier cohort data for the same group.

Half of the young people were still in education (15 per cent combining this with work), 26 per cent had left school and were working, 9 per cent were married and not working (mainly young women), and 7 per cent were not studying, working or married. Almost a third of the sample children had started university-level education, although children from economically and socially disadvantaged groups were more likely to have left full-time education, many without a secondary-level qualification. By the age of 19, 36 per cent of the girls in the sample, and 2 per cent of the boys, were married – and 107 of these already had a child of their own (almost two-thirds of the married girls already had children). Early marriage and child-bearing were most common for girls in rural areas, from poor households, or who had only completed primary education.[9]

The findings are an indication that greater focus should be paid to young people from poorer communities in ensuring access to affordable secondary and tertiary education for those who aspire to higher education, and that a specific focus on young women's poverty needs to address specific gender-related issues in education and the prevention of early marriage and unwanted pregnancy, which are directly related to poverty alleviation and autonomy for young women.

Source: Young Lives 2014b

Box 21.4 Mandela's Children – Birth-to-Twenty study, South Africa

Growing out of the desire to understand the new realities of South Africa's children following the sociopolitical change that came post-Apartheid, *Birth-to-Twenty* (BT20), initially known as Birth-to-Ten, followed a group of urban children, among the first to be born into a democratic South Africa, for 20 years. Led by the University of Witwatersrand and the South African Medical Research Council, the BT20 study took a lifecycle approach and focused studies on issues that were relevant to the specific development phase of the cohort at that given time – i.e. focusing on things such as cognitive and physical development during the younger years, and sexual behaviour and social marginalisation in the teen and later years.

(Continued)

Box 21.4 Mandela's Children – Birth-to-Twenty study, South Africa (*Cont.*)

The approach to the study was multidisciplinary, with a variety of researchers and scientists accessing the group or particular subgroups within the cohort for discipline-specific data. One potential opportunity for such a study is to have a more heterogeneous cohort of participants, so that a systematic comparison between subgroups among youth can be made – in this case, between black, Afrikaans and other racial groups in South Africa. This may facilitate disaggregation of data for young people from different backgrounds and assessing the relationship between marginality and growth/attainment factors. This in turn would provide more evidence on inequalities that may exist within subgroups and later inform intervention programmes or policies that address the real issues.

Such studies require a committed group of people dedicated to 'operations, administration, lab and data … [and systems which allow] reporting to investigators weekly, sophisticated bar code, filing, and electronic systems have been designed to print address lists, weekly appointments, tracking participants through the study components, data completeness and quality, entry, cleaning and the construction of analytical datasets'.[10]

However, the gains of investing in such youth-focused research can lead to more impactful and relevant interventions in various sectors and can be a source to inform major policy-level decisions where there is a paucity of other current data.[11]

These initiatives can be discussed to analyse youth poverty in member countries where sectors demonstrate an interest in mainstreaming youth poverty dynamics into their poverty alleviation programmes.

21.4 Implications: what enablers/disablers influenced the process?

Considering the Youth Mainstreaming Enablers Framework in Chapter 4, the societal, structural, organisational and impact factors laid out in Table 21.1 help us understand successes and challenges of youth poverty analysis.

1. Questions for member countries contemplating youth poverty studies may include:

   - Research capacity: Are there any existing studies on youth poverty? Are member countries equipped to do life-course analysis and gather longitudinal data

Table 21.1 Youth and poverty case studies: Analysis of enablers and disablers

Enablers/disablers	Elaboration
Societal	• Understanding of variant poverty drivers for young people
Structural – macro	• Institutional collaboration between universities, medical research bodies, structures etc. in place for multidisciplinary research (connected governance)
Structural – meso	• Financial commitments to long-term research and valuing of evidence-based planning
Organisational – structure	• Organisational capacity for long-term cross-sectoral collaboration, knowledge of child and youth development factors in medical and other research bodies, skills and capacities for longitudinal studies
Organisational – process	• Child and youth-focused research in broader poverty studies
Impact	• Greater understanding of poverty drivers and mitigators from childhood to young adulthood to inform policy

with the participation of young people? Does the expertise exist? Do resources exist?

• Policy directives: If not, what policy directives will support the institutionalisation of such research and analysis to ensure that a youth lens is incorporated into poverty analysis?

• Attitudes: Do the right attitudes and sufficient capacity building exist to ensure youth participation and youth analysis in poverty alleviation programmes, including analysing development outcomes for specific economic/social groups of youth?

• A visionary approach: Do we consciously build the SDGs vision into national poverty alleviation programmes, with equity at the centre?

b. Implications for the youth sector:

• Lobby with ministries/departments of poverty alleviation/economic empowerment to focus on youth poverty.

• Encourage youth-led research on youth poverty.

21.5 Conclusion

This chapter looked at the importance of systemic youth poverty analysis to understand the drivers and detractors of poverty, in order to adjust/formulate policies, programmes and projects informed by the findings. It demonstrates the requirement for investment in robust research on youth poverty, and the benefits this will have in terms of informed and effective poverty alleviation programmes for young people.

Notes

1   Moore 2005.
2   Ibid.
3   Ibid., 22.
4   Intergenerational Foundation 2016.
5   Moore 2005, 23.
6   See Young Lives website: www.younglives.org.uk.
7   See Richter et al. 2007.
8   Young Lives 2014a.
9   Young Lives 2014b.
10 Richter et al. 2007.
11 Ibid.

References

Intergenerational Foundation (2016), 'Intergenerational Fairness Commission Recommends Scrapping the State Pension Triple Lock', available at: http://www.if.org.uk/archives/8966/intergenerational-fairness-commission-recommends-scrapping-the-state-pension-triple-lock

Moore, K (2005), *Thinking about Youth Poverty through the Lenses of Chronic Poverty, Life-Course Poverty and Intergenerational Poverty*, Chronic Poverty Research Centre, Institute of Development Policy and Management, University of Manchester, Manchester.

Richter, L, S Norris, J Pettifor, D Yach and N Cameron (2007), 'Cohort Profile: Mandela's Children: The 1990 Birth to Twenty Study in South Africa', *International Journal of Epidemiology*, Vol. 36 No. 3, 504–511, available at: https://www.ncbi.nlm.nih.gov/pmc/articles/PMC2702039/

Young Lives (2014a), *Survey Design and Sampling in India*, available at: http://www.younglives_India.org

Young Lives (2014b), *Youth and Development: Preliminary Findings of the Round 4 Survey in India*, available at: http://www.younglives.org.uk/content/youth-and-development-preliminary-findings-round-4-survey-india

Chapter 22
Case Study Theme 2: Youth and Health – South Africa and India

22.1 Introduction

This chapter looks at two case studies on health provision and young women's reproductive health services from India and South Africa. The case study from India focuses on a youth-led audit of services, while the study from South Africa looks at initiatives to set up youth health centres with capacitated staff, guidelines and services. It is set against Goal 3: Good Health and Wellbeing.

22.2 The Youth-Friendly Health Services programme, South Africa

The following case study is based on a report[1] of a youth-friendly health services programme that was designed for greater access to health for young people in South Africa. It demonstrates a means of mainstreaming young people's concerns into healthcare provision. Instigated by an NGO called LoveLife, the programme was subsequently taken over by the Department of Health, South Africa.

Youth analysis of reproductive health issues and service provision: The concerns that resulted in the project included 2011 statistics in South Africa that indicated 12 per cent HIV prevalence among young women (aged 15–24 years) and 5 per cent among young men. Half of women had given birth by the

---

Box 22.1 SDG 3 Good Health and Wellbeing

Targets: 3.7 Universal access to sexual and reproductive healthcare services, universal health coverage; 10.2 mentions social inclusion

Main sector: Health

Issue: Youth access to services in health

Strategy: Youth-friendly health services, India and South Africa

age of 20 years, while two-thirds of adolescent (15–19 years) pregnancies were reported as unwanted. Nine per cent reported having had sex before the age of 15 years, with early sexual debut associated with increased risk of HIV infection, other sexually transmitted infections (STIs), adolescent pregnancy, forced sex and an increased number of lifetime partners, as well as with decreased use of condoms and other contraceptives. Knowledge about sexuality and reproductive health among young men and young women was limited, and young people reported a need for more information on relationships, pregnancy and STIs.

In this context, the response of the health sector to ensure young people's optimal access to services was less than satisfactory. Some concerns raised by young people were:

- Attitudes of health sector staff: They feared the judgmental attitudes of healthcare workers, which they saw as a barrier to their use of a range of health services in South Africa. Young people engaging in sexual activity were branded as 'naughty'.

- Violation of young people's right to confidentiality: Young people over the age of 12 in South Africa have the right to legally access health services without parental consent. These services include HIV testing and treatment, contraceptives and other reproductive health facilities. This right, however, was rarely upheld, with health officers often seeking permission of parents, or informing parents of the young person's healthcare needs, thus breaking young people's right to confidentiality.

It is in this context that the NGO LoveLife realised the importance of youth-friendly health services that provided sensitive help to young people to encourage their entry into safe, confidential spaces in healthcare where they felt valued, respected and their confidentiality protected, and where they also obtained the services they required.

The programme, called the National Adolescent-Friendly Clinic Initiative (NAFCI) and launched in 2001, targeted young people aged 10–24 and aimed to promote access to and utilisation of youth-friendly services (YFSs), improve the health status of young people, build the capacity of healthcare providers to provide YFS, and to promote services for HIV-infected and

HIV-exposed young people. It trained service providers on youth-friendly health services, improved facilities, and used multimedia campaigns and activities in the community and with other sectors. LoveLife supported the Department of Health (DoH) by developing training curricula, programme guidelines and implementation tools, and by facilitating YFS training for Department of Health practitioners at the department's request.

A set of 'adolescent-friendly' standards, which included those relating to the types of services provided, policies supporting adolescents' rights to healthcare and the clinic environment, were defined for clinics to work towards using a facilitated approach. These standards remain an integral component of the project. The DoH was an active partner from the programme's inception, and by 2005 350 clinics nationwide were involved.

A challenge with the programme has been the lack of monitoring and evaluation since the handover, which limits learning and improvement.

22.3 *Seen, Not Heard*: Youth-led audit of sexual and reproductive health services in Lucknow, India

The *Seen, Not Heard* study, youth-led research conducted by 12 young service users in Lucknow, India, in 2016, is progressive in its methodology of young people defining the research questions, designing and implementing the research, analysing the data and writing the report. The findings will inform policy-makers of issues young people face in accessing reproductive health services, as well as recommendations for improving information, services and access.[2]

The YP Foundation (TYPF) is a youth-led organisation based in New Delhi, India, that supports young people to create programmes and influence policies in the areas of gender, sexuality, health, education and governance. In the last 13 years, TYPF has worked directly with 6,500 young people to develop their perspectives and critical thinking on issues of social justice and human rights and set up more than 300 projects in India, reaching out to 450,000 adolescents and young people between the ages of 3 and 28 across 18 of India's total 29 states and 7 union territories.

TYPF's work on sexual and reproductive health is based on the recognition of the lack of adequate information on sexuality available to young people, paternalism and misplaced adult perceptions of sexual inactivity. Such populist attitudes can wrongly inform policies and provision of reproductive health services, reduce access to affordable and good-quality healthcare, and increase negative impacts on young people's physical and psychological wellbeing. TYPF's flagship programme, Know Your Body, Know Your Rights, advocates for the inclusion of comprehensive sexuality education in policies and government programmes to counter such attitudes and outcomes.

At the point of accessing services, young people's rights are legally circumscribed by laws that require parental consent for certain services, such as terminating early pregnancy for under-18s, which pushes young girls to accessing illegal and unsafe abortion services. A recently enacted law against child sexual abuse, the Protection of Children from Sexual Offences (POCSO) Act, contains certain clauses that prevent medical practitioners from providing services. Section 20 of the Act makes it mandatory for service providers to report any sexual acts between people under 18 years of age. In practice, this translates in to doctors refusing to provide sexual and reproductive health (SRH) services to young people under 18, since this then requires mandatory reporting.

The context is also one where young people are attaining puberty at increasingly early ages (as young as 8) and where, by age 16, most young people have engaged in sexual activity. Coupled with this, young people are not seen as capable decision-makers, owing to their explorative and experimental nature, and sexual education is seen as a dangerous catalyst to sexual activity.

This mind set has hindered any attempts (by government and NGOs) to make comprehensive sexuality education accessible. An Adolescent Education Programme (AEP) launched by the Government of India in 2007 is a case in point. The AEP was suspended in several states because of objections raised by teachers, parents and policy-makers on grounds that its explicit content was contrary to India's culture and morality.

This has affected young people negatively through increases in STIs, violence, early marriage, unplanned pregnancy, mental health issues etc. Increased rates of death due to HIV have also escalated so that it is in second position in the top ten causes of death among adolescents.

This is unlike in South Africa, where independent access to reproductive health services is assured legally for all youth above 12 through laws that provide them with such access and assure them confidentiality rights, which does not require parental notification (see story above). The obstacle observed in South Africa was that institutional and staff measures do not honour this legally binding right.

The research: Young people who were themselves service users led the research design, implementation and analysis. They set their own research agenda and conducted their own analysis based on their lived experiences as service users. The study was done in the above context of a lack of information and services.

The study aimed to:

- generate evidence through youth-centred processes;
- increase visibility of existing youth-friendly health services, in particular stigma-free access to reproductive health services;
- create a cadre of young leaders equipped to advocate for and assess stigma-free health services, including counselling and service provision; and
- contribute to existing information on the availability and quality of existing health services, especially for unwanted early pregnancies.

Training: A week-long training programme was designed to capture the team's collective views on what would make health service delivery 'youth-friendly'. Based on this input and that obtained from select external resources, standards of youth-friendly health services (YFHS) were delineated against which the quality of each service/health centre would be assessed. A mapping implementation tool were developed to facilitate collection of the corresponding data.

Researchers: Twelve young people trained throughout one year in sexual health and rights, with an express realisation and articulation that sexual health rights are in fact human rights. Researchers were aged between 18 and 27, with an average age of 23. Their research capacity was built through enhancing their capacity to lead a research study and conduct a social audit, enhancing their knowledge on current government schemes and guidelines that endorse YFHS, and refresh their technical knowledge on sexual and reproductive health rights (SRHR).

Sites of intervention: The study was conducted with a variety of service providers, including government, private health providers, NGOs and illegal street-side service providers, who offered varying degrees of privacy, confidentiality, affordability, accessibility etc. to service users. While unauthorised street-side services offered confidentiality, they also provided the least safe methods/services.

Findings: These included inadequate distribution of clinics, unregulated pricing by private healthcare providers, making them unaffordable for young people, lack of counselling services in private facilities and, again, unaffordability of services where they were available. Other findings included a lack of information or misinformation on SRHR, provider bias preventing access to services for single/unmarried young people, especially young girls and women, medical diagnosis overriding patient's informed choice and consent, stigmatising of HIV-related services, and absence of counselling services creating anxiety and uncertainty among young people.

Recommendations: These comprised basic SRHR knowledge for all service providers; non-judgemental and rights-affirming service delivery; wide dissemination of good-quality information on young people's sexual and reproductive health and services; affordability of commodities and services; accessible facilities and information; expanding the outreach of adolescent-friendly health clinics; fast-tracking the selection, appointment and training of peer educators; improving infrastructure to ensure privacy for patients; mainstreaming comprehensive sexuality education; and lifting the region's ban on the Adolescent Education Programme (AEP).

22.4 Implications: what enablers/disablers influenced the process?

The two programmatic and research-based initiatives above have several implications for youth mainstreaming in the health sector and demonstrate both enablers and disablers in relation to the Enablers Framework in Chapter 4 (Table 22.1).

Table 22.1 Youth and health case studies: analysis of enablers and disablers

Enablers/disablers	Elaboration
Societal	• Negative attitudes and misinformation about young people's sexual activity
Structural – macro	• Public funding constraints for additional financing of youth-friendly spaces • Private healthcare service delivery not regulated to ensure access to affordable, quality healthcare for the most marginalised
Structural – meso	• Low visibility of political will for legally sanctioning youth health rights, particularly reproductive health rights • Where rights are legally sanctioned, a lack of political will to translate law into practice
Organisational – structures	• Collaboration between youth-led organisations and healthcare facilities • Collaboration between non-governmental and governmental health sector stakeholders on youth issues • Meaningful, long-term rights-based training of staff on youth and health rights • Institutional vision and transformation • Recognition of the need for separate medical healthcare spaces for young people to ensure privacy and confidentiality
Organisational – process	• Meaningful youth participation and youth-led research processes • Integrating youth work into youth and health processes
Impact	• Greater access for young people of youth-friendly services, with confidentiality and privacy respected (South Africa) • Youth-centred knowledge provides recommendations for institutional transformation in provision of youth-friendly healthcare services (India)

Governments and other stakeholders considering mainstreaming youth in healthcare facilities need to:

- inquire into fiscal commitments for additional funding to sustain a youth-friendly healthcare structure and staff training;

- transform healthcare institutions to integrate young people at all levels of design and planning of healthcare services;

- measure impacts of young people's access to health services, and outcomes for young people of healthcare disaggregated for youth as a specific age cohort with specific healthcare needs;

- commit to legal enactments to ensure young people's access to health and reproductive health facilities; and

- ensure that legal provisions are translated into practice through staff and organisational capacity building.

The youth sector's role:

- work with the health sector to impart youth-led research skills and youth work skills; and

- work with the health sector on youth empowerment factors in relation to young people as health service receivers.

22.5 Conclusion

Both studies above demonstrate the need for institutional and attitudinal transformation to provide meaningful youth- and gender-sensitive services to young people. They also demonstrate the need for collaboration across youth-focused stakeholders, including government departments, young service users and services.

Notes

1   World Health Organisation 2009.
2   This case study is drawn from material available in the full report, *Seen, Not Heard: Youth-Led Audit of Sexual and Reproductive Health Services in Lucknow* (YP Foundation N.D.).

References

World Health Organization (2009), *Evolution of the National Adolescent-Friendly Clinic Initiative in South Africa*, World Health Organisation, Geneva, available at: http://apps.who.int/iris/bitstream/10665/44154/1/9789241598361_eng.pdf

YP Foundation (N.D.), *Seen, Not Heard: Youth-Led Audit of Sexual and Reproductive Health Services in Lucknow*, available at: http://www.theypfoundation.org/wp-content/uploads/2016/10/SeenNotHeard-English.pdf

Chapter 23
Case Study Theme 3: Youth and Employment – Kenya and Uganda

Box 23.1 SDG 8 Decent Work and Economic Growth

Targets: 8.3 Decent job creation, entrepreneurship, formalisation and growth of micro-, small and medium-sized enterprises, including access to financial services; 8.5 Full and productive employment and decent work for all, including for young people; 8.6 By 2020, substantially reduce the proportion of young people not in employment, education or training; 8b By 2020, develop and operationalise a global strategy for youth employment

Issue: Lack of access to decent and dignified jobs; and competition from larger, experienced enterprises

Strategy: Access to Government Procurement Opportunities (AGPO) - Kenya, and employment plans in Uganda

23.1 Introduction

This case study is set against Goal 8: Decent Work and Economic Growth. There is increasing political will nationally and internationally to tackle the youth unemployment crisis across the globe. The ILO's *World Employment and Social Outlook 2016, Trends for Youth* report showed that the global number of unemployed youth was set to rise by half a million, to reach 71 million in 2016. Many governments are recognising the significance of addressing this crisis. The following case studies look at enhancing economic opportunities for young entrepreneurs, through affirmative action in procurement policies in Kenya and a multi-sectoral youth employment initiative in Uganda.

23.2 Access to Government Procurement Opportunities (AGPO), Kenya

The biggest challenge for young people in building a reputation for their enterprises as entrants into the arena is competing with larger, well-established and often influential adult enterprises. Kenya's AGPO project recognises this disparity between youth and adult enterprises, and sets aside support for specific groups of people disadvantaged by highly competitive processes.

The AGPO project, initiated in 2012, is an example of how micro- and small businesses owned by young people, women and people living with disability were able to benefit from government procurement opportunities through a Presidential Directive that required that at least '30% of government tenders and procurement opportunities should be set aside specifically for these enterprises'.[1]

The initiative grew out of the Public Procurement and Disposal (Preference and Reservations) Amendment Regulations in 2013, which specify that 'a procuring entity shall implement the requirement through its budgets, procurement plans, tender notices, contract awards and submit quarterly reports to the authority'.[2] It was led by the Ministry of Finance through the Public Procurement Directorate, and partnerships included those with revenue and construction authorities, a council representing persons with disability, legal offices, and the authority representing medium-sized and small enterprises.

In overcoming challenges in the process, and to overcome the initial non-response to this enabling strategy, the implementing ministry 1) increased information and outreach to youth businesses and 2) conducted training through groups such as the National Gender and Equality Commission to sensitise women and youth on the procurement qualification and requirements, registration process, available opportunities and how to obtain information about the programme.

23.3 Multi-sectoral youth employment initiatives in Uganda

The magnitude of the youth unemployment context in Uganda has demanded that many state and non-state actors focus on national unemployment challenges,[3] especially as outlined in the National Employment Policy (2011), the Skilling Uganda Strategic Plan (2012–2022) and the Government of Uganda's 2040 Vision, among others.

Under the *Delivering as One*[4] initiative, numerous UN agencies in Uganda – from the Food and Agriculture Organization to the International Organization for Migration – worked collaboratively, and cohesively, on a Programme of Action on Youth Engagement and Employment, to ensure a holistic approach that builds on strengths but avoids overlap by the various UN agencies. This approach to mainstreaming has included interventions that support emerging and established enterprises of young people, training on labour market data, development of a *Youth Entrepreneurship Development Manual*, used to train more than 6,000 young people, and support to government for the finalisation of a National Plan for Youth Employment.

23.4 Implications: what enablers/disablers influenced the process?

Considering the Enablers Framework in Chapter 4, the societal, structural, institutional and impact factors outlined in Table 23.1 influenced these affirmative action and multi-sectoral initiatives.

Table 23.1 Youth and employment case studies: analysis of enablers and disablers

Enablers/disablers	Elaboration
Societal	• Lack of trust in relatively new, youth-led entrepreneurship initiatives may hinder procurement opportunities being provided to young people (Kenya) • Highly competitive bidding processes involving large-scale and experienced bidders and limited assessment criteria may result in inadequate attention to the quality and innovation of youth-led enterprises (Kenya) • High levels of youth unemployment (Uganda)
Structural – macro	• None identified
Structural – meso	• Recognition of specific needs of young and emerging entrepreneurs (Kenya) and unemployed youth (Uganda)
Organisational – structures	• Recognition of youth-specific challenges in entrepreneurship and creating responsive, youth-friendly bidding procedures on the part of the Ministry of Finance and the Public Procurement Directorate (Kenya) • Recognition of youth unemployment as a specific area of focus in broader unemployment (Uganda)
Organisational – process	• Design and implementation of affirmative action programmes for procurement processes, with a focus on young people (Kenya)
Impact	• Greater government business opportunities for young entrepreneurs

Where the youth sector or government is interested in providing greater opportunities for young entrepreneurs, or for youth employment, it may need to consider:

- collaboration with public procurement departments and ministries of finance and planning to advocate for youth-specific concerns in relation to young entrepreneurs/youth unemployment and partnerships with government and other stakeholders;

- highlighting youth talent/innovation/value for money in providing services to governments and other stakeholders through evidence, including innovation awards etc.;

- working through processes to influence the design and implementation of government directives around affirmative action for young entrepreneurs;

- ensuring the integration of youth unemployment issues, and youth voices and influence, in developing national employment strategies;

- supporting development of youth-friendly monitoring and evaluation tools to assess the impact of programmes such as AGPO or youth employment programmes on the lives of young entrepreneurs (stability and security of entrepreneurship programmes) and unemployed youth obtaining jobs; and

- where affirmative action for youth is combined with programmes for affirmative action for women and people living with disability, ensuring that there is equitable distribution of procurement opportunities across all three groups, where one group is not favoured.

Notes

1 Access to Government Procurement Opportunities (AGPO) N.D.
2 Government directive.
3 YouthPOL is the ILO's global online repository of information, policies and legislation related to youth employment.
4 United Nations N.D.

References

Access to Government Procurement Opportunities (AGPO)(N.D.), 'About AGPO', available at: http://agpo.go.ke/pages/about-agpo

International Labour Organisation (2016), *World Employment and Social Outlook 2016: Trends for Youth*, available at: http://www.ilo.org/global/about-the-ilo/newsroom/news/WCMS_513728/lang--en/index.htm.

United Nations Uganda (N.D.), *Delivering as One*, available at: http://www.un-ug.org/page/delivering-one

Chapter 24
Case Study Theme 4: Youth Budgets – Ghana and Uganda

Box 24.1 SDG 10 Reducing Inequality

Target: 10.2 Empower and promote the social, economic and political inclusion of all, irrespective of age, sex, ethnicity, origin, or economic or other status

Sector: Finance

Issue: Unequal financial allocations to meet young people's needs

Strategy: Youth budgets in Ghana and Uganda

24.1 Introduction

The two examples in this chapter look at how a youth perspective on budgeting can help integrate youth priorities, through young people's assessment of needs within a sector and the translation of those needs into financial value. This involves participation in budget programmes to ensure that youth-specific expenditure is costed into budgeting through evidence-based processes.

The case of Ghana is a grassroots process that influenced local government budgets, and ultimately began influencing national programmes and budgets as well.

The case of Uganda is a national-level initiative to integrate youth budgeting into national frameworks. It is set against SDG 10: Reducing Inequality, as it clearly demonstrates the importance of equitable financing to ensure equal development outcomes for young people.

24.2 Why youth budgeting?

Youth-focused budgeting and youth participation in budget assessment and planning is a central means to ensure that young people obtain equitable outcomes from development processes. The case studies below also provide an indication that there can be no meaningful youth budgeting without the participation of young people themselves in identifying their legitimate needs and scrutinising government budgets to ensure adequate allocation to achieve targeted outcomes.

These case studies focus on two initiatives:

1. An initiative by Plan Ghana in the Awutu-Senya District[1] to train and mobilise young people to understand youth rights, assess policies and programmes that translate rights into development frameworks and action, and identify allocation, expenditure and outcomes in relation to budgets. This is an example of how an initiative that began at the local government level ultimately affected national budget processes.

2. A national state initiative in Uganda to integrate youth budgeting into national planning.

24.3 What is participatory youth budgeting?

Participatory youth budgeting refers to young people's involvement in budget analysis, budget formulation, tracking expenditure against allocation and assessing the effectiveness of expenditure in relation to outcomes. The aspiration of the youth budgeting process in Ghana was that young people's involvement in budget analysis, formulation and M&E will make neglect of youth issues such as education, access to healthcare etc. in national planning a thing of the past. It was a remarkable attempt to take budgeting away from technocrats and economists and demystify the budget process, so that young people could understand government processes, and participate and contribute to make (in this case) local government budgeting more relevant and responsive to young people's needs. This would allow the mainstreaming of youth concerns into local government financial planning processes and could easily be replicated at the national level.

24.4 The youth budget initiative, Ghana

The project: Plan Ghana, in co-operation with the Social Development Centre, formulated the youth budget process as a pilot for replication in other West African countries.

The project trained young people in budget advocacy, and created the Youth Budget Advocacy Group of Awutu-Senya District (Y-BAGAS).

Method: Ten young men and women aged 12–30 were selected for the project. Analysis of budgeting was linked to a rights-based approach and the study of international human rights instruments that formed the basis of identifying state priorities for young people. Through the training, young people could understand the budget cycle, local and national budget documents, and how these can be influenced at each stage in the process. Participants also learnt means of calculating growth rates and engaging in trend analysis of budget figures. Brainstorming and group exercises highlighted the implications of budgets for vulnerable groups, especially women and children.

The youth budgeting process included the steps set out in Figure 24.1.

The youth groups also used typically youth-friendly methods of communicating their message to authorities, including putting on a role-play activity depicting how their district assembly budget could address the basic needs of children, especially for education, health and water. All these activities were interpreted in the local language, thereby reaching more participants. This activity generated a lot of interest and questions, and the youth responded with practical examples using preliminary findings from their field survey.

Subsequent engagement of these young people in a forum of civil society organisations to inform Ghana's 2011 budget statement resulted in their voices being heard at the national level. This reportedly led to the retention of critical programmes – such as the Youth in Agriculture programme – due to the advocacy of youth budget groups.[2] Local authorities, too, began attaching greater importance to young people's views, as their level of skills in data analysis and advocacy increased.

Institutionalising young people's participation in budget analysis, advocacy and assessing allocation, expenditure and impact at a much larger scale:

Figure 24.1 Youth budgeting process

- can have transformational impacts in the equitable distribution of resources for young people in development planning; and

- opens young people's eyes to inequities in development planning, and motivates and enables their agency in striving for social equity; this ultimately enhances young people's skills and confidence to participate more fully and effectively in public life.

Philomena, an 18-year-old girl, told the report writers:

> I am very glad I took part in this survey, because it helped me to be more conscious about how some children are denied access to basic educational facilities, although government and local authorities are mandated to meet these needs. This situation boosted my morale to advocate more for these voiceless children to be heard.

Mohammed A, aged 21 and a member of Y-BAGAS, evaluates himself:

> Ever since I was exposed to the concept of budgeting, I am able to write articles and contribute to some policy discussions. I am proud to call myself a budget expert, because I can without any help analyse my district budget and carry out effective advocacy for children's issues to be considered in budgeting.

24.5 Youth budgets at the national level, Uganda

The project: This national Ugandan example aims to tackle negative youth outcomes through pro-youth budgeting, which is envisaged to address high levels of youth unemployment despite consistent economic growth.[3]

The project was based on the acknowledgement by the government of the negative implications for the economy if young people are not productive. The government recognised that, to effectively address the challenges and capitalise on the benefits of youth, it must prioritise youth throughout the national budgeting process. The 'Youth Budget Prioritization – the Way to Go'[4] document is a budget analysis paper by the Uganda Parliamentary Forum on Youth Affairs (UPFYA)[5] and analyses the various sections and sectors of the budget with specific youth priority allocations.

It provides:

- specific dollar amounts allocated to youth within each sector;

- an overview of the various youth-serving programmes catered for within the budgetary period; and

- information on unfunded youth priorities to facilitate advocacy for additional budget allocations for youth.

24.6 Example observations and recommendations

Jobs: Among the recommendations provided in the paper by the UPFYA, one example of a gap identified was between amounts committed and actual spending on some programmes such as the Promotion of Green Jobs and Fair Labour Market. The planned cost for ten years was 863 billion Uganda shillings (USh), with USh86.30 billion being allocated each year. However, with only a small percentage being provided for in the 2016/17 budget, there was a gap of USh62.80 billion, which would restrict the reach of the programme.

Reflecting these observations, the UPFYA has recommended additional allocations in accordance with the previous budgetary commitment, particularly given the urgency required to address youth unemployment challenges.

Health: Another example is the analysis of the health budget. The health sector budget saw increases over a financial year which were committed to improving service delivery to adequately target new HIV infections, maternal/child/family planning and care, as well as to rehabilitate health facilities. However, the UPFYA observed that the amount allocated to health centre upgrades intended to offer improved SRH services did not have an allocation in the following year, which would mean that access to SRH services would still be a challenge for young people, particularly those in rural areas. Recommendations included funding for a national health insurance scheme to be created as a 'safety net' for young people who are unable to access health services.

Outcomes: Youth-focused budget analysis provides evidence to promote financial transparency and accountability of government spending for young people, thus enhancing government accountability towards youth. It can also act as a point of advocacy for prioritising youth-focused allocations across sectors and empower young people with information on youth budgeting.

The Ugandan example demonstrates that government will be better able to deliver outcomes for youth, as these processes facilitate:

- a comprehensive youth analysis from the planning stage, with youth budgeting as a key part of the process, whereby cross-sectoral implications are outlined from the onset;

- adequate financial allocations, which ensure effective implementation; and

- even greater allocations to ensure youth-specific planning and meeting youth targets through the years in development planning.

These youth-focused budget analyses can put forward recommendations on funding increases or decreases, based on a programme's success and impact. For example, youth budget prioritisation can highlight key unfunded priorities, such as health centres in the case of Uganda. It also raises the level of transparency and accountability on the part of the government, along with its financial commitment to youth development.

This approach helps governments answer the questions: Are we meeting the needs of youth through federal and national spending? Are the right areas being sufficiently and effectively funded? What is the impact and value of youth-specific initiatives that have been completed and assessed? and How are each of our agencies prioritising youth and delivering impacts for youth with budget support?

24.7 Implications : what enablers/disablers influenced the process?

Considering the Enablers Framework, the societal, structural, institutional and impact factors set out in Table 24.1 help us understand structural and organisational enablers in youth budgeting as exemplified in the two stories from Ghana and Uganda.

Table 24.1 Youth budget case studies: analysis of enablers and disablers

Enablers/disablers	Elaboration
Societal	• Perception of young people as partners in development
Structural – macro	• Commitments at the level of national planning and finance bodies for youth-centric planning across sectors
Structural – meso	• Political will to integrate youth mainstreaming into national planning
Organisational – structures	• A comprehension of the specific ways in which young people are affected by planning and budgeting that do not take their concerns into account • Understanding the critical role of young people in designing programmes and budgets for those programmes • Linking local processes to national planning • Setting in place youth-participatory mechanisms • Building research capacity for youth-specific programme and budget analysis
Organisational – process	• Implementing mechanisms for youth-centred planning and budgeting • Adequately costed programme commitments for young people across sectors
Impact	• Improved cross-sectoral and co-ordinated outcomes for young people

Governments and youth sector organisations planning to implement youth budgeting would need to:

- collaborate with the youth sector to apply a youth lens to inform planning and budgeting;

- set in place capacity building for finance and planning staff on youth development and building in multi-sectoral youth-specific concerns to national planning, including putting in place youth participation structures;

- work with specific sectors to ensure capacity building for youth-specific planning and budgeting;

- ensure that local government lessons are considered and integrated into national planning; and

- ensure youth-friendly approaches to working with young people through the introduction of youth work processes (Chapter 6).

Notes

1 Bani-Agudego et al. 2011.
2 Coalition of Youth Development Organisations in Ghana 2012, 4.
3 Uganda Bureau of Statistics 2010.
4 Uganda Parliamentary Forum on Youth Affairs 2016.
5 The UPFYA is an advocacy platform focusing on influencing youth mainstreaming issues and approaches 'through legislation, budget appropriations and oversight'. It has been functioning since 2008 and comprises 78 youth members of parliament.

References

Bani-Agudego, C, GC Yorke, and AA Koudhoh, (2011), *Seeing from Our Perspectives: Youth Budget Advocacy in Ghana, in Participatory Learning and Action*, 2011, available at: http://pubs.iied.org/pdfs/G03202.pdf

Coalition of Youth Development Organisations in Ghana (2012), *Youth Budget Watch: Analysis of the Youth Development Budget in Ghana*, Accra.

Uganda Bureau of Statistics (2010), *Navigating Challenges, Charting Hope: A Cross-Sectoral Situational Analysis on Youth* in *Uganda, Vol. II, The Report on the Uganda National Household Survey 2009/2010*, available at: http://www.iyfnet.org/sites/default/files/YouthMap_Uganda_Vol2.pdf

Uganda Parliamentary Forum on Youth Affairs (2016), 'National Budget FY 2016/17: Youth Budget Prioritization the Way to Go', UPFYA Budget Analysis Paper No. 1/June 2016.

Chapter 25
Case Study Theme 5: Youth and Justice – United Kingdom

Box 25.1 SDG 16 Peace, Justice and Strong Institutions

Targets: 16.6 Develop effective, accountable and transparent institutions at all levels; 16.7 Ensure responsive, inclusive, participatory and representative decision-making at all levels; 16.10 Ensure public access to information and protect fundamental freedoms

SDG 10: Reduce inequality within and among countries

Target: 10.2 mentions social and political inclusion

Main sector: Justice

Issue: Lack of restorative justice for young people

Strategy: Youth courts

25.1 Introduction

The following case study looks at youth-friendly service delivery for young people in the justice sector. The primary SDG it is linked to is Goal 16: Peace, Justice and Strong Institutions, which includes rule of law and justice for all.

25.2 Justice for young people through youth courts

If we are to achieve justice for all, particularly justice for youth in our case, how do we establish mechanisms within the justice system, or outside it, which take a youth-centric approach to resolving issues of youth crime? The approach of youth courts outlined here can significantly increase the likelihood of youth-inclusive and youth-friendly approaches to justice processes.

Young people make up a considerable proportion of those that come in contact with the justice system. In the year ended March 2016, the police carried out a total of 896,200 arrests in England and Wales, of which 88,600 were of people aged 10 to 17 years, 10 per cent of the total; this is the same as the proportion of young people in England and Wales in the general population that are of offending age (that is, those aged 10 years or older).[1]

Youth-centric analysis of crime: The rationale for youth courts has been a careful assessment of the root causes of youth crime, including lack of social connectedness, poor intergenerational relations and poverty. Its youth-to-youth resolution mechanisms are also based on evidence of young people's resistance to adult authority and natural allegiance and respect for peers, particularly given the non-youth-centric, hierarchical nature of policing and legal systems.

As Mark Walsh, a police constable who supported the institutionalisation of youth courts in the UK, puts it:

> To a youth, the officious criminal justice system which often focuses on procedures rather than restorative outcomes can produce lack of understanding, uncomfortable surroundings and can make things difficult for the young person to be able to relate to the people they are dealing with. This can make the opportunity to learn from mistakes and rehabilitation so much harder, often resulting in non-compliance and further offending. This is something which is acknowledged by professionals as the 'revolving door' of the criminal justice system.[2]

What are youth courts? Youth courts are a part of restorative justice systems that focus on rehabilitation and reconciliation, rather than traditional systems of punishment and incarceration. They often form an integral part of state justice systems: they need not be outside the system and may rather be adjunct to it. There are many models for youth courts. Overall, they present an alternative to the traditional justice system – one in which young people are heard and questioned, and the consequences of their actions, are judged by other young people. In most youth courts, members of the public are not allowed into the hearing, and young people are addressed by their first names to make the atmosphere friendly, informal and non-threatening.

The youth court is considered a crime-prevention mechanism that bonds young people to their communities and friends, and encourages reflection and regret for their actions; here young people feel respected by those listening to them. In addition, the youth court helps young people who perform the role of judges to understand how government and the justice system works or should work.

Youth work in the justice system: There are explicit and implicit references to the role of youth work in this context, in developing young people's sense of belonging in their communities and developing structured activities that give them a sense of purpose in the long term to avoid their entry into crime in the first place. Solutions include providing greater support to families (young people often engage in gang activity and drug selling to generate income to feed their families and pay bills) and support education systems, which often bear the brunt of youth crime.

What difference does it make? The UK government commissioned a seven-year study into restorative justice, which showed 27 per cent fewer crimes were committed by people who had experienced restorative justice approaches. Eighty-five per cent of victims and 80 per cent of people defined as offenders stated they were either 'very' or 'quite' satisfied with the process. For every 1 pound sterling (£) that was spent on restorative justice, £9 worth of savings were delivered to the criminal justice system in England and Wales.[3] While similar benefits of restorative justice processes may exist in other Commonwealth member countries, more scientific research needs to be conducted to assess these.

Young people's own assessment of their experiences in youth courts are testament to their success.

Young offenders from the Time Dollar Youth Courts in Washington, DC, say[4]:

> I ain't got no father, so I could say youth court is like my father.

> I have 250 hours of community service on my resume because of this youth court process. That has been really helpful for College or getting a job … we are not bad people, we just make poor choices.

A young offender in the youth court system says:

> Why I like youth courts is because it gives you a second chance, maybe you make a mistake, you regret what you did, you get a second chance …

25.3 Implications: what enablers/disablers influenced the process?

Considering the Enablers Matrix in Chapter 4, the societal, structural, institutional and impact factors set out in Table 25.1 influenced the initiative for youth courts.

Governments and the youth sector, or other stakeholders wishing to build youth court/youth restorative justice programmes into their justice systems, would benefit from:

- working with the youth sector and groups working with young offenders in designing youth court/ restorative justice processes;

- training justice sector staff and police on restorative justice and youth court processes, with a specific focus on youth development and youth engagement;

- from the outset, setting in place meaningful monitoring and evaluation mechanisms to evaluate and disseminate the outcomes of restorative justice/ youth court programmes.

Table 25.1 Youth and justice case studies: analysis of enablers and disablers

Enablers/disablers	Elaboration
Societal	• Young offenders being seen in the same light as adult offenders
Structural – macro	• State commitments to financing youth courts
Structural – meso	• Youth-specific commitments in resource allocation for youth courts, restorative justice and rehabilitation programmes
Organisational – structures	• Building staff capacity for, and implementing, youth-centric analysis of crime • Staff and youth training on juvenile and general justice systems, court proceedings and working with young people • Enhancing justice sector staff knowledge of youth work approaches in youth justice
Organisational – process	• Youth-centred approaches to redressing youth offending cases, with youth participatory structures
Impact	• Lowering incarceration of youth, with a greater focus on rehabilitation programmes • Decreased recidivism • Young people build trust in society and the state • Enhanced institutional trust built between young people, the court system, the police etc.

Notes

1   Ministry of Justice, UK 2017.
2   Walsh 2014, 8.
3   Prison Reform Trust 2013, quoted in Walsh 2014, 8.
4   TimeBanksUSA 2009.

References

Ministry of Justice, UK (2017), 'Youth justice statistics 2015/16, England and Wales', *Statistics Bulletin*, London, available at: https://www.gov.uk/government/uploads/system/uploads/attachment_data/file/585897/youth-justice-statistics-2015-2016.pdf

TimeBanksUSA (2009), *TimeDollar Youth Court: Thoughts from Participants* [Online Video], 3 September 2009, available at: https://www.youtube.com/watch?v=bIL1Ch9OET0

Walsh, M (2014), *Restorative Justice for Youth, Administered by Youth*, Winston Churchill Memorial Trust, available at http://www.wcmt.org.uk/sites/default/files/migrated-reports/1194_1.pdf

Chapter 26
Case Study Theme 6: Youth and Urban Planning – Nepal and Kenya

Box 26.1 SDG 11: Sustainable Cities and Communities

Targets: 11.1 Housing and basic services; 11.2 Transport for all; 11.3 Inclusive and sustainable urbanisation through integrated and sustainable human settlement planning and management; 11.7 Safe, inclusive and accessible green and public spaces

Issue: Lack of youth inputs to urban planning

Strategy: Minecraft for youth involvement in urban planning

26.1 Introduction

Young people are often marginalised in urban planning. This means that their needs – in terms of housing, basic services and public spaces – are not considered in urban planning policy and implementation. UN Habitat's Youth Unit ensures creative, fun ways for young people to get involved in urban planning and influence youth-friendly urban design. Citizen participation is important for city governments to consider the needs, interests and knowledge of different stakeholders, something requiring collaborative design and participatory decision-making processes.[1]

This case study is set against SDG 11: Sustainable Cities and Communities and particularly focuses on its targets on inclusive and sustainable urbanisation and safe, inclusive public spaces.

26.2 Minecraft – introduction

UN Habitat piloted an approach to inclusive urban design and governance which targeted young people and incorporated information and communication technologies (ICTs) through the popular computer game of Minecraft as a tool for community participation. The initiative builds on the theory that ICT can be more effectively used to 'increase levels of participation, efficiency and accountability in public urban policies … and [its] use by youth can have a direct impact on increasing civic engagement, giving them new avenues through which to become informed, shape opinions, get organised, collaborate and take action'.[2]

Young people informing the design of public spaces is critical in a context where such involvement 'promotes social inclusion and diversity, improves urban safety, provides a space for democracy, improves health, creates a positive environment and provides more space to businesses and markets'.[3]

With UN Habitat's projection that the world's population living in urban areas will move from 10 per cent (in the early 2000s) to 50 per cent by 2030,[4] the approach integrates youth participation and technology into urban planning processes to tackle the inequalities and stratification which exist within urban centres,[5] to particularly benefit the growing youth population who are constantly excluded.

The game is one of the most popular in the world and provides a virtual space for players to interact and build their virtual environment and cities in a 3D space. Using available resources such as images, Google Maps and community maps, UN Habitat creates a basic model of the actual targeted space before organising training for community members on using Minecraft.

In the process of engagement, an inclusive community participation workshop is held to provide training on creating models, and to encourage collaboration and 'idea-storming' among a diverse group of young people from the community. It is essential to bring as many different voices to the table to ensure that the final design of the space meets a variety of needs. The community members work in groups of two to four to collaborate and visualise the various design elements, and bring their ideas to life.

26.3 Minecraft – Nepal

UN Habitat was able to bring together the local municipality, a local development NGO and local communities to work together to improve public spaces, so that it could better meet the needs of the public in this setting in a Nepali city in 2015.

Public spaces in Nepal, as anywhere else, play a culturally significant role in providing a space for community members to not only interact recreationally, but carry out their daily activities. The Minecraft workshop brought together 37 young people to design proposals. From the impact evaluations conducted in Nepal, the strategy was recognised as being one of a very limited set of opportunities young people have had to participate in urban planning and engage with experts and officials.

Most young people were also attracted to the project because of their interest in video games, which highlights the importance of integrating fun and youth-friendly ways of working with young people to engage them productively in public decision making spaces.

26.4 Minecraft – Kenya

UN Habitat's work with young people in urban planning in Kenya was initiated in 2012. This work focused on a location called Kiberia, the largest informal settlement in Kenya's capital, Nairobi. It houses around 200,000 to 300,000 people, who live in congested conditions and with few public spaces, a critical requirement for young people's leisure, recreation and sense of freedom.

The primary contest in the restructuring of spaces and facilities for these communities was between a group of 14- to 22-year-olds and a group of elderly women on the reshaping of functions for the Silange Sports Field, one of the few proper public spaces available for young people.

The use of Minecraft enabled these groups to resolve their disagreements over the use of the area. It was used as a tool for dialogue in working with young people to ensure that their play space was not compromised in the new design for the community. This was particularly in relation to ensuring that a new access road that cut across the market did not result in a major loss of play space.

'When we introduced *Minecraft* in these workshops it was like a light had been lifted', says Pontus Westerberg, of the United Nations Human Settlements Program. 'You could see and feel a different atmosphere'.[6]

Table 26.1 Youth and urban planning: enablers and disablers

Enablers/disablers	Elaboration
Societal	• Attitude that young people can influence urban planning positively
Structural – macro	• None identified
Structural – meso	• Governance structures enabled multistakeholder engagement, including youth engagement
Organisational – structures	• Staff capacity to integrate youth as experts through their lived experience in urban planning
Organisational – process	• Young people involved in planning through visual, youth-friendly methods
Impact	• Youth-friendly urban spaces as a result of youth participation in urban planning

The partners in this case study were the Nairobi City County Government, Undugu Society of Kenya, the Kilimanjaro Initiative, Project for Public Spaces and Kounkey Design Initiative, which initiated a comprehensive community engagement process to identify public space improvements.

26.5 Implications what enablers/disablers influenced the process?

Considering the Youth Mainstreaming Enablers Framework in Chapter 4, the societal, structural, organisational and impact factors set out in Table 26.1 help us understand successes and challenges of such programmes.

Notes

1   Von Heland et al. 2015, 2.
2   Ben-Attar and Campbell 2012, 34.
3   Crecente 2014.
4   UN Habitat 2015, 24.
5   Ibid.
6   Crecente 2014.

References

Ben-Attar, D and T Campbell (2012), *ICT, Urban Governance and Youth*, UN-Habitat, Nairobi.
Crecente, B (2014), *How Minecraft Is Helping the United Nations Improve the World*, available at: http://www.polygon.com/2014/4/22/5641044/minecraft-block-by-block-united-nations-project

von Heland, F, P Wesberg and M Nyberg (2015), *Using Minecraft as a Citizen Participation Tool in Urban Design and Decision-Making*, Ericsson Research, Stockholm.

UN Habitat (2015), *Using Minecraft for Youth Participation in Urban Design and Governance*, UN Habitat, available at: http://unhabitat.org/ books/using-minecraft-for-youth-participation-in-urban-design-and-governance/#

Annex 1
Definitions of Youth

Youth, in Commonwealth educational material, is not a 'natural category', and it cannot be a 'universal concept'.[1] Young people's life chances are determined by their age, and change across time, place, economic, social and political contexts. Young people's experiences are also defined by physical and psychosocial developmental phases such as early and late adolescence, and by youth-adult relationships and resultant power dynamics. These conceptions have implications for our planning for them.

Perhaps the most dominant means of perceiving youth is as an 'age category'; the Commonwealth refers to young people as those between 15 and 29 years of age. The United Nations refers to young people as those between 15 and 24. Country definitions range from a lower limit of 13 to a higher limit of 40. Age ranges for minors and majors also differ within cultural and regional laws and legal instruments within states.[2] But clearly chronological markers are of limited use in a world of continual flux for young people, across time and space. Chronological markers do, however, assist in defining specific needs and rights that are priorities for specific age groups of youth, such as those in early and late adolescence, early adulthood and so on.

While it is clearly recognised that **transitional markers** are not particularly unique to youth, specific, generalised transitional markers – such as leaving school, entering employment, owning a house, experience of first impressions such as love, initiation to sexual practices and experimentation – are all associated with youth. However, experiences such as entering employment or owning your own house are constantly delayed for young people, given contexts of poverty, austerity, war and so on.

In this regard, Commonwealth learning material links economic and social policies as markers that define youth and points out how structural adjustment continues to create extended periods of unemployment, which **extends the period of life experiences** generally ascribed to 'youth'.[3] Similarly, in some cases, there are also arguments for extending the lower age limits for youth to 12 or 13 years of age, considering the increasing overlap of older children's needs, such as sexual and reproductive needs, with those generally ascribed to the 'youth' category.

In recent youth rights discourses, however, it has been abundantly highlighted that young people are not just 'becoming', 'in transition' or 'the future', but that **young people are the 'present'**. This concept of young people as fully formed citizens has important implications for the way in which we see their role as agents in their own growth and empowerment and in national/global development.

The Commonwealth also highlights the need to pay attention to the 'problems of **class and gender inequality** among young people … for instance, they may define the social unrest that is caused by poverty as something that *young* people do. By doing this, they are able to ignore the fact that it tends to occur among *poor* young people'.[4] Clearly, class, race, sexual orientation and so on multiply the marginalities of young people.

The definition of 'youth' is also **transient through time**; 'the social meaning of youth one hundred years ago was not the same as it is today'.[5] Indeed, it changes from generation to generation. In generalised descriptions, Generation X (born in the mid-1960s to early 1980s) was seen to be inclusive and individualistic, whereas Generation Y (born 1980s to 2000), or millennials, are known for their engagement with technology, connectedness and pushing for change and disruption based on values. Generation Z, or post-millennials, are assumed to be a generation that will build more aggressively on generations past, but their reality may also be informed by growing inequality and global insecurity. As generalised as these categories are, however, generational experiences through time are often a useful way of understanding youth groups in specific contexts. These generational experiences differ in each national/local context, given the history of Commonwealth member countries, and need to be formally researched prior to planning for them in youth mainstreaming.

Notes

1   Commonwealth Youth Programme 2007, 47.

2 Age of criminal culpability, minimum age of marriage etc. also set acknowledgement of maturation across cultures and nations, and are separate from child/youth categories.
3 Commonwealth Youth Programme 2007, 49.
4 Ibid., 45.
5 Ibid., 47.

Reference

Commonwealth Youth Programme (2007), 'Module 2', *Young People and Society: The Commonwealth Diploma in Youth Development*, Commonwealth Secretariat, London

Annex 2
Youth Social, Political and Economic Empowerment

Young people's social, political and economic empowerment

Social empowerment is understood as the process of developing a sense of autonomy and self-confidence, and acting individually and collectively to change social relationships and the institutions and discourses that exclude social cohorts (in our case, young people). Young people's empowerment, and their ability to hold others to account, is strongly influenced by their individual assets (such as land, housing, livestock, savings) and capabilities of all types: human (such as good health and education), social (such as social belonging, a sense of identity, leadership relations) and psychological (self-esteem, self-confidence, the ability to imagine and aspire to a better future), which can also be termed as their capabilities.

These strengths are translated into **political empowerment** when they are organised to inform representation and voice in decision-making. This involves representation and voice not just through party politics, but through community organisation and building collective strength to influence change.

Economic empowerment is thought to allow young people to think beyond immediate daily survival and to exercise greater control over both their resources and life choices. For example, it enables households to make their own decisions around making investments in health and education, and taking risks in order to increase their income. There is also some evidence that economic empowerment can strengthen vulnerable groups' participation in decision-making. Economic power is often easily 'converted' into increased social status or decision-making power. More generally, the discourse on economic empowerment centres around four broad areas: 1) the promotion of the assets of poor [in our case young] people; 2) transformative forms of social protection; 3) microfinance; and 4) skills training.

– Adapted and rewritten from GSDRC Applied Knowledge Services 2014

Reference

GSDRC Applied Knowledge Services (2014), *Social and Economic Empowerment*, available at: http://www.gsdrc.org/topic-guides/voice-empowerment-and-accountability/supplements/social-and-economic-empowerment/.

Annex 3
Youth Participation Practice Standards

The following practice standards, developed by the Commonwealth/UNICEF, may be useful in framing your own organisation or sector's youth participation standards.

1. Is it voluntary? Real participation is voluntary, not forced.

2. Is it accessible? Too often only urban or better-off young people are involved. Too often only the boys get to speak.

3. Is it respectful? Real participation takes place in a climate of respect, where no one is laughed at or ignored.

4. What's the point of it? Unless all participants have tackled this question themselves, they will see the exercise as confusing or a waste of time.

5. Who wants it? Real participation is based around issues that young people themselves care about and need to give their attention.

6. Does it make a difference? Real participation is where young people contribute and have real influence on the outcomes.

7. Is the language right? Real participation requires young people to feel competent in the language and vocabulary spoken.

8. Are the participants prepared? If older adults have all the information, whereas the young people are pulled in at short notice, results will be poor. Young people need to build their skills and confidence to participate effectively.

9. Is it open-ended? Real participation allows young people to follow ideas through – it isn't all decided in advance by the older adults.

10. Is it honest? Is everyone being honest with each other, as partners? Are they being honest with themselves?

11. Is it safe? Real participation takes every effort to ensure participants are not endangered by what they do or say.

12. What happens afterwards? Real participation means people are clear about who is responsible for follow-up actions.

    – Source: Commonwealth Youth Programme and UNICEF 2005a–c

References

Commonwealth Youth Programme and UNICEF (2005a), *Adolescent and Youth Participation: Adults Get Ready!*, Commonwealth Secretariat, London.

Commonwealth Youth Programme and UNICEF (2005b), *Adolescent Participation and the Project Cycle*, Commonwealth Secretariat, London.

Commonwealth Youth Programme and UNICEF (2005c), *Participation in the Second Decade of Life: What and Why?*, Commonwealth Secretariat, London.

Annex 4
Marginality Mapping

Marginality Mapping is an exercise that appeared in the Commonwealth document *Co-Creating Youth Spaces – A Practice-Based Guide for Youth Facilitators.*[1] It is adapted from an exercise called Poverty Mapping derived from Dhruva, the consultancy wing of Concerned for Working Children (CWC), a rights-based organisation working on children and governance, located at Bangalore, India.

Why Marginality Mapping?

In order to ensure meaningful representation in youth participation, it is important to identify who is marginalised and why they are marginalised. Social groups and individuals are marginalised because of several factors such as economic, social, cultural, political and geographic status. For example, a young person belonging to a certain religious group (cultural) may be marginalised because of his or her religious identity, or a young person could be marginalised for simply having a view on a subject that is different from the majority view (political) etc. Marginality is an ever-changing process, and a group's level of marginality can change over time and place. For this reason, it is possible to work with stakeholders and young people not only to analyse marginality, but also to discuss how marginalisation can be challenged and minimised.

Each sector may have to re-adapt this tool to study particular forms of marginality in their specific contexts – e.g. the health sector would need to assess who is most marginalised in terms of accessing and benefiting from health services in a specific context.

The tool

This mapping tool covers five areas of potential marginality for young people:

- **Social marginalisation:** Includes aspects highlighted in the Equality Matrix for Youth (Table 3.1) under social equality – i.e. marginality pertaining to education, literacy, housing, equal status for those with disability, women, minorities etc.

- **Cultural marginalisation:** Includes marginalisation pertaining to creative expression, religion etc.

- **Economic marginalisation:** Includes marginalisation due to unemployment, low income, inequitable income for commensurate work, lack of voice in the work place etc.

- **Political marginalisation:** Includes lack of ability to express opinions on, and influence decisions that affect, young people and society – including in party-political spaces, in global, national and local governance, in the family, and all other personal and public spaces young people are associated with such as communities, schools, universities, work places etc.

- **Geographic marginalisation:** Includes remoteness and influence on quality of life because of environmental effects, either human-made or natural environmental crises such as global warming, landslides, infertile soil, drought etc.

Figure A4.1 shows:

- how different forms of marginality can often intersect, through the levels of overlap; and

- the gravity of each form of marginality, through the size of the circle.

Figure A4.1 Marginality mapping Venn diagram

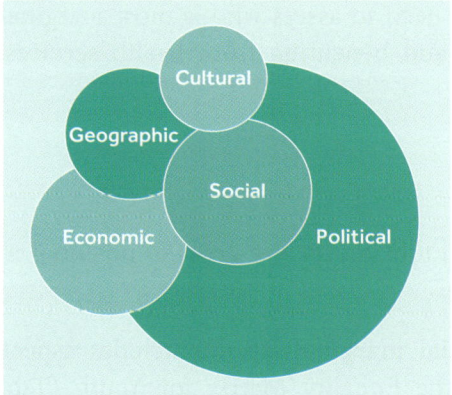

Young people and stakeholders can change the size and placement of the circles in ways they see as applying to their contexts.

This tool not only serves the identification of forms of marginality and their intersections, but also helps dialogue and discussion among young people and adult stakeholders on the issue.

A detailed tool pertaining to this is available in Co-creating Youth Spaces, pp 135–6 for you to adapt.

Note

1   Commonwealth Youth Programme et al. 2014.

Reference

Commonwealth Youth Programme, Nehru Yuva Kendra Sangathan (NYKS) and Pravah (2014), *Co-creating Youth Spaces: A Practice-Based Guide for Youth Facilitators*, Commonwealth Secretariat, London, available at: http://thecommonwealth.org/sites/default/files/inline/Co-Creating_Youth_Spaces_web.pdf

Annex 5
Sarah White's 'Interests in Participation' Model

Sarah White's model of 'Interests in Participation', as highlighted in her article 'Depoliticising Development: The Uses and Abuses of Participation', demonstrates transformational youth participation as defined in this publication. It recognises various **forms of participation** – from nominal to transformational – and indicates what **interests** drive these forms of participation from two perspectives:

1. That of the originator – i.e. the organisation/ government.

2. That of the participants – communities, and in our case, youth. (Of course it has to be remembered that communities/youth can also initiate participatory processes, and often transform orthodox processes in unexpected ways.)

Finally, it highlights the **function** or result of this participation. Of course, White points out that 'interests' in reality are far more complicated than a chart can suggest. In Table A5.1, we try to provide some examples from youth participation for each of White's forms of participation.

Table A5.1 Interests in participation

Form Degree of participation (less to more)	Top-down Interests of those who design development programmes	Bottom-up Participants' view of, and expectations from, their participation	Function The result of such participation
Nominal To show that an agency is 'doing something' about participation to tick a box; i.e. have youth 'groups' on paper with random involvement in meetings.	**Legitimisation** To enhance the legitimacy of the agency. Seen to be participatory.	**Inclusion** Communities want to be part of process, want to gain leverage, but not always successful. Also, individual gain.	**Display** To 'show' outwardly that participation is taking place.
Instrumental For example, 'youth for development' programmes, where young people in communities are used to implement development programmes, not necessarily with their views considered.	**Efficiency** Creates efficiency and cost-effectiveness by replacing paid labour with community labour etc.	**Cost** Community members/youth feel it is costly in terms of their time and engagement in pursuits such as education, and their regular work, in the case of youth, often as entrants into employment.	**Means** Participation is a means to an end that does not necessarily benefit young people.
Representative Youth groups or communities develop their own by-laws/p ans for development, thus enabling their voice in development planning for sustainability.	**Sustainability** Involvement of youth and communities enables more responsive planning.	**Leverage** Communities and youth want to leverage their interests in public planning.	**Voice** Youth and communities get the opportunity to integrate their voice in planning.
Transformative Participation as empowerment. Considering options, making decisions, collective action. Creates greater consciousness of power relationships, and of youth and community ability to make a difference. Controlled 'from below'.	**Empowerment** Agencies work in solidarity with marginalised communities and youth to consciously empower them, not just to create responsive programmes.	**Empowerment** Communities and youth realise their own potential as agents of change in critiquing, making decisions and acting for change.	**Means/end** Participation is a means to empowerment through greater access to services and resources/obtaining rights and as an end in itself (see bottom-up).

Annex 6
The power cube: Levels, spaces and forms of power

Gaventa's power cube (see Figure A6.1) represents three dimensions that determine power levels, spaces and forms.[1]

Levels are levels of governance – global, national, local etc.

Forms refer to different levels of visibility of the wielded power. Visible power refers to the more observable aspects of the political process; hidden power is where certain key actors (e.g. economic powers) may exercise control through shaping what issues and decisions enter the public arena in the first place; and invisible power (norms of beliefs of legitimacy) includes the psychological aspects of power such as how it can influence people's perceptions of what constitutes a legitimate grievance or issue for action.

There are three types of spaces where power is exercised. These are closed, invited and claimed/created spaces. In closed spaces, deliberations are closed to the public and decisions are made

Figure A6.1 The power cube: the levels, spaces and forms of power

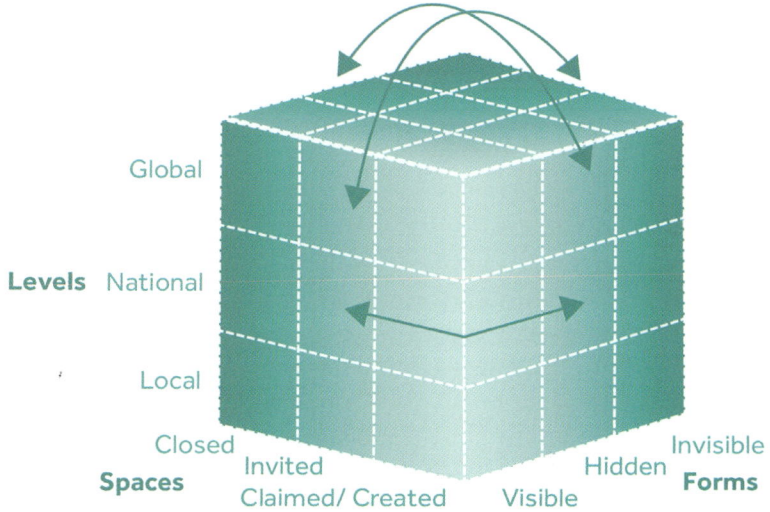

Source: Gaventa and Martorano (2006). See also www.powercube.net for other presentations.

by bureaucrats or economic elites. In invited spaces, the public and policy-makers come together for consultation and public dialogue. In claimed spaces, citizens exercise power through small-scale acts of resistance or larger-scale protests and social movements,[2] or indeed by claiming, rather than being invited to, spaces in formal policy domains.

Notes

1   Gaventa and Martorano 2016.
2   For a fuller discussion, see Gaventa and Martorano 2016, 14–22.

Reference

Gaventa, J and B Martorano (2016), 'Inequality, Power and Participation: Revisiting the Links', *IDS Bulletin*, Vol. 47 No. 5, 11–30, DOI: http://dx.doi.org/10.19088/1968-2016.164.

Annex 7
Example Youth Analysis Frameworks

Table A7.1 shows some forms of analysis that the Commonwealth articulates in the Commonwealth Diploma in Youth Development Work.[1] We either implicitly or explicitly engage in assessing the realities of young people through one or several of these frameworks. These forms of analysis can be either deficit- or asset-based.

Table A7.1 Example analytical frameworks

Analytical framework	Example as applying to youth analysis
1: Analysis based on social order (functionalist): This analysis sees society as an organism composed of many parts, each with its own function. These functions are specific but interrelated and help maintain *social order*. Parts of society are considered to be *institutions*, which are family, politics, education, religion and the economy, and each has its own functions – for example, a family would reproduce and train new members of society. Functionalists focus on social order and, if change is to occur, this is gradual, so that the whole society maintains order. Dysfunctional institutions, such as the drug trade, must be eliminated, according to functionalists, and action will be taken to restore equilibrium.	Efforts to *conform* youth to subscribe to the 'social order' in the youth sector would belong in this category. This is evident in youth development work that focuses on attitude and behaviour change in young people, at the cost of limited or no focus on other approaches to asset-based youth development. The inference here is that young people should 'fit into' the status quo and this is a broad premise of most youth policies.[2] This may be seen as a framework that is based on a model of social control.
2: Analysis based on social conflict: While the functionalist model stresses organisation, order and stability, the conflict model stresses that 'social order' is superficial; that, underneath, there are deep conflicts of interest between the various social groups, and that this suppressed conflict is what leads to social change and development. They also stress the use of coercion based on power. These differing ideas lead to social change, such as the Marxist class struggle or the feminist struggle for social equality for women.	Many social political education aspects of analysing young people's contexts rely on references to identities of gender, class, caste etc., the conflicts created because of these identities, and action for social equity that attempts to minimise the impact of these conflicts.

(Continued)

Table A7.1 Example analytical frameworks (*cont.*)

Analytical framework	Example as applying to youth analysis
3: Analysis based on social interactions: This analysis examines the processes by which small groups of people interact with each other and build symbol systems that get converted to social roles, and thereon to social structures. This maintains that, within a particular society or culture, the members always share a common set of symbols, so that they can communicate the same meanings to each other. Language is one way of embodying these symbols, as is our house, our school or our dress sense. This analysis focuses on small groups of people who are really the actors who construct dominant social values. We often accept the social structure that the elite have formulated. Language and icons are means by which the elite may maintain their power invisibly.	If you keep telling a young person that he or she is a 'troublemaker', then the young person will tend to *become* the troublemaker they have been labelled (labelling theory). Therefore, in modern youth development work, we highlight the need to help young people build positive images of themselves in the way we interact with them, so that youth symbolically represent positivity rather than negativity.
4: Analysis based on social exclusion: Social exclusion refers to systematic ways in which individuals or communities are obstructed from fulfilling their rights, and from accessing opportunities or resources by virtue of their gender, class, ethnicity and other identities, thereby marginalising them from mainstream society. The Commonwealth Diploma looks at social exclusion in relation to structural adjustment policies, where lower levels of investment in public spending and greater reliance on the free market to drive wealth creation and employment have resulted in many forms of social exclusion, including in employment trends.[3] However, there are many other root causes of social exclusion, including racial discrimination, forms of violating disability rights, gender discrimination etc.	If data from Country X demonstrate that a minority ethnic group in that country has lower secondary school enrolment, this trend will be analysed in terms of the laws and policies, social, cultural and political norms, and institutional rules, cultures and practices that exclude certain groups from education.
5: Analysis based on human rights: The Commonwealth Charter is based on the principles of human rights. Rights pertain to entitlements in relation to human rights conventions/protocols, including the Commonwealth Charter itself, the Universal Declaration of Human Rights (UDHR) and the United Nations Convention on the Rights of the Child (UNCRC), and other regional and national instruments. Outcomes for young people are analysed here in terms of their ability to realise rights in relation to rights frameworks. This could refer to sexual discrimination, access to justice, protection, the right to participation, the right to freedom of expression etc., where young people are **rights-holders** and the state and other parties responsible for young people are **duty-bearers**. Young people therefore may have claims against those who do not fulfil rights obligations.	Young women are often denied access to information and services on reproductive healthcare in public health institutions. In a rights-based analysis, this context will be analysed in terms of international conventions on the right to health and the right to information and any existing country legislation. Young women are seen as rights-holders in this context and the state as duty-bearers accountable to young women. Young women will also be at the centre of such an analysis, as determined by the centrality of participation and agency in rights language.

A7

Notes

1 Commonwealth Youth Programme 2007.
2 Ibid., 34.
3 Ibid., 41.

Reference

Commonwealth Youth Programme (2007), *The Commonwealth Plan of Action for Youth Empowerment 2007–2015*, Commonwealth Secretariat, London.

Glossary

Activism: Taking action to effect social change. It can be conducted by individuals, but is most often a collective effort. In the case of youth, activism in its most visible form is undertaken by youth movements which focus on addressing social injustice. Activism can be mainstream, such as lobbying the government, participating in public meetings etc., or less mainstream, such as forms of civil disobedience, protests, occupations, campaigns, boycotts, demonstrations etc.

Development planning: All aspects of development, including policy and strategy development, legislation and implementation/service delivery (programming).

Developmental rights: Human rights that define rights to physical, mental, moral and social development, and associated responsibilities of society and institutions.

Diversity: Understanding and recognising that everyone is unique and different. Regarding youth, this means designing ways to capture different 'youth voices', e.g. young women's, or those from a particular ethnic group etc.

Equality for youth: Equal enjoyment of human rights for youth. Equal social and development outcomes for young people, including intergenerational equality, respect and understanding, non-discrimination, and equality of access to services and resources, irrespective of age or other attributes. It means that young people are given the same as their elders in terms of fulfilment of human rights.

Equity for youth: Fairness in the treatment of young men and women that considers their specific rights and aspirations and prevents age-based and other inequalities caused by social class, gender, caste, sexual orientation and other identity markers. Equity measures must consider this intersectionality. Equity is about giving young people what they need.

Intersectionality: The study of overlapping or intersecting social identities and related systems of oppression, domination or discrimination, e.g. examining how gender, caste, class, ethnicity, age and so on can reinforce and compound exclusionary practices, and then seeking ways to address this.

Good youth mainstreaming approaches, for example, never treat young women and men as a homogeneous group.

Safeguarding rights: Human rights that define young people's right to safety, security and confidentiality in their interactions with society and institutions.

Sociodemographic focus: A demographic focus relates to analysis, planning and implementation based on implications for variables such as age, sex, ethnicity, caste, class, religion, education status etc. Sociological data refer to group affiliations, household status, interests, values etc.

Unaffiliated youth: Young people in all social groups who are not part of organised groups such as youth clubs, youth councils, youth movements and so on. They may also be classified as young people in informal employment, migrants, refugees etc., whose needs are not articulated formally as youth interests and therefore are not met by policy processes. They may, however, have informal means of gathering which are not consciously organised.

Youth: The chronological, social, political, economic and cultural attributes and opportunities that are associated with being at a transition stage between childhood and adulthood. Age definitions vary from culture to culture.

Youth-adult partnerships: Ethical partnerships where young people and adults work with each other in professional settings as equal partners. While the responsibility is with both parties, there is an additional onus on adults to ensure equality and respect.

Youth agency: Young people exercising autonomy in expressing opinions and taking action for change.

Youth-centric analysis: An analysis that centres around evidence-based, collective youth interests, most often pegged against international conventions relating to youth rights. This analysis emerges from a keen understanding and knowledge of young people's lived and experienced realities, particularly in the context of marginalised youth groups. A youth-centric analysis is not possible without the involvement of young men and women themselves.

Youth empowerment: Enhancing the status of young people, helping them empower themselves to build their competencies and capabilities for life. This involves social, political, cultural and economic empowerment. It will enable them to contribute to, and benefit from, a politically stable, economically viable and legally supportive environment, ensuring their full participation as active citizens.

Youth-led: Young people lead and design research, programmes and civic action. Where adults are involved, they play a supportive, guiding role.

Youth mainstreaming: Strategies for intergenerational equity and justice that enable young people's capacities, participation and human rights to be an integral dimension of the analysis, design, implementation, and monitoring and evaluation of policies and programmes in inter-sectoral planning across all social, political and economic spheres. It enables young people and adults to benefit equally from, and contribute equally to, development outcomes.

Youth participation: Young people's involvement in their families, communities, education institutions, work places and institutional governance at all levels and in all sectors in influencing attitudes, policies and practices that affect their lives and society.

Youth work: A profession that involves competencies of youth engagement. The Commonwealth defines it as youth engagement approaches that build personal awareness and support the social, political and economic empowerment of young people, delivered through non-formal learning within a matrix of care.

Further Reading

The following resources were referred to in the development of the handbook, and are likely to be of further interest to the reader.

Barrow, R (2012), 'What Should Be Taught in Our Schools, and Why?', in *Commonwealth Education Partnerships 2012/13*, Nexus Strategic Partnerships, Cambridge, 101–102.

Boumphrey, S (2012), 'Key Points', in *Special Report: The World's Youngest Population*, Euromonitor International, available at: http://blog.euromonitor.com/2012/02/special-report-the-worlds-youngest-populations.html.

Charles, H and J-C Madgerie (2012), 'School-to-Work Transition in the Caribbean: Social Efficiency or Active Citizenship?', in *Commonwealth Education Partnerships 2012/13*, Nexus Strategic Partnerships, Cambridge, 228–230.

Clark, N (2012), 'Education in the Community: Learning to Live with Environmental Change', in *Commonwealth Education Partnerships 2012/13*, Nexus Strategic Partnerships, Cambridge.

Committee on Standards in Public Life (2013), 'Standards Matter: Ethical Standards in Public Life, Best Practices and Current Threats', in *Commonwealth Governance Handbook: Democracy Development and Public Administration 2013/14*, Nexus Strategic Partnerships, Cambridge, 46–53.

Commonwealth Secretariat (2014), *Gender Mainstreaming Guidelines for Project Planning*, Commonwealth Secretariat.

Commonwealth Students' Association Steering Committee (2013), 'The Commonwealth Students' Association Encouraging Students to Form a Collective Voice', in *Commonwealth Education Partnerships 2013/14*, Nexus Strategic Partnerships, Cambridge, 124–127.

Concerned for Working Children (N.D.), *Children's Citizenship*, available at: http://www.concernedforworkingchildren.org/empowering-children/childrens-citizenship/.

Crowley, A (2014), 'Evaluating the Impact of Children's Participation in Public Decision-Making', in J Westwood et al. (eds.), *Participation, Citizenship and Inter-Generational Relations in Children and Young People's Lives*, Palgrave Macmillan, Hampshire, 29–42.

Davis, T (2012), 'How Might Open Data Contribute to Good Governance?', in *Commonwealth Governance Handbook: Democracy Development and Public Administration 2012/13*, Nexus Strategic Partnerships, Cambridge, 148–150.

Department for International Development (DFID) (2009), *Political Economy Analysis How-To Note*, July, available at: https://www.odi.org/sites/odi.org.uk/files/odi-assets/events-documents/3797.pdf.

D'Souza, F (2013), 'Gaining Momentum through Women's Political Leadership', in *Commonwealth Governance Handbook: Democracy Development and Public Administration 2013/14*, Nexus Strategic Partnerships, Cambridge, 37–39.

Elder, S (2011), 'Transitions from School to Decent Work: Introducing the ILO's Work4Youth Programme', in *Commonwealth Education Partnerships 2011/12*, Nexus Strategic Partnerships, Cambridge, 44–46.

Engmann, M, S Jayaram and M Thomas (2013), 'Strategies for Supporting Youth Employment and the School to Work Transition', *Commonwealth Education Partnerships 2013/14*, Nexus Strategic Partnerships, Cambridge, 28–31.

European Commission (2008), *Manual for Gender Mainstreaming: Employment, Social Inclusion and Social Protection Policies*, European Communities, Luxembourg.

Goldsworthy, D (2013), 'Improving Accountability: Strengthening Public Audit across the Commonwealth', in *Commonwealth Governance Handbook: Democracy Development and Public Administration 2012/13*, Nexus Strategic Partnerships, Cambridge, 103–104.

Goulds, S (2012), 'The State of the World's Girls: Learning for Life', in *Commonwealth Education Partnerships 2012/13*, Nexus Strategic Partnerships, Cambridge, 39–41.

Ministry of Youth and Culture, Government of Jamaica (2015), *National Youth Policy 2015–2030*, available online at: http://jis.gov.jm/media/Final-Green-Paper-2015_April-9.pdf

Green, D (2011), 'The Democratic Developmental State: Wishful Thinking or Direction of Travel?', in *Commonwealth Governance Handbook: Democracy Development and Public Administration 2011/12*, Nexus Strategic Partnerships, Cambridge, 40–43.

Hosking, G (2012), '"A Trusted Partner" – but What Is Trust?', in *Commonwealth Governance Handbook: Democracy Development and Public Administration 2012/13*, Nexus Strategic Partnerships, Cambridge, 126–129.

International Labour Organization (ILO) (2013), *Global Employment Trends for Youth 2013: A Generation at Risk*, ILO, Geneva.

Joint UN Programme on HIV/AIDS (UNAIDS), UN Population Fund (UNFPA) and UN Women (UNIFEM) (2004), *Women and HIV/AIDS: Confronting the Crisis*, United Nations.

Kadaga, R (2013), 'Women's Political Leadership in East Africa with Specific Reference to Uganda', in *Commonwealth Governance Handbook: Democracy Development and Public Administration 2013–2014*, Nexus Strategic Partnerships, Cambridge, 32–36.

Knight, L (2011), 'Employability Skills: A Gap in the Discourse', in *Commonwealth Education Partnerships 2011/12*, Nexus Strategic Partnerships, Cambridge, 79–80.

Maphatia, A (2011), 'Are Public-Private Partnerships the Way to Achieve the Right to Education in India?', in *Commonwealth Education Partnerships 2011/12*, Nexus Strategic Partnerships, Cambridge, 21–23.

Mcnallly, S and S Telhaj (2007), *The Cost of Exclusion: Counting the Cost of Youth Disadvantage in the UK*, Prince's Trust, London.

Mishra, RK (2012), 'Putting Youth at the Heart of HIV/AIDS Prevention Efforts', in *Commonwealth Education Partnerships 2012/13*, Nexus Strategic Partnerships, Cambridge, 206–207.

National Adolescent-Friendly Clinic Initiative (N.D.), 'Adolescent Health South Africa', available at: http://www.ppdafrica.org/docs/southafricaadolescent.pdf.

Office of the Secretary General's Envoy on Youth, United Nations (2014), *Crowdsourcing Initiative on Youth in the Post-2015 Development Agenda Launched Today*, available at: http://www.un.org/youthenvoy/2014/02/crowdsourcing-initiative-on-youth-in-the-post-2015-development-agenda-launched-today/

Ogunsanya, K (2013), 'Equitable Governance and Women's Leadership in the Commonwealth', in *Commonwealth Governance Handbook, 2013/14*, Nexus Strategic Partnerships, Cambridge, 26–29.

Oyelaran-Oyeyinka, O (2013), *State of Urban Youth Report 2012–2013: Youth in the Prosperity of Cities*, UN Habitat, Nairobi.

Paolini, G (N.D.), *Youth Social Exclusion and Lessons from Youth Work*, European Commission, Education, Audiovisual and Culture Executive Agency.

Patel, G and D Devaiah (2012), 'Promoting Equality with Life-Changing Learning for Disadvantaged Groups', *Commonwealth Education Partnerships 2012/13*, Nexus Strategic Partnerships, Cambridge, 172–175.

Poirrier, C (2012), 'Unlocking the Budget's Development Impact: The Role of Citizen-Led Accountability Initiatives', *Commonwealth Governance Handbook: Democracy Development and Public Administration 2012/13*, Nexus Strategic Partnerships, Cambridge, 109–111.

Population Reference Bureau (2013), *The World's Youth 2013 Data Sheet*.

Pringle, I (2012), 'Widespread and Participatory Learning about Health', in *Commonwealth Education Partnerships 2012/13*, Nexus Strategic Partnerships, Cambridge, 208–210.

Salto-Youth Cultural Diversity Resource Centre (N.D.), *Understanding Youth: Exploring Identity and Its Role in International Youth Work*, European Commission, Brussels.

Sharra, S (2012), 'Respect, Understanding and Human Rights Education: A Fair Exchange?', in *Commonwealth Education Partnerships 2012/13*, Nexus Strategic Partnerships, Cambridge, 121–122.

Siurala, L (N.D.), *A European Framework for Youth Policy*, Council of Europe Publishing.

Staunton, M and S Goulds (2011), 'Because I Am a Girl – Invest in Me', in *Commonwealth Education Partnerships 2011/12*, Nexus Strategic Partnerships, Cambridge, 32–33.

Stöd, J (2007), *Gender Mainstreaming Manual*, Swedish Government Official Reports, Stockholm.

United Nations (2013a), *A New Global Partnership: Eradicate Poverty and Transform Economics through Sustainable Development – The Report of the High-Level Panel of Eminent Persons on the Post-2015 Development Agenda*, United Nations, New York.

United Nations (2013b), *UN World Youth Report, 2012, Summary*, October, United Nations, New York.

United Nations (2013c), *UN World Youth Report, 2013, Youth Migration*. United Nations, New York.

United Nations (2014), *Youth Employment: Youth Perspectives on the Pursuit of Decent Work in Changing Times*, Summary Report of UN World Youth Report 2011, January, United Nations, New York.

United Nations (2015a), *Sustainable Development Knowledge Platform, SDG 10*, available at: https://sustainabledevelopment.un.org/sdg10.

United Nations (2015b), *We the Peoples: Celebrating Seven Million Voices*, available at: https://myworld2015.files.wordpress.com/2014/12/wethepeoples-7million.pdf.

United Nations (N.D.) *Delivering as One*, Uganda, available at: http://www.un-ug.org/page/delivering-one.

UN Children's Fund (UNICEF) (2012), *Children in an Urban World*, UNICEF, New York.

UN Children's Fund (UNICEF) (N.D.), 'U-Report', available at: https://ureport.in/.

UNDP/PRIO (2016), Expert Meeting on Measuring SDG 16, Report, Oslo, 28–29 January 2016, Voksenåsen Conference Centre, Oslo, Norway.

UNESCO, Section for Education and HIV & Aids (2011), 'HIV and Education', in *Commonwealth Education Partnerships 2011/12*, Nexus Strategic Partnerships, Cambridge, 50–52.

UNESCO (2006), Section for Youth. *Youth Mainstreaming Training Kit*, UNESCO, Paris.

Unwin, T (2013), 'Good Governance in the Commonwealth: Many Cultures, One Agenda', in *Commonwealth Governance Handbook: Democracy Development and Public Administration 2013/14*, Nexus Strategic Partnerships, Cambridge, 41–44.

Westwood, J, C Larkins, D Moxon, Y Perry and N Thomas (Eds.) (2014), *Participation, Citizenship and Inter-Generational Relations in Children and Young People's Lives*, Palgrave Macmillan, Hampshire.

White, S (1996), 'Depoliticising Development: The Uses and Abuses of Participation', *Development in Practice*, Vol. 6 No. 1, 6–15.

World Bank (2011), *World Development Report*, World Bank, Washington, DC.

World Conference on Youth (2014), *Colombo Declaration on Youth: Youth Mainstreaming in the Post-2015 Agenda,* Colombo, available at: http://www.cfa-international.org/userfiles/files/colombo-declaration-on-youth-final.pdf.

Wright, C (2011), 'The Commonwealth Local Government Forum (CLFG): Strengthening Local Democratic Government to Deliver Development', in *Commonwealth Governance Handbook: Democracy Development and Public Administration 2011/12*, Nexus Strategic Partnerships, Cambridge, 57–59.

YouthPolicy.org (N.D.), *International Youth Sector, Overview.*